W9-CCA-539

THE
Energy
OF
Money

A Spiritual Guide to Financial and Personal Fulfillment

Maria Nemeth, Ph.D.

Ballantine Wellspring™
The Random House Publishing Group | New York

Portions of this work originally appeared in *You and Money*, published by Vildehiya Publications in 1997, and in an audio cassette course titled *The Energy of Money*, published by Sounds True in 1997.

Grateful acknowledgment is made to the following for permission to reprint previously published material:

Crown Publishers, a division of Random House, Inc.: excerpt from *Silence, Simplicity, and Solitude: A Guide for Spiritual Retreat* by David Hannoch Cooper. Copyright © 1992 by David Hanoch Cooper.

Doubleday, a division of Random House, Inc.: excerpt from *The Story of Psychology* by Morton Hunt.

HarperCollins Publishers, Inc.: excerpt from *The Enlightened Mind* by Stephen Mitchell. Copyright © 1991 by Stephen Mitchell.

HarperCollins Publishers, Inc., and Rigpa Fellowship: excerpts from *The Tibetan Book of Living and Dying* by Sogyal Rinpoche. Copyright © 1992, 1993 by Rigpa Fellowship.

Alfred A Knopf, Inc.: excerpt from *Death Comes for the Archbishop* by Willa Cather. Copyright © 1927 by Willa Cather. Copyright renewed 1955 by the Executors of the Estate of Willa Cather.

Random House, Inc.: excerpt from *Letters to a Young Poet* by Rainer Maria Rilke, translated by Stephen Mitchell. Copyright © 1982 by Stephen Mitchell.

Shambhala Publications, Inc., Boston: excerpt from *The Wisdom of No Escape* by Pema Chödrön. Copyright © 1991.

W.W. Norton & Company, Inc.: excerpt from *A Theory of Personality: The Psychology of Personal Constructs* by George A. Kelly. Copyright © 1955, 1963 by George A. Kelly, renewed 1983, 1991 by Gladys Kelly. Reprinted by permission of W.W. Norton & Company, Inc.

www.ballantinebooks.com

Library of Congress Card Number: 99-91878

ISBN 0-345-43497-8

Text design by Debbie Glasserman
Cover design by Min Choi

Manufactured in the United States of America

First Hardcover Edition: March 1999
First Trade Paperback Edition: April 2000

To Rita and Aunt Anna

CONTENTS

ACKNOWLEDGMENTS

Nothing is created without the support of others, especially anything that moves the heart and educates the soul. We all seek to make a contribution to the lives of those around us. So it is with this book and the work from which it derives.

Thousands of participants of the You and Money Course have contributed to clarifying the concepts and insights contained here. For years this work has spread by word of mouth. In a leap of faith, Tami Simon from Sounds True, the premier purveyor of transformational tapes, provided national exposure to these ideas by producing the Energy of Money tape series. Jennifer Woodhull, Sounds True talent scout and producer, made the introduction. I met Jennifer at a Pema Chödrön meditation retreat. I went to the Sounds True studio and sat for three days in a small sound recording room, while food was shoved under the door. Tami's skillful questioning allowed me to take the You and Money material more into its present conceptual framework.

Tami introduced me to Kim Witherspoon, an intrepid and persistent agent, who decided to take me on. I am so grateful. Tami was right: she is one of the most brilliant people around. Thanks to her and the staff at Witherspoon Associates, Gideon Weil and Josh Greenhut, for holding my hand through the process of negotiating our way with publishers to a final contract with Ballantine. Thanks also to my literary attorney, Laurie Emerson, who looked out after my interests every step of the way.

I couldn't have asked for a better editor than Leslie Meredith at Ballantine Wellspring. The project was on such a tight timeline. We laughed, gasped, worried, and rejoiced together. And always she had faith that we'd get it done. She kept me going. Cathy Elliott, her assistant, was always available for my concerns and questions.

Thanks to Rhoda McKnight and Margarita Camarena for their generosity, creativity, and persistence in working on the illustrations.

This book and the You and Money work has gotten a lot of spiritual support. Thanks to Reverend Wayne Manning, Reverend Mary Tumpkin, Reverend Diane Sickler, and Reverend Shay St. John. Special thanks to my best friend, Reverend Beth Ann Suggs, who has always helped me to keep true to my spiritual center.

Three people helped me write this book: Rita Saenz, Carol Costello, and Donna Frazier. First, I want to thank Rita. She has been my business partner for twenty-two years and has held my kite string. None of this work would have been possible without her brilliance, courage, compassion, and faith in me. She has always known who I am, even when I forget. She is a true manifestation of abundance in my life.

Carol Costello, editor extraordinaire, incisive writer, true friend, gifted thinker, helped bring precision to this manuscript. She jumped in with a gentle hand, helped me separate everything that the book was *not*, thereby leaving the principles in their pristine form.

Donna Frazier, editor on the first phase of this book, helped me give it form. Her consistency, creativity, and guidance were invaluable in helping me clarify the Twelve Principles.

There would also have been no book without the support of people who were eager to lend a hand in a compassionate and empowering way. First, Charlotte Higgins, a busy author, actor, and playwright, and coach, helped me keep my promises in writing this manuscript, and never gave up on me. Wendy Jordan, through her generosity, has continued to support this work. Thanks to Sharon Taymor for enthusiastic encouragement in getting this book published. I deeply appreciate Lori Pelliccia and Walter Steinlauf for all the time they put into reasearch and copyediting for the book. My deep gratitude to all the Sacramento, San Francisco Bay Area, and Austin You and Money coaches for all they've done to keep this work going.

Finally, to my family, who has always sustained me, I owe a debt of gratitude. Thank you for your love: Aunt Gloria, Uncle Arnold, Lisa, Chuck, Rachael and Bea Simon; Susie and Andrea Saenz; Bruce, Judy, Margot, and Natalie Parks; Nancy and Robert DeCandia; Toni and Jerry Yaffe.

INTRODUCTION

Money is an uncomfortable subject for most of us. Many people would rather talk about their sex lives than about their bank balance. We love money, and we hate it. We can't live with it, and we can't live without it. Money can be a source of great joy and creativity, or it can bring frustration and misery, depending on our relationship with it. And we bring all these doubts and fears, hopes and expectations with us every time we deal with money—not just when we visit a financial planner or a loan officer, but in every area of our lives.

Money touches almost every aspect of living: work, leisure time, creative activities, home, family, and spiritual pursuits. Everything we do and dream of is affected by our relationship with this powerful form of energy. Whether your dream is to travel around the world, pay for a house, establish a food bank, buy a Corvette, get out from under a mountain of debt, or take a year off to write a novel, that vision is intertwined with the possibilities and pitfalls bound up in the energy of money.

This very discomfort is what makes our relationship with money such fertile ground. Whatever is potent for us, whatever elicits strong emotions, whatever seems to "hold on to us" in life has the power to bring forth our greatest strengths and most remarkable qualities. Our relationship with money calls on us to wake up, to see how we are handling *all* kinds of energy—not only money but time, physical vitality, enjoyment, creativity, and the support of friends—and to use those lessons to enrich every aspect of our lives.

THE HERO'S JOURNEY

In my twenty-five years as a clinical psychologist and seventeen years of leading the You and Money Course, I have been inspired by how willing people are to learn and apply these lessons in ways that enrich their own lives and contribute to others'. In fact, I have come to see our relationship with money as a hero's journey. It is a path fraught with trials and triumphs, tribulations and treasure.

The hero's journey is often thought of as a classic "coming of age" story. We all undergo such a journey, consciously or unconsciously, in our individual lives. And we all go through the same basic stages of this journey as we undertake new pursuits and goals throughout our lives: we depart from our familiar routines, lives, or families; we enter into unknown territory where we encounter fears, mysteries, dragons, and mentors; we are initiated into new understandings, pursuits, or skills; and, finally, we gain mastery over our newfound skills, ourselves, and our particular part of the world.

The hero's journey calls on us to bring forth the power of "being," which *Webster's* defines as "the complex of spiritual qualities that constitutes an individual." In working with the energy of money, we think of our being as that ineffable, indescribable part of us that remains constant and courageous, regardless of what is happening around us. The power of being emerges in moments of extraordinary insight or heroism. It is our authentic self, the essence of who we are, apart from our personality traits or the drama that sometimes surrounds our lives. The hero strives to bring the qualities of being to whatever he does, including his relationship with money. Working with money from the source of your true being will give you power and ease and a sense of interconnectedness.

The main goal of the hero's journey is to make your dreams a physical reality—and to learn from all the challenges along the way. In doing this, we see and appreciate our own true nature more clearly—which is where our dreams come from—and we share ourselves and our accomplishments as a contribution to others. I believe that this is the purpose of being human.

In this book, you will discover that you are a hero—and you will start bringing those natural strengths and virtues to your relationship with money. You'll be able to do the things you've always wanted to do, and bring forth and refine—or redefine—your purpose in life.

We will lay out the exact route to a powerful relationship with money. You will see how to bring your goals and dreams into physical reality, and how to ground them in the Life's Intentions and Standards of Integrity that reflect who you really are. Ultimately, this book is about the richness and fulfillment of living life as a hero's journey.

In the You and Money Course, I've coached more than 4,500 people toward breakthroughs in their relationship with money. One by one, I've held each person's hand as he or she stood in front of a group, took a deep breath, and began talking about his or her money life and monthly take-home pay. This was desperately uncomfortable for some, but these people had a vision for themselves. They realized that they had achieved certain goals, and some had come a long way from where they began, but they also sensed that something was keeping them from going further. They all had intentions and dreams, and the desire to know that they had made a difference. They had inner Standards of Integrity, even if they had temporarily lost sight of them, and they were willing to experience the momentary discomfort of revealing themselves and their concerns to the group if it might help them experience miracles.

I have worked with people in every walk of life, wealthy men and women and those on welfare, as they grappled with their relationship with money. I saw them look at how they had been "shooting themselves in the foot," at where they had stopped themselves in the past, and at what they could do to keep moving forward toward their goals and dreams despite great discomfort.

I saw these people succeed at bringing their dreams into reality with ease and joy—building a business that contributed to the community, getting their pilot's license, having an art exhibit or publishing the book they'd always wanted to write, taking their children on a vacation, being a successful entrepreneur. Finally, I watched them see themselves clearly, sometimes for the first time, and experience themselves as courageous, wise, loving, powerful, and compassionate individuals who had learned to release and use the energy of money.

This journey always began with being willing to look within, and then to bring forth into physical reality that which had heart and meaning. These people have inspired me, and shown me what was important in my own life. They have also pointed me to certain questions, and one of these is: Why is it that we don't use all the information and resources available to us to achieve what we want in life?

KNOWLEDGE + WISDOM = POWER

Today, we are surrounded as never before by all manner of information, knowledge, and advice—but something stops us from using it. Have you ever read a financial magazine or gone to a money-management seminar, but then didn't put all that good advice to use in your life? As one woman said, "I have some of the world's greatest money books sitting on my nightstand gathering dust. I wish I could close my eyes and absorb them all through osmosis or something. I never seem to do anything with the information."

Acquiring information and advice about how to manage or invest our money is easy. The trick is to act on the information, to do something that improves your life and the lives of those you love. That's what wielding the energy of money is all about. The woman with the stack of unused budget and investment books was not experiencing a powerful relationship with money. Her situation had nothing to do with her skills, talents, ability, or intelligence. It had everything to do with her own personal money obstacles—obstacles that she eventually cleared away using the principles in this book.

If you could take all the information available and put it to work in your life—if you could translate all that knowledge into behavior—would you do it?

All of my work as a clinical psychologist and in the You and Money Course has been aimed at giving people the tools both to use all the information and knowledge available, and to access their own inner wisdom—because I believe that *knowledge plus wisdom equals power*.

USING THE ENERGY OF MONEY

To use the energy of money successfully, you need to operate in both physical reality and the metaphysical reality made up of, among other things, dreams, visions, and your Life's Intentions.

Our inner visions inspire us, but we can't be content merely to "metafizzle" our ideas without taking any action in the real world. I can dream forever about taking a trip to Paris, but nothing will happen until I call the travel agent, book a ticket, go to the airport, and gather the funds to pay for all this. If I don't do these things in physical reality, that goal of a Paris trip will languish on my "wish list" forever, the subject of endless talks with friends and perhaps even discussions of how I limit myself. Psychological insight, positive thinking, and reading travel brochures may help me clarify what I really want, but only the energy of money will help me get on the plane.

How do I make it happen with ease? And how do I apply the lessons I learn in my relationship with money to all other areas of my life? That is the subject of this book.

I promise that when you learn to work freely and easily with the energy of money, your life will become what psychologists and counselors call "intentionally" satisfying. You will know precisely what you want, what brings you joy and meaning, and you will see how to get it with ease. It will not be a hit-or-miss proposition. For example, when you understand your true Life's Intentions, apply your personal Standards of Integrity, and learn to release the energy of money within your company, you will do business differently and probably with greater success. You will make the important decisions in your life consciously, never again abandoning your dreams by default because you "can't afford them."

In these pages, I won't be telling you how to invest your money, or where to put your savings. Instead, I will help you clarify what you really want out of life and give you the tools to act powerfully when you use money to move toward those dreams.

MY OWN STORY

If you had asked me to talk about my relationship with money seventeen years ago, I would have been mortified. That year, I gambled and lost. I invested $35,000 on an unsecured promissory note to a man I had known for six months. It wasn't even my own money. I had borrowed it from a family member.

The man to whom I loaned this money promised I would get a 30 percent return on my investment. The money was supposed to be used to make short-term loans to buyers who needed to close real estate escrows. It was a fraud. There were no escrows, and within a few months all the investors lost everything.

Like many of you, I had read investment books and attended

money seminars. I had a financially sound private practice as a clinical psychologist. But in the case of this $35,000 investment, what I knew didn't influence my behavior.

When I lost the money, I felt terrible. I have since repaid my relative, but at the time I still felt stupid. It was bad enough to have lost the money, and equally humiliating not to have listened to my friends, who told me to reconsider, that the deal sounded too good to be true. And worst of all was a haunting memory: just as I was about to sign my name to that $35,000 check, I distinctly heard a small voice—my internal voice of reason—say, "Don't do it!" Did I listen? No.

I hoped no one would find out what had happened. I thought that for the next several months, I could just hide in my office, make lots of money, and hope my friends would forget to ask me about my investment. However, Fate had other plans for me. Two weeks after I discovered my money was gone, I got an unexpected phone call from a local newswoman.

"Dr. Nemeth," she began, "the university gave us your name because you're an associate clinical professor there. We know you're a psychotherapist, and I need your help on an article I'm writing for the *Sacramento Bee*."

Now, as many of us would, I found her inquiry a great boost to my shaken state of mind. Here, at last, was a chance to recoup some of my lost self-esteem. After all, I was still a competent psychologist!

"Yes, I'd be glad to help in any way I can," I said with my most dignified, yet humble, professional voice.

"Well, you may not be aware of this, but Sacramento has been having a run of investment frauds lately. I'm doing an article on it. We need to know if there is any type of personality or character flaw that allows people to get taken in these schemes. You must see lots of these types of people in your practice. What exactly is wrong with their thinking process?"

Oh, my God! I was caught! At first, I wanted to say that I was way too busy to talk. I wanted to hang up the phone before she asked another question. I saw my reputation going down the drain. But the worst was yet to come.

I'm an extrovert. In order to know what I'm thinking, I have to hear myself say it. So, before I knew it, I heard the following words slipping out of my mouth: "*I was one of those people!* I lost $35,000 on that scheme!" I stared into the receiver, feeling my heart going right down through those little black holes. I was horrified.

After a long pause, the reporter asked kindly, "Are you sure you want to tell me this? Do you really want me to print this?"

As I regained my breath, I considered her questions. She might as well, I thought. Maybe others can learn from my mistakes.

At one point, the reporter tried to find excuses for my actions. "He played upon your trust and relationship with your friends who were also investing," she said.

"Well, maybe. But do you want to know the real reason I invested with him without reading the fine print?" By now, the relief from telling the truth was making me feel a little heady.

"Yes. Tell me," she gasped.

"It was greed."

The instant the words were out of my mouth, I knew it was true. Greed. Wanting to beat the system and make a quick profit. I hadn't listened to anyone who warned me about how risky the investment was. I had been blinded by the possibility of a fabulous outcome. I had not wanted to bother with the finer details, such as knowing the long-term track record of the company. I did not even ask to see the actual escrow papers of the deals I was supposed to be financing!

The reporter's interview was lengthy. The article she wrote detailed how people from all walks of life can experience moments of money madness. Greed was the form this madness took with me.

Soon after the publication of the interview, my friends and colleagues started calling to reveal their own financial nightmares. They had stories of scams, bankruptcies, and unexpected losses. People told me about their spending binges, or how they hid money from their spouses. I heard stories of families being torn apart because some were left more money than others when their parent or loved one died.

People told me about goals they had abandoned. They spoke about dreams delayed or unachieved because of the fear of taking even the slightest chance with their money. A bank vice president told me about a couple who kept more than $250,000 in a low-interest, simple savings account because they were too afraid to invest in money-market certificates.

Soon I had a big file of personal stories that showed how upset we can get in our relationship with money. Some of the people who told the truth about their worries and difficult money experiences were bankers, real estate brokers, certified financial planners, and stockbrokers. These were individuals one would expect to know better. The truth was, they did know better. *Their knowledge was simply not getting translated into Authentic Action.*

A well-known financial consultant confided, "When it comes to other people's money, I know just what to do. But I can't follow my own financial advice. I'm like the child of the shoemaker going without shoes." I have since found that this is not an unusual experience, and it's especially difficult for those who are experts in financial fields. If their relationship with money is less-than-powerful, they worry that they are frauds. Nothing could be further from the truth! Interacting with the energy of money is an opportunity for all of us to learn lessons—no matter how much information we have. The trick is to identify and learn those lessons before they get bigger and more demanding.

I spoke with other people who, rather than having a disastrous relationship with money, were simply bored with the tedious predictability of their money lives. They made enough to pay the bills and make necessary major purchases. Their credit-card debt was too high, but they felt they would get around to paying it off—someday. Many of their goals and dreams had been delayed until their lives settled down—one day. This "someday/one day" mantra had captured their attention and was draining their creative energy.

THE YOU AND MONEY COURSE BEGINS

Prompted by everything I was hearing about people and money, I decided to start an informal workshop on money, scarcity, and abundance. Friends joined me. We set aside time when we could get together and focus on looking at our relationship with money. Eventually, these first efforts to bring clarity into our own lives evolved into the You and Money Course.

The first question we looked at was how to confront our unconscious beliefs and feelings about money. That's a paradox, because if it's unconscious, how do you know what to confront? We plunged right in and began by asking, "What don't I want to look at regarding me and money?"

Old fears, unfulfilled dreams, and financial mistakes took shape before us. Repeatedly, we faced the hard choice of telling the truth— or trying to look good. We found that relief and change came with telling the truth.

A competent administrator of a multimillion-dollar program confided, "It would be easier for me to fly to the moon than to balance my personal checkbook to the penny." Even as she said this, she began to notice other areas of her life that were out of balance and hadn't been "reconciled"—like her low energy because of chronic headaches and the fact that she kept putting off seeing her doctor. For another participant, balancing the checkbook was a piece of cake, but the thought of actually having fun with money while reaching satisfying financial goals seemed like a bad joke. And this lack of enjoyment seemed to be echoed in his personal relationships as well.

We discovered that money is so central to our lives that, whether we are rich or poor, we have a relationship with it as soon as we are old enough to count. Money provides us with security, stability, a way to take care of our families, make a contribution, and have fun. These are some of the same reasons we seek relationships with other people. As in our relationships with loved ones, we often get mired in anxieties.

One woman laughed and said, "My relationship with money is like a one-night stand—here today, gone tomorrow, and it doesn't even know my name."

"I don't have enough money" was a common thread running through most of our discussions. Money was frequently named as the number-one cause of stress. (In 1996, a Louis Harris and Associates survey for the Lutheran Brotherhood found that one-third of the adults who responded said they have trouble sleeping or relaxing because of financial anxieties. Decisions they had delayed because of financial obligations included: buying a house, changing careers, having children, and getting married.)

Almost everyone's solution to the money problems they were having was simple: "Just give me more money. Then things will get better for me."

I even talked with people who questioned whether they had the right to continue living if they couldn't afford to meet their basic needs. Others believed that winning the lottery could solve all their problems. Some worried that their desire for money conflicted with their spiritual beliefs. Many felt victimized or helpless, as though money were an outside force controlling their lives. They felt they would never be free of its tyranny.

As each of us looked at our own particular brands of money madness, telling the truth to ourselves and one another, an unusual phenomenon occurred. We all felt that, suddenly, we had more breathing room in our lives. What we genuinely wanted in life became more clear. We also gained the fortitude to pursue goals that had seemed impossible. This happened no matter how old or young we were, or what shape our finances were in before the seminar.

BREATHING ROOM

Let's talk about breathing room for a moment, since you'll be hearing that term used frequently in this book. When we talk about money, many of us feel jammed up against life, as if our face is being pressed against a pane of glass. We feel pressured or blocked, and wish we could just get away from this particular subject. It is as if we had a weight on our chest that kept us from breathing easily.

If you want to test this for yourself, think for a moment about this question: "Do I have enough money?" Ask the question aloud to yourself three or four times. Where does your body register a reaction? Maybe in your stomach? In your chest region? At your throat? Not much breathing room, right?

Breathing room occurs the moment you get into what I call the *observational position.* From this vantage point, you feel space between yourself and what you are experiencing. It happens when you tell the truth about something that's been bothering you. If you pay attention the next time you do it, you may find yourself automatically taking a deep breath. You calm down. You are not so upset. In that moment, you might even see options for action where previously there seemed to be none. The program you're about to follow in this book is specifically designed to give you this kind of freedom. Breathing room brings clarity and creativity to your relationship with money.

Breathing room occurred for Dorothy, who took the You and Money Course a few years ago. She was in her seventies, a retired librarian who had given up her cherished dream to join the Peace Corps and teach English in a faraway place because she thought she was "too old." In addition, she was worried about leaving her grown son, who had special needs and required care. After she faced and told the truth about these concerns in the course, she saw that her own hero's journey was far from over. Dorothy made appropriate financial arrangements for her son, applied to the Peace Corps, and was accepted. Not long after the last meeting of her group, I received a postcard from Sri Lanka, where she was organizing libraries and teaching English as a Second Language.

Another woman, Jane, had a successful restaurant in California. She wanted to expand, but never seemed to have the impetus or wherewithall to do so—and it was becoming a problem for her. In the You and Money Course, she saw that one of her practices was to pay some of her servers under the table, not declaring them as employees for state workers' compensation. She wasn't paying them any more or less than she paid other servers, but she was trying to escape paying withholding taxes. Jane saw in the course what a drain this practice was on her energy. Not only was it not a sound business practice, but it also went against what she knew to be right.

In the course, she told the truth about it and got some breathing room. She didn't *like* telling the truth about it, but she did. She then took action and made the situation right. She put all her employees on the payroll officially. That gave her a clean slate to see what it really took to run her business, and the restaurant prospered and expanded. This simple shift to telling the truth was powerful for Jane.

I am not the ethics police, and I don't tell people what the rules are. The purpose of this work is for you to discover your own rules, the rules that you've always had, the rules that are reflections of your being. When you don't operate in accordance with those rules, you don't have any breathing room. Jane found that bringing her business practices into alignment with her own rules not only made her feel more whole but made her business prosper.

Doris also experienced the benefits of breathing room. She was the East Coast representative for a major manufacturing firm that had a very popular product. The company wanted to get information on it out very quickly—and in the rush, Doris dropped some details and a fancy brochure was sent out with erroneous information on it. Reprinting the brochure would cost a fortune, but because of the nature of the information, the company would face legal problems if the brochure was not corrected.

Doris's breathing room came when she saw that she'd been so driven that she hadn't attended to the details. Ordinarily, she would have rushed to do another brochure immediately, but she realized that in that panicky state, she might have gotten other information wrong. When she was able just to sit and observe the situation and her reactions to it, instead of rushing ahead to do the same thing she'd done before, she had some breathing room to develop a better strategy, and it worked.

Graduates of the You and Money Course have freed themselves from crippling debt, built successful businesses, purchased dream homes, and written screenplays. They have located and accomplished their hearts' desires, and so can you.

The first courses, gatherings with friends who were willing to share their experiences with money, represented a turning point in my life. I clarified some of my own beliefs about money and got in touch with some hidden feelings about it. But there was more. When I saw how my own and others' lives were changing for the better, I felt that I had been given a life's purpose to fulfill. It was like being handed an invaluable gift. I could give my own life expanded meaning and purpose, and at the same time create a setting and provide tools that others could use to gain clarity and power with money. I wasn't the only one to be given such a gift. Others in these early groups found that they, too, were uncovering a deeper sense of purpose in their lives.

I offered the seminar outside my circle of friends, and it caught on. Within a short while there was a great demand for this work. Soon I was getting requests from other parts of the country, and within a few years I found myself traveling to other states. Today I am teaching these principles internationally.

The You and Money Course continues to evolve as courageous people step forward to unleash the energy of money in their lives. Each time we present the course, I am moved by how willing they are to be present to their lessons, and to contribute to the process and to those who come after them. Over time we have developed twelve guiding principles for this work.

THE 12 PRINCIPLES

The *Energy of Money* presents 12 Principles for personal fulfillment. Through them you will begin to develop mastery with the energy of money. You will uncover the hidden landscape of beliefs, behavior patterns, and habits that underlie and sometimes subvert how you use money and other forms of energy. You learn to unleash and focus the energy of money, how to express your Life's Intentions through meaningful goals, how to handle the difficulties that inevitably arise as you approach the border between dreams and physical reality, and how to live in forgiveness, support, and abundance.

Webster's Third International Dictionary tells us that a principle is a "general or fundamental truth; a basic or primary source of material or energy." A principle is not an action step that you do once, and then it's over. A principle is an ongoing guide for living. Each of these 12 Principles is designed to help you access your own inner wisdom, so that you move with ease and clarity toward your goals and dreams. The 12 Principles may surprise you, and some may even seem counterintuitive. But if you work with them, I promise you clarity and ease beyond your wildest dreams.

You may notice that these are universal principles for successful living, and you may be tempted to use them in areas of your life other than money. That's fine, but I suggest that you focus on your relationship with money, because doing so will give you the most measurable, immediate, and potent results.

The Principles are presented in four parts. Part One, "The Hero's Purpose," invites you to see how willing you are and have always been, define your Life's Intentions and Standards of Integrity, and develop goals that express who you are in your hero's heart. In Part Two, "Identifying the Inner Blocks to Progress," you will learn about Monkey Mind chatter, what scarcity really means, and how we waste the energy of money with driven behavior. Part Three, "Clearing the Path," is about releasing old beliefs, unleashing the energy of money through forgiveness, and making and keeping promises that move you along your path. In Part Four, "Staying the Course," you will learn how to deal with external obstacles to your goals, use the support of others to increase your ability to handle money energy, and embrace gratitude as the gateway to abundance.

A FINAL WORD

In coaching people along their paths, I have found that money is neither spiritual nor nonspiritual. It's simply energy. It is here to be used wisely, consciously, and with enjoyment. In our culture, there is much discussion of whether you can be on a spiritual path and still have money. Of course you can! The question is: *What are you using the money for?* Does it further your Life's Intentions? Are you contributing to the lives of others? Does it bring lasting satisfaction, or are you using it for instant gratification because your life is off-kilter? These are the questions that bring clarity to your hero's journey, and they are the questions we will explore in this book.

One more thing before you begin the first chapter: To get the most from this book, be sure to keep a notebook or journal to take notes and do the exercises. Keep a record of the journey you are about to take. Your notes may become your own private seminar. You may also decide to read through this book with friends, and to support one another as you engage in the exercises. If you do either of these things, you will follow in the footsteps of the You and Money graduates who have turned their dreams into realities.

Congratulations! In reading this book, you are taking a big first step. I applaud how willing you are to embark consciously on the hero's journey, and I wish you well along the way.

WHAT IS THE ENERGY OF MONEY?

Imagine being able to approach your finances with a sense of optimism, clarity, and openness, instead of dread. For seventeen years I have traveled around the country coaching people who have not been able to do or get what they want and shown them how they could become successful; and I have coached successful people to become even more so. By "successful people," I mean people who have succeeded in using money to realize their hearts' desires as well as people who have used money to become comfortable or wealthy personally and professionally.

These successful people with whom I have worked do not have any particular natural aptitudes or attributes that set them apart from other people whose dreams have never materialized. The successful people do have one learned skill that distinguishes them from those who don't succeed. It is this: *they have learned how to handle energy.*

WHAT MAKES PEOPLE SUCCESSFUL?

Successful people know how energy works. They know how to focus the various kinds of energy—money, time, physical vitality, creativity, among others—to convert their ideas, dreams, and visions into reality. And they know how to do this with ease. They have realized their particular dreams, gone through their personal challenges, vanquished their individual dragons or fears. While they may not always be successful in their ventures, in general they have mastered how to use energy, and particularly how to use the energy of money. I consider these people heroes, for, to me, the hero's journey is to use energy consciously to make goals and dreams real in the physical world.

It is a heroic task to keep moving forward in the face of all the thoughts, feelings, self-judgments, and assessments that we attach to money. It requires courage and creativity and a genuine longing to express who we truly are in the world.

In *The Hero with a Thousand Faces*, Joseph Campbell, the noted mythologist and philosopher, describes the hero's journey. During our life's progress, as with every hero's quest, we have to suffer certain losses, leave the predictable comforts of our home, and set out into unfamiliar terrain to realize our dreams and goals. Along the way, the hero inevitably meets with dragons that block the way. Usually, his or her quest takes the hero into dark places to do tremendous battle with unseen forces for hidden treasure. Out of these struggles the hero emerges with a grail or jewels or wisdom that he shares with others.

It is his or her contribution to others and to the larger world that makes the hero into a hero, for the ultimate task of the hero is to bring knowledge, energy, and power back to the people he or she loves and to share it with them. Each of us has unique talents to contribute to the world, and we make our contribution by turning our individual dreams—the ones that truly excite and inspire us—into reality. Our task may be to nurture a family or to create a business that helps a community thrive. Whatever the vision that calls to us, accomplishing it is a heroic mission.

When we are engaged in that mission, when we know that we are making a larger contribution, when we know that our personal goals are also helping our business succeed, or when we know that being financially successful will also put our children through college, we are using the energy of money heroically.

This chapter gives you a map of the hero's journey on which you will embark to learn exactly how to master the energy of money. You'll learn what heroes do, what their challenges are, where they learn their lessons, and how they wield energy to bring forth their goals and dreams.

You will see that you are a hero, as well.

Actually, you will begin pretty immediately to see that you already have all the qualities and abilities you need to use the energy of money to make your dreams come true. This kind of mastery requires no special talents or intelligence. You don't even have to rid yourself of fears, doubts, and worries.

We are all born with the ability to bring our dreams into reality. In fact, this ability may be our best evolutionary tool. We humans don't have the fur, fangs, fleetness, or fighting capacity that helped many animal species survive and thrive—but we do have the ability to focus our consciousness on an idea, then translate that idea into an actual form or a behavior that enables us to protect ourselves, remove ourselves from danger, or make our lives easier. We can make ideas into physical reality.

We do this all the time, but many of us don't do it consciously. Successful people, however, are *conscious conduits* of energy. In general, they behave according to twelve principles that free up energy in their own lives and in the world. This book will tell you what these principles are and how you, too, can use them. It will help you become conscious of the energy of money in your own life, which increases your money power—and your own personal power.

YOUR MONEY IS YOUR LIFE

Joseph Campbell said, "Money is congealed energy, and releasing it releases life's possibilities." We can hold money in our hands, touch it, feel it, and use it for any purpose we choose.

Try this exercise. Take out a dollar bill and hold it for a moment. Imagine everywhere this dollar bill has been, and everywhere it will be going. Think about the people who have held this dollar bill, and what they have used it for. Think of the people who will hold it in the future, and what they will use it for. This bill may find its way into the hands of a mother who needs one more dollar to buy her kids the food they need. Or it could transport a businessperson in a taxi on the way to make a deal that will provide jobs to thousands of people. Or it could become part of a down payment on a first home, a car, a dream vacation. Do you sense the energy? The energy of this single dollar can flow from your hands into many people's lives.

We live in a universe made up of energy and surrounded by energy. Because we all share in the universal energy that unifies us, no compartment of life is shut off from another. The smallest parts of life and matter reflect the properties of the universe as a whole. Physicist David Bohm called this the holographic universe: every aspect of our lives has a reflection in every other aspect. This means how you do money is how you do life. Our relationship with money is a metaphor for our relationship with all forms of energy: time, physical vitality, enjoyment, creativity, and the support of friends.

These energies empower our lives. Without any one of them, life becomes difficult. But improving the flow in any one of these forms of energy usually makes our lives easier. You will discover how interdependent these forms of energy are as you do the exercises in this book. Your money breakthroughs will be echoed in your personal life; in your health, which will improve; in your creative energy, which will also increase; and in your relationship with time, which will be friendlier, easier. When you learn to use money energy, you can use *any* form of energy with ease.

Think about it for a moment.

• Do you ever have enough money? (Do you have enough time? Physical vitality?)

• Must you hoard money to feel secure? (Must you reserve your support of others in order to feel safe?)

• Do you waste your money? (Do you fritter away your time?)

• Do you know exactly how much money is in your checking account right now? (Do you have an accurate picture of your current physical health?)

One of the purposes of being human is to wake up and become conscious. Traditionally, the pursuit of consciousness has been done on solitary retreats or meditations, which is certainly an important and valid pursuit. But what if waking up really means seeing how to conduct yourself powerfully in your everyday, regular life in the real world? The congealed energy of money gives us that opportunity. When we know, for example, exactly how much we spend on "incidentals" every week, or how much money is in our wallet at any given moment, or what our monthly take-home pay is, to the penny, we demonstrate in a concrete way that we have mastered the conscious use of energy.

You may flinch at the feelings that come up when you answer such questions, or blanch at the notion that the way you handle your finances gives a true reflection of who you are. But I encourage you to keep your eyes open as we go along, no matter how uncomfortable it may be to look at tough issues like debt or fear or unsatisfied desires. I know it's not easy to talk or think calmly and consciously about money. As we go through this process, I encourage you to jot down in your notebook any feelings that come up or realizations that you have. Later we'll return to these initial observations and see how much your attitudes have changed.

THE MONEY TABOO

If successful people are those who understand how to use the energy of money, and if our relationship with money is a metaphor for our relationship with all kinds of energy, then why aren't the 12 Principles of money energy better known?

The main reason is that talking about money is desperately uncomfortable for most of us. I learned that discussing money was taboo at age seven, when my cousins came over for dinner. I wanted to sound grown-up, so I asked my grown cousin Irwin, "How much money do you make?"

Everyone stopped talking. It was alarming, given the usual noise level at our dinner table. Mother looked at me, clearly embarrassed.

"Maria," she said sternly, "that's something you should never ask people."

All the adults laughed. Me? I had just learned something important about money: it is too personal to talk about. You may have had a similar experience as you were growing up. That's one reason it's sometimes uncomfortable to wake up to our relationship with money. We have to violate the taboo. But if we take the leap and start asking ourselves some questions about how we relate to money, we might discover how we use it to further or frustrate our dreams, or to define our worldview. In doing this, we begin our personal journey toward consciousness. With this consciousness comes clarity, focus, and the ability to accomplish what we genuinely want in life, for ourselves and for others.

What is my relationship with money? How well have I used its energy? How is this a mirror for the way I handle other forms of energy in my life? These may be the most important questions you will ever ask. When you know the answers, your path to a fulfilled life will become clearer, as if a knowledgeable, kindly guide had forged ahead of you into the wilderness, clearing a road just for you.

The rest of this chapter describes that path.

METAPHYSICAL AND PHYSICAL REALITY

We've said that the hero's journey involves using the energy of money to bring goals and dreams into physical reality. The diagram below is a map of that process. Let's look at it, one element at a time.

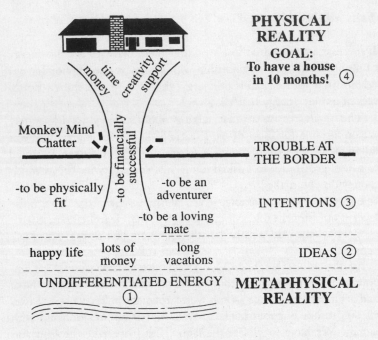

Let's suppose that reality as we know it is divided into two parts. One aspect, the top portion of the diagram, is called *physical reality*. In this realm, energy is coalesced into objects that have form, density, and size. You can see, taste, feel, or smell these things. You can measure them and observe that they are subject to the constraints of time and space. One law of this domain is impermanence: things grow, die, and are replaced. Change is the unalterable norm. To move or change objects in this domain, you have to focus energy on them. For instance, your lawn doesn't get mowed simply by your dreaming about it; somebody actually has to push the lawn mower.

If you were to look at the physical domain from the perspective of physics, you might say this is the Newtonian level, where the laws of cause and effect seem clear. For example, everyone knows that if you hold a glass of water and then let it go, the glass will fall and shatter, splashing water everywhere. There is a sense of certainty in this linear connection between cause and effect, since you can predict at least some outcomes on the basis of prior action. Saving $30 a month will net you $360 at the end of a year.

Unfortunately for many of us, the simplicity and obviousness of the physical domain seems tiresome and pedestrian. Most people will agree that it's important to balance their checkbooks to the penny, but it's so booooring! If we were to look more closely, however, we might find that some of our most powerful lessons in life are those that, at least in the beginning, we considered mundane and somehow unworthy of our attention. We know we should fasten our seat belts, for instance, but it sometimes seems tiresome and stuffy. We think about the value of seat belts only when we see or hear about an accident in which people weren't wearing them. Even knowing how much we are owed in accounts receivable (or by our children) can seem nitpicky, but going numb or unconscious about this kind of information can be disastrous. "Small" and "mundane" things count for a lot in the physical domain.

A second aspect of reality (the bottom portion of the diagram) is called *metaphysical reality*. In this realm, energy has not been solidified into form. It is free-flowing and unbounded. Whatever exists here is intangible and cannot be measured by the usual physical means. This is the home of what early Western philosophers have called Pure Ideas. Elements in metaphysical reality are immune to the law of impermanence. As we experience this realm through our imagination, visions, and intention, we become excited at possibilities that don't yet exist in physical reality.

We can think of the metaphysical realm as having various layers of organization. At the deepest level, we find undifferentiated energy, or what metaphysicians have called Substance, or pure potentiality (see point 1 of the diagram).

We interact with this plane all the time, and the first forms that emerge are ideas (see point 2 of the diagram). An idea is like a dream or vision. It usually starts with words like "Wouldn't it be great if . . . I had all the money I needed . . . I didn't have to work fifty hours a week . . . we had a great sports program for the kids." There is a lightness to these ideas because the energy is still so free-form and fluid. This is the realm of brainstorming, when ideas just spark up in us. It's exciting and fun. These ideas don't have any promises attached to them yet; they are simply "puffs" of energy, starting to take form and floating around us as we think about them.

Every day, you and I go about the drama of giving physical form and density to the pure energy of our ideas. We do that through the creation of Life's Intentions, the third level of metaphysical reality, which is closest to the line between metaphysical and physical reality (see point 3 of the diagram).

A Life's Intention is a direction, aim, or purpose that comes from deep within us. It reflects who we are in our hearts and elicits an emotional response. Life's Intentions are things such as "I want . . . to be an author, to be a great mom, to be a healer, to be financially successful, to be a successful entrepreneur, to be a contribution to my community." We all have many Life's Intentions. They bring us closer to physical reality because they "tell" us where we might want to direct our energy. They are blueprints for where our energy will flow, and they act as "energy shunts" from metaphysical to physical reality.

Different "rules" apply in the physical and metaphysical domains. In the metaphysical realm, our cause-and-effect ideas about time and space don't apply. Things work more as they do in quantum physics. In the quantum realm, matter is made of both energy and matter, electromagnetic waves and particles. Energy and matter communicate with each other instantly, simultaneously, synchronously. Quantum physics can change our notion of the usual laws of cause and effect.

We experience the metaphysical realm in odd moments, as when you think about your favorite song, for example, then turn on the car radio and hear it playing. How did that happen? You couldn't say that your thought about the song actually caused it to be playing, could you? That would be superstitious. But what's going on here? It can be confusing. To deal successfully in the metaphysical realm, you need the ability to suspend logic.

Some of our biggest mistakes in life come when our minds try to make Newtonian-like rules about how the metaphysical realm affects the physical. They do not work. "Rules" such as "If I hold positive thoughts about prosperity, money will just start pouring into my life" are just too simplistic to work. This kind of thinking is "metafizzling."

The bottom line is that money exists in the physical domain.

Money doesn't come as the result of thoughts in the metaphysical realm; it comes as the result of *actions in the physical domain.*

Another mistake is to try jumping directly from the realm of Ideas ("Wouldn't it be great to have a sailboat!") to the goal of buying a sailboat—without first seeing what specific Life's Intention having a sailboat fulfills. It might be "to be an adventurer," "to be a master sailor," or some other Intention. Regardless of what it is, grounding your goals in specific Life's Intentions is important, because your Intentions are the blueprints for what happens in physical reality, the living spirit behind your goals and dreams. Your Life's Intentions keep you energized and focused whenever you encounter challenges on the path to your goals. They keep you heading in the direction of what has heart and meaning for you.

Those of us who "metafizzle" operate under the delusion that there is a cause-and-effect relationship, a linear causality, between what happens in the metaphysical and physical realms. We think, or hope, that if we think positive thoughts, positive things will happen to us in physical reality.

The more useful interpretation of the relationship between metaphysical and physical realities is that we can expend efforts in the metaphysical realm to *clear ourselves* to be available to what can happen in physical reality. Then we have to do the *footwork* in physical reality. We have to be willing to clear ourselves in the metaphysical realm by doing such things as letting go of limiting beliefs and knowing our true Life's Intentions, but then we have to get to work in the physical domain to produce the result.

Here's how it works. Barbara is a graphic artist. In doing this work, she realized that she had an old, limiting belief, a firmly held idea, that $500 was as much as she could ever charge for a project. She was willing to go beyond that belief, but she still had to make sales calls to potential clients who might have larger jobs, update her portfolio, and go meet with people to sign contracts for the work. She cleared herself in the metaphysical realm, then took action in the physical realm.

That is the essence of the hero's journey. In this book I will show you exactly how to clear yourself in the metaphysical realm so that you can take Authentic Action in the physical realm to manifest your goals and dreams. When you know how to do this, all the wonderful information and advice that surrounds us today becomes useful to you, because you're freed up to use your inner wisdom.

We are all happiest when we are demonstrating in physical reality what we know to be true about ourselves, when we are giving form to our Life's Intentions in a way that contributes to others. Each of the Principles in this book is designed to create this kind of opening. The Principles are not pieces of advice. They are guides for living, and for clearing your way to mastering energy. In each chapter there are ways to put the principles into practice, but these steps are just the beginning of a lifelong process in which these guidelines can help you live the life of your dreams.

GOALS: PROJECTING OUR LIFE'S INTENTIONS INTO PHYSICAL REALITY

How exactly do we know that we are manifesting our Life's Intentions, and how do we go about doing so? To know that we are manifesting our Life's Intentions, we need to see results in physical reality. If our Life's Intention is "to be an artist," we need to see a painting. If our Life's Intention is "to be a successful entrepreneur," we need to see the business and the books.

We propel our Life's Intentions into the physical realm by creating goals. A goal is, literally, a projection of a Life's Intention into physical reality (see point 4 of the diagram). It is a promise we make ourselves about how we will fulfill that Life's Intention. In this work, we use the dictionary definition of a goal: "an area or object toward which play is directed in order to score."

Without goals, our Life's Intentions remain unfulfilled, and unfulfilled Life's Intentions often result in frustration and resignation. Conversely, our greatest joy comes from achieving goals that have real meaning and heart for us because they are anchored in the metaphysical realm.

These are some goals, and the Life's Intentions that they manifest:

GOAL	INTENTION
to buy a house	to be financially successful
to climb Mt. Shasta	to be physically fit
to move into beautiful new offices	to be a successful entrepreneur
to take my kids to Disneyland	to be a great dad

Here's an example of how I have used goals. More than a decade ago, I was working as a psychologist at a hospital, and I decided to leave and start a private practice. The Life's Intention I wanted to fulfill was "to be a successful businesswoman," and my goal was to have thirty clients and one group within six months.

Now, being a psychologist had also fulfilled my Life's Intention "to be of service to others," but actually putting together my own practice was a business venture. I could see in my mind's eye how the practice would look, how much money I'd be making, how many people I'd be seeing each week. It was exciting to think about all the ways I could get my business off the ground.

TROUBLE AT THE BORDER

When I thought about starting my practice, I was "pumped" and ready to go. But something happened at the moment that I actually tried making the jump from the metaphysical—the world of ideas—into the real-life world of the physical plane.

I was immediately faced with decisions that weren't inspiring at all. I had to find an office, get an answering service, and get a business license. There were dozens of questions to answer: How was I going to find my clients? I couldn't just walk the streets of Sacramento suggesting that people visit me for consultations (I might have gotten myself arrested for that!), so I scheduled talks all over town to let people know who I was and that they could use me as a therapist. Some of my appearances were fun, but some were pure hell.

It was slow going. I'd promised myself that in six months I'd have a full practice, but when six months had passed, I was seeing a total of five people a week. That wasn't even close to the thirty people I'd counted on. I kept thinking, "Is this all I have to show for that tremendous investment of energy?"

On one level I was happy with the progress I'd made in my fledgling business. But I was also terribly disappointed with myself. I'd thought that it was going to be much easier to take my idea of the perfect private practice and put it into reality, and I couldn't figure out what I was doing wrong.

What I didn't know was that I was experiencing what I have come to call "Trouble at the Border." When you begin to move an idea from the metaphysical realm into physical reality, you must cross the Border between these two very different worlds. And at the Border, the inspiration and fun of the original idea encounters the energy requirement of physical reality.

Sometimes, encountering the Border between metaphysical and physical reality is a real shock. Energy in the physical realm is, extremely dense. It is a dramatic change from the fluid, loose, free-floating energy of the metaphysical realm. This change in density can be quite dramatic, as though you'd been standing on the shore of a beach, enjoying the sunshine, and were suddenly hit by a solid wall of ice-cold water.

At the Border, we may meet doubts and fears so strong that they seem to stop us in our tracks almost before our journey begins. We experience inertia. That happened to me when I was trying to find an office for my business. I looked everywhere. No luck. Nothing fit the picture of what my office should look like, and after a couple of weeks of searching, my enthusiasm for the whole enterprise seemed to die.

Suddenly I was completely uninspired by my dream of starting a solo private practice. It was taking too much energy in the form of time, physical vitality, and creativity, not to mention the money I wasn't earning during this search. Just at the point when I needed the energy to reach escape velocity and get going, everything became just too hard to do.

You may have experienced this same phenomenon when you've moved from the idea stage to the realm of schedules, resources, details, and people. Things don't always work out the way you'd hoped.

I know something now that I didn't know then: *Trouble at the Border is inevitable.* If you really recognize the truth of this statement, you can start to relax. There is nothing wrong with you or your dream. *Whenever* you bring a creative idea to the Border between metaphysical and physical reality, you will experience this energy shift. Everyone from Da Vinci, to Mother Teresa, to your uncle who never put his dreams on the line runs into the heavy, disheartening feeling that what they were about to do was much harder than antici-pated, and that it was taking more time, money, or stamina than anyone thought it would. Stories of Trouble at the Border abound in the biographies of successful inventors, researchers, movie directors, and entrepreneurs.

Physical science provides the perfect metaphor for Trouble at the Border: liftoff. We all know that a rocket burns most of its fuel during the first few moments of flight, as it overcomes inertia and the gravitational pull of the earth. That's what it's like for us as we launch our dreams into physical reality.

The Principles in this book will guide you in making your own journey from the metaphysical to the physical more exciting and productive. When the going gets rough, you won't need to lose courage, or to question your goal or the Life's Intention behind it. You won't have to try to muscle it through on your own. In fact, you may come to see that any distress you experience in the face of difficulty is a measure of your courage as you move outside your comfort zone. It's a sign of how much you're stretching beyond your present capacities or place in life. It shows that you are expanding both your skills and your strengths.

MONKEY MIND

In my early attempts to start a private practice, I was dealing not only with the greater-than-expected energy requirements at the Border, but also with a running commentary in my head, a little voice that provided judgments and critiques about my every action:

- "It wasn't supposed to be this hard."
- "Maybe now isn't the right time to be doing this."
- "If I were really meant to be doing psychotherapy, I wouldn't be having so much trouble."
- "I just know the universe is telling me something."

I now call this inner dialogue the Monkey Mind. The concept of Monkey Mind comes from Buddhism, which describes it as a self-criticizing aspect of our mind that swings us from doubt, to worry, and back to doubt. Monkey Mind chatters the most loudly when we threaten to change the status quo—even if the status quo is something we long to leave behind.

Monkey Mind is designed to solve problems, to expect danger, and to brace us for trouble. It's a kind of survival instinct, so it likes the familiar. It doesn't like change, it doesn't like to take risks, and it doesn't appreciate any steps we take toward the Border, because right across the Border is brand-new territory. Monkey Mind doesn't care if what lies in that territory is the goal that's closest to your heart. It's new, so it's off-limits.

In psychology, we might say that the Monkey Mind is a product of the frontal lobes, the place in the brain where problem-solving takes place. It's almost as if these lobes get startled into action when the energy requirements shift. They get loud and insistent, often calling for us to stay put.

In my case, when clients didn't show up in droves as I'd hoped, Monkey Mind had a compelling analysis: "See? I *knew* I wasn't going to make it in this field. I should have stayed at my steady job at Long Beach General Hospital. This is a disaster!"

Later in this book, we will look deeply at your own Monkey Mind conversations regarding money. Monkey Mind goes crazy when you think about money, and if you doubt this for a moment, notice your internal dialogue as you contemplate the following words: net worth, credit rating, retirement savings, credit-card debt. Breathe! I'll stop using those terms for now. However, once you see your particular medley of Monkey Mind symptoms, they won't surprise, deter, or frighten you when they appear. You'll be able to give yourself some breathing room and continue toward your goals.

In *The Tibetan Book of Living and Dying*, Soygal Rinpoche compares Monkey Mind with a beehive. He says we can easily provoke the bees into chasing and stinging us, or we can leave them alone. We have the same choice when it comes to our active mind chatter. We can stir it up by trying to analyze it, suppress it, or argue with it, which only makes it louder. Or we can refrain from turning our energy toward the mind in this way. If we turn our attention away from the chatter, Monkey Mind won't hinder us. The buzz won't go away, but it won't be aimed in our direction.

Successful people have learned not to poke at the beehive. They hear Monkey Mind reminding them daily, even moment to moment, of their doubts, fears, and worries, just like the rest of us. But they recognize that these anxieties are always going to be there when they're at the Border. They also see that Monkey Mind's activity is not relevant to who they are or to their aims in life. They focus instead on energizing their goals.

ENERGIZING YOUR GOALS

Have you ever found yourself in a flow of energy that was so creative, so productive and exciting, that you felt you could do what you were doing forever? You knew you were making something wonderful, that your work was superlative, that you were performing at your optimal capacity. You probably could feel energy moving through you and animating your efforts. I felt that way when I was a guide on an outdoor "ropes course" designed to help people confront and surmount their fears through rock climbing. I was on the belay team, holding the safety line for one of the events: the vertical rappel. Most of the participants had never done any form of strenuous exercise, let alone a sheer vertical descent down hundreds of feet of granite.

Many balked at the start. Some cried as they looked at the pine trees far below. All day we steadied the ropes for them. We directed the energy of support toward each person before us as he or she faced down the cliff. We cheered them on, assuring them that they could do it. And everyone went over the edge, energized by our encouragement. One hundred and ten people bounded down the wall that day.

That night, as people shared their experiences, one thing was clear: they had felt the vitalizing effects of our support. Many said it had made the difference in their completing the event. That was one of the first times I clearly felt like a conduit. Throughout the day I had felt as though the river of energy carrying people down the mountain had come not from me, but through me.

We all have the ability to connect with that incredible flow and direct it toward whatever we want to accomplish. When I say that our task as humans is to wake up and become conscious conduits for energy, I am being very literal: We are channels that move money and other forms of energy in the direction of our dreams so we can bring them to fruition.

The six primary forms of energy that we talk about in this work are:

Money
Time
Physical vitality
Enjoyment

Creativity
Support of friends

We use these forms of energy to energize our goals, to help them across the Border between metaphysical reality and physical reality. To develop my practice, I ultimately used all six. I invested money and time. I used physical vitality to stay healthy and keep up my stamina. I loved what I was doing and developed creative approaches to getting clients. I had the support of many friends who held my hand, gave me pep talks, and even referred friends to me.

How do we know when we are successful with our goals? In the You and Money Course, we say that "success is doing what you said you would do—with ease." I knew I had been successful with my practice when I had thirty clients and one group a week, and when I had done that with ease.

DOING LIFE THE EASY WAY

For many of us, doing what we said we would do is nothing new. The challenge for us is to do so *with ease*. When I say that success is doing what you said you would do, with ease, people's faces don't clench up until I get to "with ease."

I'd like you to take a deep breath right now and ask yourself this question: "Would it be all right with me if life got easier?" This is something I've asked myself for many years—and am still asking.

You might think that it should elicit an automatic "Yes!" But guess again! When I ask people, there is sometimes a moment of hesitation as the question sinks in. Perhaps we get used to doing things the hard way. Remember the slogan "No pain, no gain"?

Or we think that if we relax our guard, things will get worse. For example, don't you really believe, in your heart of hearts, that the best way to succeed is to do things on your own, without depending on the support of others? Haven't you thought that asking for help is a sign of weakness, that heroes don't ask for help? If you think of yourself as a loner, join the crowd! Most of us have been taught to be Lone Rangers, rugged individualists who are proud of our ability to tough it out. Doing it alone, depleting our energy instead of magnifying it by working with others, is definitely doing it the hard way.

We have a variety of ways to make life harder than it need be.

Sometimes we are afraid of failing, and worry that it means the end of the world. We've heard familiar sayings such as "If you are not failing, you are not aiming high enough," but we say to ourselves, "Yeah, sure! Whoever said that has never been in my position." So we go through life playing it safe, or taking it personally every time we do fail at something. The energy cost is tremendous as we divert the time and attention that could be energizing our dreams into concerns about failure. When fear of failure becomes a topic for the Monkey Mind, it can stop us in our tracks.

I am not recommending that you deliberately seek out failure or have a cavalier attitude about it. But becoming preoccupied or perfectionistic in an effort to avoid mistakes and never looking at failure as positive feedback is doing life the hard way. Failure-phobia can gobble up all the breathing room for creativity, spontaneity, and learning in your life. You become old before your time when you trade your dreams for illusions of security, huddling in your familiar huts and ruts forever, not venturing forth on your hero's path.

Helen Keller, blind and deaf from the time she was nineteen months old, said something that I have carried with me for the days when all I want to do is retreat into the simple security of no mistakes: "Security is mostly a superstition. It does not exist in nature, nor do the children of men as a whole experience it. Avoiding danger is no safer in the long run than outright exposure. Life is either a daring adventure or nothing."

Life is hard when you don't do what you truly value because you are putting all your energy into trying to get rid of your fears rather than into materializing your dreams. When you're stuck within your comfort zone, life becomes stifling—and therefore, very uncomfortable! In a paradoxical way, the easy life includes the experience of discomfort. It is when we try to avoid naturally occurring pain or discomfort that life becomes difficult.

DEALING WITH DISCOMFORT

Discomfort is a worthy companion at the Border. And anytime you examine the blocks and leaks in your life that dissipate your money energy, you're going to feel uncomfortable. In the You and Money Course, the director of a large county agency told me that she would sooner walk over hot coals than figure out how much she owes in back taxes. If this sounds silly to you, I guarantee that there is some aspect of your relationship with money that you have not looked at because it is painful for you. This is a natural response.

The key to an easy life is to learn to use fear and discomfort as teachers. Fear may be a sign for you to explore another path. Discomfort may indicate that you are at the edge of your predictable territory. Another woman in the You and Money Course reported these discomforts the day she promised to add up her credit-card debt. But instead of running back to a familiar place of avoidance, she faced the dragon and confronted a major block to her money energy—and as a result was able to free up more energy in her life.

Let me give you another example. Roger had a dream of opening a bagel bakery. He worked for a state agency and was comfortable in his job. But he had a vision of owning a bakery that made the best bagels around. He even visited Chicago and New York to check out the best bagel flour, one that had just the right amount of gluten.

When he came back home and looked seriously at opening his store, Roger panicked. Should he really leave a comfortable job with benefits and go out on his own? Maybe he should put off his dream until after retirement, seven years down the line. To cross these borders, he decided to look squarely at his fear and turn it into an ally. He brought in a friend to form a business partnership, and worked at the store himself only part-time at first. Roger also made sure he had the support of his wife and friends. Two years later, he left his regular job to open another bagel outlet, and both stores are doing well.

Roger's decision may not have worked for you and your dream. Only you can see what lessons are at your border. But everyone's decision requires that he or she be clear about what his or her choices are, and be willing to face discomfort and analyze its source.

DOING LIFE WITH STRUGGLE

The opposite of ease is struggle—not, as many think, working hard.

You can work hard with ease. Let's say you've decided to switch careers from architecture to fine art, and you're working on a sculpture. You have a vision of the shape you'd like the stone to take, and you set aside time to work on it, finding that you're engrossed and focused as you do the hard physical and mental work of chiseling and polishing. You spend hours on the project, but the time passes quickly. You may emerge hours later, having lost track of time, covered with marble dust but with a smile on your face. You're pushing your limits, but there's a sense of fun as you immerse yourself in the process of creating. You're working hard, but it's filled with a sense of ease.

The struggle occurs only when you begin to heed the Monkey Mind conversations that arise as you sketch out the project. You're energized by your vision and even buy a slab of marble, but as you begin, doubts and worries assail you: "Do I really have enough talent to do this right? Can I finish it well? I don't really have the time to do this now. How can I pull away from a well-paying job to do something frivolous like this? I must be nuts."

The more you dance with these conversations, repeating them, or even analyzing why you're feeling this way, the more your energy is sucked into fighting with Monkey Mind—*instead of sculpting*. You might postpone the project, deciding to wait until you feel comfortable before picking up the chisel. Or you may abandon your sculpture, and your dream, completely. This is true struggle.

Monkey Mind's chatter can be a siren's song. As we move toward our financial goals and dreams, we can lose ourselves if we listen to Monkey Mind telling us, "Next year, when things clear up, when I get my life together, then I'll go for it. There's just too much on my plate right now." I've found that things do not usually "clear up"—and that even if they do, something equally distracting generally takes their place.

Monkey Mind is not your cheerleader. It doesn't tell you, "Listen to those people who are encouraging you to take a risk. There's been a lot of care put into making this a safe ropes course. Go for it!" It won't whisper in your ear, "You *do* have what it takes to be financially successful! Just be willing to wake up and learn something new. You can do it!"

The hero's journey is not about abolishing Monkey Mind, because it will never really go away. It's always at the Border between metaphysical and physical reality. You don't cross the Border just once to manifest a Life's Intention in the form of a physical goal. This is an ongoing process for the hero, and Monkey Mind will be waiting for us each time we approach the Border. We will cross the Border often, and Monkey Mind will be there every time.

This is why we say that enlightenment may be nothing more than a simple shift of attention and energy, away from Monkey Mind and toward your goals.

TRAINING FOR SUCCESS

You cross the Border toward success when you take what I call Authentic Action—even as Monkey Mind continues to whisper in your ear. Authentic Action happens in physical reality, but it is aligned in metaphysical reality with your true nature. It reflects your true Life's Intentions. Authentic Action moves you closer to your goal—or cleans up a mess like back taxes so that you are free to move toward your goal.

Speaking engagements were Authentic Actions toward my goal of a successful practice. Getting a pedicure might have been a positive, nurturing action, but it would not have been an Authentic Action toward that goal.

When I say to take Authentic Action, I'm not saying, "Just do it!" Much of what we "just do" keeps us busy but leaves us spinning in place. If we want to give our dreams physical form, we must take actions that *focus* energy.

In each of the following chapters, you'll be asked to act on one of the 12 Principles that serve as guideposts for your journey. You'll know you've truly learned the energy lesson when you see the principle in action in your daily life. You are the gatekeeper who opens the way in front of you. Action turns the key to the next level of energy, and then the next. If you keep taking Authentic Action that reflects what you've learned, you will succeed.

Remember, success is doing what you said you would do, with ease. Period. Success shows up only in physical reality, through taking action. As my friend Reverend Johnnie Colemon says, "How do you spell success? W-O-R-K!"

You are being successful when you consistently keep your word over time. The promises don't have to be enormous. If you take on too much, you may scatter energy and deter yourself from demonstrating financial success. Most of us have to start small, gain confidence, and then make bigger promises. It's like weight training. You start out with very little weight, and add weight as you gain strength. Start by learning to make small promises—and keep them. When you do that consistently, over time, you can start making bigger ones. Meanwhile, you experience success at each level.

I always think of Sally, who had no idea what financial success meant when she came to the You and Money Course, but who learned to start small and get big. Sally told me, "I remember wanting to have a financial portfolio. But I was just off of welfare. No one in my family ever invested in anything. We didn't have the money. Then I thought: 'Okay, if being successful really means keeping promises over time, then what happens if, as a housecleaner, I save $100 a month out of my paycheck?' Well, I did that. At the end of the first year, I had $1,200 to invest, and I started the portfolio with some mutual fund."

I saw Sally two weeks after she made her initial investment. She was walking on air. She was so excited that she decided to save even more every month, starting with $150. Today she has a sizable portfolio. She is demonstrating what it is to be financially successful. Her self-esteem is way up.

Sally is a walking manifestation of an important lesson I learned a few years ago: *Don't wait until your self-esteem is high enough before you take Authentic Action. When you take Authentic Action, your self-esteem will rise naturally.* Sally is an example I use for myself whenever I'm tempted to doubt this.

The work we do together may be challenging or uncomfortable, and it won't always come at the perfect time for you—when there are no distractions or stress in your life. But if you stick with it and let me coach you in this, you will feel the lightness and relief that come from clearing away the obstacles that have stood between you and your heart's desire. The energy you'll unleash as you master each of the 12 Principles is the delight and satisfaction of seeing your dreams come true.

THE HERO'S CONTRIBUTION

It is challenging to face the "dark side" of how you handle money—or the doubts, fears, worries, and thwarted hopes that may appear. Sometimes it's hard to see the hidden treasure, but when we tell the truth about what we see, even when we don't want to see it, we're given even more strength.

In some early myths, the hero makes no attempt to slay the

dragon. He merely turns to face it, neither running from it nor fighting it, and sometimes even asks the dragon what it has to teach him. The dragon then becomes an ally that helps him along his path.

The heroic myth is enacted time and again in contemporary fiction and movies. In the *Star Wars* trilogy, for example, Luke Skywalker travels through all the stages described above as he learns to become a conscious conduit of energy—The Force. In the final scenes of *Return of the Jedi*, he at last throws down his sword and turns to face Darth Vader, saying, "I will not fight you, Father." His nemesis becomes his ally, and Darth Vader then saves Luke from the evil Emperor. Once more the dragon is transformed into a powerful ally, this time in the form of a loving father.

By facing the truth and making allies, we gain energy and power. By seeing and acknowledging difficulties, we enable ourselves to face our obstacles and attain our goals and dreams.

When we don't succeed, it is sometimes because our goals are not connected to our Life's Intentions, our Standards of Integrity, or our deep desire to contribute. They are not inspired by a larger purpose, and without that context we become myopic. We are uninspired. Our goals languish, and so do we.

To complete the hero's journey, we must awaken to our own power and potential to manage energy. By becoming more conscious of who we truly are and what we truly want in life, and by bringing those powerful metaphysical elements through Authentic Action into physical reality, we will discover our personal mission and simultaneously find happiness, success, and fulfillment.

The first step is fairly simple. You need to be willing to attain all this and to deal with any challenges in your way. In the next chapter you'll learn how to be willing and open your heart and mind to energy.

PART I

The Hero's Purpose

YOUR GREATEST POWER IS TO BE WILLING

Being willing is simply the power to say "Yes"—even in the midst of doubts, worries, fears, dislikes, objections, and all your Monkey Mind conversations. It gives you everything you need to develop a powerful relationship with money.

Being willing could be called the one true act of "being." It calls forth who you are in your heart and transcends the chattering of Monkey Mind. Being willing is your ticket to a life of creativity, power, and fulfillment. It will change the course of your life.

Sometimes we think that power comes with the ability to say "no," but it's actually the other way around. Developmental psychologists point out that "no" is the first word a two-year-old learns to differentiate himself from others, primarily from Mom. Some of us learn later in life to say "no" in an assertive way—and pride ourselves on doing it.

But the next phase of development for all of us is learning to say "yes" to whatever is on our plate, and realizing that everything we find in our lives today is here to wake us up.

WILLING VS. WANTING

You can be willing to do something you don't want to do. You can have all sorts of opinions and distracting thoughts and still be willing to take action when it's necessary. A pregnant woman does not want to go through the discomfort of childbirth, but she is willing.

You may not want to balance your checkbook to the penny, and it may even seem pointless to do so if you haven't balanced it in years. But the true power of the hero is unleashed when you say, "Yes, I'm willing to do it. I'm willing to wake up in any area where I may have been asleep, including this one." You can have all kinds of opinions about why it would be impossible for you to balance your checkbook, or why it's unnecessary to go to a financial planner or create a will, and still be willing to do so.

Just knowing that you are willing can energize you. When you are willing, you call upon something inside you that is enormously powerful and much larger than Monkey Mind. You tap into the core of your being. For many of us, gaining access to that core is an empowering and sometimes spiritual experience. And the more you operate from being willing, rather than from the surface complaints and nattering of Monkey Mind, the more conscious you become and the greater the transformations you'll have in your relationship with money and in your life.

We all have witnessed or heard about inspiring stories of people who are willing to do what they don't want to do. One example for me is Margaret, a computer programmer living in Silicon Valley. She had a home with an extra bedroom that she rented out to a friend. For months she collected the rent, pocketed it "under the table," and went about her business. She decided not to tell her CPA about this arrangement, because she didn't want to pay anything extra to the IRS. One day after the You and Money Course, she wrote me:

> MARGARET: I didn't want to report that income—but when I saw I could be willing to do what I didn't want to do, something shifted inside of me. I decided to report it after all, because it seemed like the right thing to do. The strangest part of this is that, after doing some simple calculations, my CPA determined that I'd actually get some income tax *deductions* by having this renter. I was going to get money back! By being willing to do what I didn't want to do for fear of *losing* money, I actually *made* money. But even more important, the moment I became willing to clean up my "money act," a big weight lifted off of me. Now it's clear to me that I'm willing to be financially successful with ease.

Successful people are willing. I have found that people who are successful are willing to look at the important questions and learn the important lessons that are before them. Such questions might include:

- What do I really want to do with my life?
- What do I really want to use my money for?
- What are the talents that I want to develop?

Successful people may not want to look at these kinds of questions. They may be afraid of what they'll see or what they'll need to do, but they are *willing* to look. They are willing to do what they don't want to do. They don't wait until they are in the right mood or until Monkey Mind quiets down—and that's what makes them so successful.

When we discuss Principle 9, I'm going to suggest that you write down any unfinished money business that occurs to you as you read, so that you can clear it up. This might include paying neglected loans, getting appropriate insurance, or making good on any promises you have made regarding money. Do you want to do this? Probably not. Monkey Mind will encourage you to skip this one. It will suggest to you that this is make-work nonsense. But despite not wanting to do such exercises, *are you willing?*

The answer to that question is either yes or no—not maybe or probably. Saying "yes" gives you power. It cuts off the alternatives. That's how being willing works. Are you willing to discover your relationship with money and to be successful at handling the energy of money? The answer is either yes or no. Listen beyond your Monkey Mind doubts and worries to the still voice within you. What do you hear?

BEYOND THE PSYCHOLOGICAL APPROACH

You may notice that I am not using the word "willingness." That's because willingness is something you *have*. It seems to exist outside of you. It is something you possess, not something you are. To be willing, however, is a state of being. It is something that exists inside you, and is part of you.

It is the difference between saying that I *have* something, which can be diminished or withdrawn, and depends on circumstances, and I *am* something. Would you rather *have* financial success or *be* financially successful? With the second option, you own the quality as something that you generate. It is part of who you are. It comes from your center, your inner core, your personal strength.

Fate can give you financial success when you win the lottery or pull the handle of a winning slot machine in Las Vegas. But to *be* financially successful takes qualities that endure whatever the external circumstances. That's why, when asked what would happen if they lost all their money, many people who are financially suc-- cessful say that they'd have it back in a few years. Lottery winners can't say that.

This distinction may seem trivial, but it is important because this whole book is based on a spiritual as well as a psychological approach. The spiritual approach is based on knowing our true being, on knowing who we are. Rather than probing and analyzing our thoughts and feelings, as a psychological approach does, the spiritual approach says, "Notice these thoughts and attitudes. They may never go away. They are part of being human. Don't analyze them, just observe them. We're going to move forward, whether they remain or not."

Many other books take only a psychological approach to financial success. They look at why you are doing what you are doing, and why you have the attitudes and thoughts you do. With a spiritual approach, you go beyond psychological interpretation. You observe how you have things hooked up within you. The operative principle here is that when you can observe something, it no longer has a hold on you. Nothing in this book, even the exercise in writing your money autobiography in this chapter, will ask you to analyze yourself. Instead the process of this book is designed for you to get a bird's-eye view of the whole terrain of your relationship with money so that you can see its richness. Seeing yourself is part of waking up, and that is the first step to mastering the energy of money.

Under some circumstances, psychological understanding can be an impediment. Some people can become so distracted by their own psychology that they never take Authentic Action to keep moving along the hero's path. Instead of just seeing, they get bogged down in the whys and wherefores of how they became as they are. Just take note of your thoughts, record them in your notebook, and move on.

The 12 Principles in this book will ask you again and again to go beyond your psychological processes and insights. When you have cleared yourself enough to be willing, you'll be better able to use all the information at your disposal to realize your goals and dreams.

All you really need is to be willing.

BEING WILLING COMES FIRST

The reason we put this Principle first is that being willing is your ticket of admission to the hero's journey. You cannot be on the hero's journey as a victim, as a martyr, or because somebody forced you to do it. You must be on that journey of your own volition. And nowhere in life is this more necessary than in your relationship with money, because money is an area where we often feel victimized and "made to do" things like balance our checkbooks.

The purpose of this book is for you to see how willing you are and have always been. I have seen that this is true of people in my work with more than 4,500 You and Money graduates, and you will see it about yourself by the end of this book.

We need the power to be willing when we look at our relationship with money because money is absolutely pervasive in our lives. And this relationship drives all of us a little crazy.

Being conscious of how we interact with money sounds straightforward enough: read the bills, look at the bank statement, and voilà! But the energy of money reaches way beyond our wallets and our checking accounts. It's so pervasive, in fact, that it's actually hard to see. We're so immersed in the culture of currency that asking us to look at our relationship with money is like asking a fish to look at the water it's swimming in. It seems almost impossible to remove ourselves to get an objective view of what we're actually doing with it. That makes being conscious about money quite a challenge.

So that you get a clearer picture of what I'm talking about, I'd like you to try a short experiment. For one twenty-four-hour period, carry a small notebook, and write down every time you think about money. Include everything: the ads you read in the morning paper, the number of times you hear commercials on radio or TV, the times your attention turns to ads on billboards as you drive down the freeway. Jot down times that you think about your salary or income, the times you sell something to a customer, the times you make a purchase, the thoughts you have about investing.

You might think this would be easy, but actually most people who've tried it have had to stop after just an hour or two—because otherwise, they'd have to put their lives on hold and write in that notebook nonstop. You will find that money is always right there in your face, or at least lingering at the periphery of your mind, demanding that you give it your attention.

Doing this experiment was enlightening for me. Between the time I got up and read about interest rates in the morning paper and the time I sat down an hour later to watch my favorite morning TV show, I had thought about money at least sixty times. I'd considered buying about forty different items, from a van to a special credit card, from joining a CD club to a Caribbean cruise.

Even more disconcerting was that I felt a perpetual tug—an urge to spend money I didn't have to buy something I didn't need. For most items, the impulse lasted about one minute before an inner voice said, "You really don't need that." But the truth was, I had *felt* I needed something—at least forty times. If you track the times you think about money in one hour and then multiply this by sixteen—the number of hours you are awake—you can get a sense of how much mental energy you pour into this phenomenon called money.

Notably, not a single voice in that morning cacophony ("Buy me! Spend me! You need me now!") urged me to step back, connect with my dreams, and direct my attention and money energy toward my genuine goals. Instead I felt buffeted, fragmented, and pulled among competing desires and demands. That same scattered feeling, and the confusion it creates, fills our lives unless we take steps to build a powerful and focused relationship with money. No wonder we have trouble sorting out what we want and where all our money energy is going!

Yes, we are crazy about money.

MONEY MADNESS

Much as we'd like to pretend that it doesn't happen, we all know that we get nuts around money, or even the promise of it. Remember when we talked about life being a hologram? You can just tell from the following stories that the person's money life is affecting everything else.

ALEX: I'm afraid to admit this, but I'm putting off trying for my goals and dreams until after my parents die, when I'll inherit the money they left me. Don't get me wrong, I love them. But I just realized that I have this thought in the back of my head that I don't have to look at my relationship with money right now, or pay down my debts. That one day I'll have lots more, and that will make everything all right.

CLAIRE: I have this need to give all my money away. It's like I don't deserve it, even though I work hard as a school administrator to earn it. Last year I cosigned and put a down payment on a car for my sister. Looking back, I see I insisted on doing this because I thought she really needed me to. Friends told me to let her figure out how to get the car for herself, since she's twenty-eight years old. But I didn't think she could do it. Anyway, three months ago we had a fight. She's not talking to me. She's stopped paying on the car, and it's showing up on my credit rating.

NAOMI: I hide what I buy from my husband. I love to shop. He says I spend too much on clothes. Well, I know what I want. I buy it, take it home, cut off the price tags, and put it on the top shelf of my closet. Six months or so later, I take it out. If he asks whether or not it's new, I can say "No" without lying. After all, I bought it quite a while back, didn't I?

All of us, at some time in our lives, have acted in bizarre ways where money was concerned. As Jacob Needleman, author of *Money and the Meaning of Life*, says, "We don't even know what it means to be normal with money."

Many of us begin acting crazily with money when we are very young. For example, when you were a child did you ever do something like eat a bug for a dollar? Steal money from your parents' wallets? Take candy, toys, or comic books from the market without paying for them? In your teens did you ever practice "mooning" from your friend's car, up and down your main street, because someone bet you $20 you wouldn't do it? If these examples do not sound familiar, I'll bet you can remember something similar! Just find that old videotape in your mind and play it back for a moment.

Even today, there may be something you would do for money

that would be totally out of character for you. Try the following thought experiment and see. The only requirement is that you tell the truth.

If someone offered you $10,000,000 cash, tax free, would you be willing to run down the main street of your city absolutely naked at high noon on a weekday?

If you are tempted to say "No" quickly, wait a moment. Imagine a suitcase filled with ten thousand $1,000 bills. Think about what you could do with that money. Now answer the question. If you still answer no, then think about something totally out of character for you that you would do for money.

Taking this a bit further, if you answered "Yes" to running naked, would you be willing to do this if someone offered you $1,000,000 cash? What if it were only $100,000? $10,000? Do you notice how your modesty and sense of reluctance increase as the amount of money decreases?

Of course, there are many things we would not do no matter how much money we were offered. But there are many things that the promise of money, or the threat of losing it, induces us to tolerate. Look at this for yourself:

• Are you hanging on to a job that is psychologically, emotionally, and physically draining because it provides you with good health or retirement plans (both of which you will need soon if you continue too much longer at this job)?

• Are you holding on to a relationship because it provides you with financial security, even though it is clear to both of you that separation would be the best for your emotional and spiritual well-being?

• Have you ever stayed awake at night, wondering where you'll get enough money to pay the bills, only to go out on a buying binge when some money finally does come in?

• What kind of decisions have you made in life because you thought that if you didn't say yes to something you didn't want to do, you wouldn't have the money you need?

These are tough questions to consider because they, too, reflect a potent form of money craziness. It is not easy to admit to ourselves that when presented with the question "Do you want joy and fulfillment—or would you prefer money?" we have often calmly answered, "I'll take the cash."

Is it any wonder that we want to change the subject when faced with the opportunity to get a true picture of how we're using money's energy in our lives? When the important questions come up, we may get tired. Or we'll have a sudden impulse to make those phone calls we've been putting off. Or we'll become consumed with "more urgent" questions like where to take a vacation or how to get higher interest rates on our savings or lower rates on our credit cards. These may be important tasks in their own right, but when they continually act to push us away from what we need to know, see, and do, they function just like the other distractions created by our Monkey Mind. They keep us stuck and unconscious, right where we are.

The central question is this: What exactly do you need to be willing to do in order to transcend money madness and Monkey Mind, and bring your goals and dreams into reality?

You need to be willing to take four steps. I've organized these four steps into what I call the Coaching Model.

THE COACHING MODEL

The Coaching Model is your key to being greater than your mental chatter, and having what you want in life even when Monkey Mind gets very loud. The four steps of the Coaching Model are:

- Look
- See
- Tell the truth
- Take Authentic Action

We will use this model repeatedly in the course of this book. It is one of the most powerful tools I can offer you. The more you practice these four steps, the more easily you'll proceed along your path toward your goals.

Take a moment now and write them in your notebook before we go any further.

Now let's look at the steps of the Coaching Model one at a time.

Step #1: Look

When you look at something, you direct your attention toward it. When you look, you focus energy. In *The Holographic Universe*, Michael Talbot cites studies that seem to indicate that the consciousness of the physicist conducting a given experiment on quantum particles affects the way they appear. Our own consciousness changes the way we perceive our life and the world around us.

In biofeedback, when a person brings her attention to her cold hands with the intention of warming them, blood and energy actually flow to her hands. In clinical studies of visualizations done by patients with broken bones, the energy generated by visualizing the image of bones knitting together helped the actual bones heal faster than those of patients who did not visualize.

Looking at something is simple, but it's not always easy. That's because we get interference from our traveling companion: Monkey Mind.

Suppose I asked you to look at whether or not you leak money. Leaking money is allowing it to trickle through your hands without knowing where it is going—or even *that* it is going. You may, for example, start out the day with a $20 bill in your wallet and end the day with $2.97, not knowing where the other $17.03 went.

It's enlightening to see just where your wallet springs a leak, but this experiment can sometimes be unexpectedly difficult. All too often Monkey Mind chimes in, and you may notice that even as you turn your attention toward the question of leaking money, Monkey Mind's voice tells you:

- "I really don't have to do this."
- "This is meant for other people. My money life is fine."
- "I know I don't have time to do this work. What's the point, anyway?"
- "It's a great idea, but this is really a bad time. Why don't I look at this when I'm not so stressed out?"

All I ask is that when your Monkey Mind begins to chatter, you say to it, "Thank you for sharing"—and continue to look.

The question becomes: *Are you willing to look at how you leak money, despite the onslaught of objections from your Monkey Mind?* The moment you answer, "Yes, I am willing to keep my attention focused on what I'm doing—no matter how inconvenient or uncomfortable it seems," you have taken a huge step toward conscious action. You are, in fact, at Step #2.

Step #2: See

To see means to notice, examine, or discern. The act of seeing can bring into the foreground thoughts and actions that have been there all along but that may have been outside your awareness. For instance, once you look thoroughly at the money leaks in your life, you may see that you love to buy quick snacks on the way to work every morning, or that you have a "Velcro hand" every time you pass the magazines at a checkout stand. Or you may see that you do not leak money and in fact you do not spend enough money on yourself.

It takes courage to hang in there long enough to "see" what's going on in your relationship with money. At the very least, it takes energy and persistence to penetrate the shroud of confusion that often surrounds our relationship with money. In large seminars, when I ask people if they know their net worth, I see eyes glaze over. If I follow up by asking them if they know how they really want to use money in their lives, the room goes dead altogether. Two hundred people looking like zombies! It's quite an experience, sedation by Monkey Mind.

Whenever you are asked to see some aspect of your relationship with money, Monkey Mind begins to chatter. It invites you to stop by telling you, "There's nothing there. Don't bother. And anyway, if there were something there, it would be too hard to see." But if you concentrate long enough, a picture will begin to take shape despite Monkey Mind's advice.

This process is like looking at stereograms, those computer-generated dot patterns that reveal a three-dimensional image if you shift your perception and see it in a particular way. I saw an image like this for the first time on a poster in a card shop. The caption said something about a school of dolphins, but all I could see were dots. I thought it was a joke until I noticed the seven- and eight-year-olds who'd pass by, stare at the dots for a moment, and then turn around a yell, "Mom, look at the dolphins!"

I stood there a long time, trying to figure out what was going on. Then gradually the background in the picture receded and I saw three dolphins leaping toward me.

It took energy to stay with the confusing design until a shape emerged, and that's what you'll notice as you try to see patterns in your relationship with money. Where are you conscious about money? Unconscious? What are your personal criteria for financial success? What goals excite you? Write down some of your answers to these questions in your notebook.

If you're having trouble determining your answers right now, don't worry. It will get easier. The only requirement is that you be willing to see the patterns in your behavior that present themselves. Thank Monkey Mind for sharing any observations it may have, and shift your attention back to what is at hand.

Step #3: Tell the Truth

To act powerfully with the energy of money, you have to be willing to tell the truth about what you see.

Telling the truth is different from being honest. The distinction we make in this work is that honesty includes all your thoughts, feelings, judgments, emotions, and even your body sensations. For instance, as you begin to see how you leak money, you may notice thoughts and feelings like:

• "I know I do leak a lot of money. But I work so hard, I need treats."
• "I hate to leak money. I'm surprised at how much I do spend unconsciously."
• "I probably learned this from my father."

These are honest responses. They are a candid, frank, and sincere reporting about the experience. It takes courage to be honest, especially when we own up to thoughts or feelings that we consider to be weak, silly, or embarrassing. But it's important to go a step beyond honesty.

Honesty clears the way for the truth. When I use the word *truth*, I mean the accurate facts or reality of a situation. The truth is what happened in physical reality. It's what is so. The truth is measurable and objective, without embellishment. For example, telling the truth might be: "I spend $70 a month on cappuccino and scones before work." This is not an interpretation or a personal evaluation. It is a fact.

When it comes to emotionally charged matters, telling the truth is definitely easier said than done. Monkey Mind goes wild.

> RON: My son left his new, radio-controlled miniature race car in the driveway. I told him to stow it in the garage so it wouldn't get wrecked, but he didn't do what I said, and it got run over when I pulled my car out of the driveway this morning on the way to work. I got out and told him what I thought of this—how careless he was, how angry he made me. When will he learn?

No one would fault this irate father for the way he felt. His thoughts and feelings are absolutely fitting. His son may need a verbal wake-up call. The only thing absent from his statements is the truth: He was the one who ran over the toy. Now, this does not excuse his son's carelessness. But unless Ron tells the truth, all he will get from this situation is a sense of righteous indignation. Telling the truth, at least to himself, might give him some breathing room. He could even ask himself if he's been in such a hurry lately that he doesn't notice what's in his environment—in this case, a small race car parked on the driveway.

Honesty does not, in and of itself, relieve a difficult situation. You know this instinctively when someone comes up to you and says, "Can I be honest with you about something?" You sense that they are about to tell you what they think or feel about you, and that it may not be a pleasant experience. Sure enough, you often walk away from the conversation irritated, guilty, or angry at the other person's honest opinions or feelings.

Honesty usually does not create breathing room. For example, remember my story about the $35,000 check I wrote in exchange for an unsecured promissory note? I felt angry, resentful, humiliated, foolish, and guilty when I lost my money, and I wanted to blame the other person for manipulating me into this position. But even as I repeated this scenario to friends and family, I noticed that telling the story gave me no relief. I got angry over and over again. The story was an honest reflection of what happened, but it was not entirely true. What was missing? I was leaving out my part in the matter.

It was only when I told the truth, *that I had willingly written the check*—and that no one had forced me to do it—that I began to experience some breathing room. My friend Rita helped me look at the truth in a conversation that went something like this:

ME: This guy, he just took my money. I could kick myself for trusting him.

RITA: He took your money? How did he take it?

ME: He had me write a check. He promised I would see a 110 percent return on my money in three months.

RITA: Who wrote the check?

ME: I did! (Growing irritated.)

RITA: Are you sure?

ME: What do you mean, am I sure? Yes. I wrote it! (As you can tell, I wasn't defensive at all.)

RITA: Well, did he make you write it? Did he force you or something?

ME: Don't get cute. No, I wrote the check. I remember writing out thirty-five thousand and 00/100 dollars.

By then I was starting to get the idea. I did it. I was not excusing the con man's actions, but the fact of the matter was that I had written that check. I had listened to the Monkey Mind conversation in my head: "Don't pay any attention to the people who are suspicious about this deal. They don't know what they're talking about." I even recalled having sensed at one point that this was a risky proposition. I had not listened even to myself! I recognized that this situation was my wake-up call.

People often ask me if the truth can always be stated simply. Aren't there circumstances in which fact is difficult to separate from interpretation? Yes, there are. However, I'd like you to be willing to ferret out the simple truths about your relationship with money as you work with this book. Looking for the truth, instead of spinning in interpretations, is empowering and will bring you great relief.

Here is a chart to help clarify the difference between honesty and telling the truth:

HONESTY	THE TRUTH
I feel guilty about spending so much at the mall today. (Feelings)	I spent $45 for a scarf, $50 for a blouse, $10 for lunch: $50 more than I said I would.
I don't think I should have to pay so much in self-employment taxes. (Thoughts and judgments)	I didn't pay all the taxes I owe.
I just don't have the money to open a Christmas savings account. (Justification)	I haven't opened the account.
It's your fault we don't have enough money for a vacation. (Blaming)	I didn't ask you to participate in saving for our trip.

When you tell the truth, please do so with liberal doses of compassion for yourself. If you don't you may send yourself the message that looking at reality will only lead you to grief, and that you're better off remaining in the "comfortable discomfort" of blaming others, external circumstances, or "society." In fact, telling the truth brings enormous breathing room and freedom to take Authentic Action, the next step of the Coaching Model.

You can only take Authentic Action as a result of genuinely looking, seeing, and telling the truth.

Step #4: Take Authentic Action

Authentic Action moves you forward on your hero's path. It does one of two things:

1. It cleans up a mess, like credit-card debt or other unfinished money business that traps energy.

2. It moves you closer to your goal. Do you want to open a new business? Travel to Tahiti? Write a screenplay? Study comparative religion? Take a cooking class in France? One step at a time, Authentic Action will get you there.

Authentic Action concentrates and amplifies the energy of money. All the insight and inspiration in the world means nothing if you don't take action that brings you closer to your goals and dreams. That's why we say in the You and Money Course, "Insight is the booby prize." Authentic insight may be nice, but it produces no results in the physical world, where the hero's journey begins.

I use the word "authentic" because action alone is not sufficient. Action alone may well result in driven behavior, which has the noisy, busy quality of a fly buzzing around a room. It is like running in place. It uses a lot of energy, but it doesn't take you any nearer to your destination. People who are successful take *Authentic Action*— purposeful action that moves them toward manifesting their goals.

There is an obviousness about Authentic Action that makes it unappealing to those of us who see ourselves as being more "complex characters." We want to take actions that speak of our effort, our intelligence, our cleverness. But Authentic Action is much simpler than that. It asks us to attend to the obvious, to answer the question: "Who's Buried in Grant's Tomb?" An Authentic Action for someone with a toothache would be to call a dentist. For the person who wakes up with a New Year's spending hangover, an Authentic Action might be to open an automatic-deposit Christmas savings account. For someone wanting to go back to school, it might be to get an application for admission.

Simple. Yet between telling the truth and taking Authentic Action is Monkey Mind, advising us that we don't have the time or energy to do anything right now. The toothache's not that bad. That savings account can wait until the tax return shows up in April. We don't have time right now to visit the college admissions office.

The question that confronts all of us is this: *Are you willing to take action, even if it seems obvious or simple?* The woman who spent $70 a month on cappuccino saw that she had developed a habit of buying food whether she really wanted it or not. She decided to use $35 a month for morning treats and put the other $35 into a travel fund.

The good news is that every time you take Authentic Action with money, *whatever that action is,* you are being financially successful.

Financial success is doing what you said you would do with money, with ease. It's something you demonstrate in the moment, not a goal out in front of you. You could start being financially successful today, just by taking one small step, and then another, toward changing your relationship with money. Are you willing to look, see, tell the truth, and take Authentic Action? The next section is your opportunity to begin.

Exercise: Your Money Autobiography

I'd like you to spend some time looking at your own relationship with money. This may be your first foray into uncharted territory, and what we're about to do may seem like an odd way to begin. But this exercise will put all the work we'll be doing in the pages ahead into a personal context for you.

Your experience with money's energy began when you were very young, and it has shaped the way you handle money today. When do you remember first hearing about money? Whom was it from? What was the emotional climate like at that time? When did you first earn money? When did you lose it? The answers to these and other questions in the exercise will give you a clear picture of the associations you bring to any discussion of your personal finances, goals, and dreams.

Get out the journal you are using to record the exercises in this book. Label this exercise "My Money Autobiography." Give yourself at least forty minutes for this exercise. You may want to divide the time into ten-minute sections. Make sure you are in a place where you won't be disturbed. You can do this at your computer, but I strongly recommend that you use pen and paper, because they are portable and accessible.

Begin by telling the story of your life using money as the theme. Begin with your earliest childhood memories and continue right up to the present. Write in narrative form, like this: "I first learned about money when I was . . ."

Let the questions below spark your recollections. You do not need to answer them all in your money autobiography. They are listed here to make your task easier. But keep in mind that when you feel a strong urge to avoid a question or label it as insignificant, it's probably one worth seriously considering.

Remember, you may not think you have the time or energy to do this. Monkey Mind has probably already come up with a dozen good reasons to skip on to the next chapter. But if you are willing, you will create real breathing room for yourself— space for miracles in your life regarding money. Please allow yourself to be willing, and proceed.

1. What were your family's financial circumstances when you were born?

2. When did you first learn about money? Was it from your father or your mother? How old were you? What were the circumstances?

3. Did you have an allowance? Did you have to work for it, or was it given to you even if you didn't do chores to earn it? If you have children, does this affect how you handle allowances with them?

4. When was the first time you bought something with money you had saved? Where were you? What did you buy? Was it money you earned or money someone gave you?

5. Do you remember your first paycheck? How did you earn it? How much was in it? What did you do with it?

6. Do you remember ever losing money? When was the earliest time? What happened? Has this happened to your children? How did you handle it?

7. Did you dream of one day having a particular job or career? Have you achieved this? Why or why not? Was the amount of money you could earn a factor in your choice of careers?

8. If your relationship with money were a personal relationship, how would you describe it? Do you fear, love, hate, depend upon, feel possessive of, or feel generous with money? Just write whatever comes to mind in this area.

9. How do you relate to people who have more money than you? Less money?

10. Do you recall your mother's or father's relationship with money? If you didn't live with them, then pick people who were your primary caregivers for this question.

11. How did the above people's relationship with money affect you? Did they have expectations of you? What were they? Were there some aspects of money that were not dis-

cussed? Even though they were not discussed, you may have known what they were. If you have children, do you have similar expectations of them? Do you treat them the same way you were treated? If you are married or in a committed relationship, do these expectations affect your partner?

12. Have you ever accomplished an important task or project involving money? What was it? What did you do that made you successful?

13. Was there a time when you tried but did not accomplish a task or project regarding money? What was it? What did you do that made you unsuccessful?

14. Have you ever given or received gifts of money? If yes, how much? For what reason(s)? How did you feel about this?

15. If you were to characterize your own brand of "money craziness," how would you describe it?

16. Where do you want to see yourself ten years from now regarding money? How much in savings? How much in investments? How much do you see yourself making ten years from now?

17. Regarding money, for what do you want to be known? If people were to talk about you and your relationship with money, what would you want them to say?

18. Are you afraid that money is not spiritual enough for you or that your spiritual path isn't compatible with financial success?

19. What do you spend money on?

20. What do you not spend money on?

Don't limit yourself to the questions on this list. If there's something I've omitted that gets to the heart of your relationship with money, please write about it.

When you've finished, give your autobiography a title that pinpoints what you've discovered about your relationship with money. Is this title a theme that reflects your relationships with other forms of energy, like love, time, physical vitality, and creativity? If so, what's similar? What do you notice? Are there issues and themes that keep coming up? Are there events and accomplishments you're proud of? And are there things you hope no one ever finds out about? What was the most difficult question on this list for you to think about? Why?

Please be compassionate toward yourself as you look over your life with money. We all make mistakes, and we all have good times. Remember that any painful material you've turned up is pointing you in the direction of what needs to be healed—and we will do plenty of healing in this process. If possible, share what you've written with a friend or loved one.

No matter how long or short your autobiography, congratulate yourself for being willing to write it. You have begun some important work by allowing yourself to see facets of your relationship with money that, though they're rooted in the past, strongly influence your present decisions in life. Just allow yourself to sit with the insights and revelations that have come from the work we've just done. They may seem important now, but I guarantee you that you'll go way beyond even these insights to a new way of relating to money.

Remember, the power to be willing will open any locked doors that have restricted the flow of money's energy into your life.

YOUR INTENTIONS AND INTEGRITY HARNESS THE ENERGY OF MONEY

In this chapter I'll show you how to look at your true nature and see it for what it is. You will also learn to work with a pair of navigational tools to guide your hero's journey.

The first tool is a list of your personal Standards of Integrity. These Standards of Integrity are your reference points for personal power. When you act in accordance with them, life is sweet, easy, and exciting. The second tool, a list of your Life's Intentions, helps you define the meaningful purposes you have for your life. These insights will keep you focused on what you are here to be, do, and contribute.

When your efforts to prosper reflect who you are and what you're meant to do in life, you are increasingly powered by joy. As George Bernard Shaw put it, "This is the true joy in life: being used for a purpose recognized by yourself as a mighty one. Being a force of nature instead of . . . complaining that the world will not devote itself to making you happy."

You were designed to be a force of nature, and to enjoy success and fulfillment with ease!

YOUR TRUE NATURE

Your Life's Intentions and Standards of Integrity capture and harness the energy of money. They are the crosshairs in which you can see who you really are. When you create goals with your Life's Intentions and Standards of Integrity in mind, those goals are sumptuous. When you create goals in any other way, you tend to act in driven or unconscious ways. Such goals leave you always hungry—both spiritually and creatively.

If we are here to be conscious conduits of energy, then what drives energy through the conduit in a powerful and heart-filled way are our Life's Intentions and Standards of Integrity. The hero channels the energy of money through his or her true nature. You, too, can learn the nature of your heart's desire and how to power your goals.

Who are you inside? In my work I've noticed that people are sometimes more willing to look at their shortcomings than they are to take in their greatness. As Marianne Williamson said, "It is not our darkness that we most fear, but our light." What if you were to see clearly the strength, integrity, intelligence and goodness that are inside of you? Seeing these qualities might just give you the power and courage to take the first step toward your goals and dreams, and the next and the next.

Can you remember a time when you were having a hard time but knew you would be all right? I remember coming home from a vacation in Hawaii to find that our house had been burglarized. As I walked through my home and saw what was taken, I was able to say to myself, "It's not so bad, I can live without that TV, stereo, ring . . . Ring? That was my mother's amethyst ring! This isn't fair! The most sentimental of the things I ever had. Why this?" After my fit of crying, I realized something that made no sense to me at that moment. I was okay. I was breathing. In fact, I was joyful, and glad to be alive!

In the middle of loss or crisis, we may have an awareness that there is something much bigger inside us than we had realized. Our core remains intact, and putting ourselves in contact with it can bring feelings of joy and liberation, even when we are grieving.

While leading the You and Money Course, I realized that it is just this power that we need to face the obstacles that arise along the road to our goals. And as we learn to honor and express it, we begin to create a life that is a direct reflection of our deepest selves.

The only thing that keeps us from wanting to know who we are is the fear of who we might be. A teacher once explained to me that we live as though there are three aspects to our being:

- Who we pretend we are
- Who we are afraid we are
- Who we really are

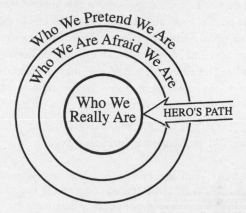

The hero's journey begins at the outer layer and works toward the core. You can think of this as a labyrinth. As you move inward, you encounter unexplored pathways.

Memories or incidents from the past regarding money may spring forth to be recognized. Each step brings you closer to the center, where your power lies. Are you willing to proceed? If you do, you'll have the opportunity throughout this book to release pretense and fear so that you can be free to use the energy of money however you wish.

WHO WE PRETEND WE ARE

This is the face we show to the world, the outermost of the circles. When it comes to money, pretending is expressed in many fascinating ways.

In 1989, 1,100 people responded to a survey I conducted for a metropolitan magazine. Many reported that they pretended to their friends and colleagues that they had more money than they actually did. They wanted people to think they had their financial lives together, that their debts were under control and that their financial futures were secure. Others wrote that they pretended to have *less* money than they actually did, so that others would not be envious or take advantage of them. Our "pretend" selves are crafted from what we think is expected of us and how we perceive the norms in our culture.

It's not easy to be clear about who we're pretending to be, because we are the people most affected by the sham as we justify or ignore the truth of certain situations in our lives. For example, one participant in the You and Money Course introduced herself as the owner of a gardening business. She told me that the business was doing well, though revenues were down at the moment because a few workers had just quit. The dialogue went something like this:

ME: Tell us about your business, Sylvia.

SYLVIA: Well, like I said, it's successful. I was able to buy a great car this year, and I'm planning a trip to the south coast of Spain. We're just having a temporary downturn.

ME: How long has your business been losing money?

SYLVIA: Not long.

ME: Do you know how long?

SYLVIA: Look, do you want me to give you the exact figures?

ME: No, you don't have to. When was the last time you looked at your books with a friend or bookkeeper?

SYLVIA: Now you want me to show my books to a friend? I could never do that!

ME: Well, how about a bookkeeper? Do you have one?

SYLVIA: (softly) No.

ME: Okay, I know this is hard. Take a deep breath (Sylvia breathes). I'm not saying that there is anything wrong with you. I know you want to be successful, and I can tell you're capable of having a great business. You're smart and energetic. Still, something is not working here. I can tell that you really know that yourself, don't you? Just take a look. You'll make it a lot easier on yourself in the long run.

SYLVIA: Yes. (Pauses) The truth is I've been losing money in this business for a year. My dad gives me money, but I'm tired of asking him to bail me out. I hate this! I feel like such a loser! (She begins to cry, but there is a great sense of relief in her tears.)

This story has a happy ending. Sylvia got through the pretense that she was being a "successful entrepreneur" and let herself be coached to see what was true about her circumstances. She paid down her credit cards, the interest on which was eating into her profit, and left her big office to work out of her apartment. Today she is successful. With one other trustworthy employee, she now supports herself consistently and has bought the home of her dreams.

As you read about this pretense level, does anything come to mind about you and your relationship with money? In thinking about this, I remembered my thirty-fifth high school reunion. Aside from all the weight I just had to lose to fit into the same size I wore at sixteen, I also felt this need to impress my classmates with what a successful psychologist I'd become. It may have been true for everyone else who was there. I don't know. I do know how uncomfortable I felt. There wasn't much room for joy.

WHO WE FEAR WE ARE

Take another look at the circle diagram. The inner circle represents the person we're afraid we are. You may get anxious when you begin to consider this part. All of us remember money-related incidents we'd rather forget, and things we've done that don't make us proud. We may have failed in a business because we were careless. We may have dropped out of school, stolen money, or intentionally failed to pay someone what we owe them. These acts, if not rectified, are harmful enough. But what's worse is what we think about ourselves for having done them and not cleaned them up. We accuse ourselves of being lazy, crazy losers. We may believe we don't deserve what we want in life. Sometimes we hide these feelings from ourselves by blaming others for our predicaments. We seldom examine our own self-recrimination, because it brings up a lot of pain. Yet it is even more painful, on a subtle level, to live with the energy that is blocked and bound up in the fear.

As you start to examine this circle, you may discover where you have been deluding yourself. And like Sylvia, you'll find that acting to change your situation gives you some freedom to have what you authentically want in life.

WHO WE REALLY ARE

Inside the inner ring, at the heart of the circle, is who you really are. As you will see time and again in this book, the discomfort associated with the second layer is the result of actions that do not reflect your authentic self, or being. Remember, pain is a great teacher. Knowing who you really are—what you value and what gives you joy—can help you face whatever discomfort arises on your journey. Don't let it make you so uncomfortable that you go unconscious. Write down your observations, note your discomfort, and move on.

Your true nature exists as potential, like a seed that contains all the qualities of a lush tropical plant or the stalk of corn it will become. The root of "potential" is "potent," so to speak of potential is to talk about power. Potent means "to be vigorous, capable, powerful and effective." Potential refers to power that may not yet be manifest. When we say, "She has great potential," we are usually referring to someone who shows the signs of doing great things in the future.

In fact, we never reach our full potential. The formless, immutable nature of potential places it squarely in the metaphysical realm. This poses a serious challenge: If your true self is pure, as-yet-unshaped potential, then seeing yourself exactly is impossible. How can you claim, or even identify, your true nature if you can't see it? How can you begin to identify your unrealized potential?

Let's look again to quantum physics for an analogy. Quantum physics studies particles that are so small and elusive that it's difficult to measure them. It's also difficult to tell whether they have mass, or are really just vibrations of energy, or whether they share the properties of both. One way scientists get a bead on them is by watching for their reflections on highly sensitive photographic surfaces.

That's essentially the method we'll use to see the formless pure potentiality at your center. You can't see your potential in the mirror, but you can study it on a highly reflective surface that is keenly sensitive to your true self—your heart.

When I talk about your heart, I don't mean the center of your emotions. Instead I mean the steady place inside you that lets emotions and thoughts wash over it like waves but remains essentially unchanged. This core is where your wisdom resides, and its shining surface reflects aspects of life that inspire you and bring you happiness. This is your true nature.

YOUR STANDARDS OF INTEGRITY

Your heart recognizes and is drawn to people who possess qualities you admire. You cherish or delight in these attributes because you know what they are. They reflect your own potential. When you see these qualities in others, you experience joy, inspiration, and gratitude. That's the signal that your heart is responding to them.

Take a moment and think about someone whom you admire. What qualities do you prize in them? Below the surface of physical attributes or possessions, which traits reflect their basic goodness? Do you admire their courage, loyalty, or creativity? Do you honor their love, compassion, or truthfulness? Even as you are thinking about the person, do you notice a certain warmth in your heart?

Your heart warms in response to these qualities because they are *inside you*. You can't appreciate a trait unless you've experienced it—whether or not you are currently experiencing it. In order to value loyalty, for example, you must know what loyalty is. You must sense what it means to be dependable, steady, faithful, and dedicated—and you must also know the pain of disloyalty. This is true for any other attribute to which your heart responds. To use a physiological metaphor, if you respond to the trait you must have a receptor site for it, a location in your heart that recognizes and reacts to the quality when you see it in others. To be moved by a trait in another person, you must have that quality inside yourself as a possibility.

Remember the old saying that you don't like certain people because they have some traits that you dislike in yourself? What if the opposite were true as well, that you value traits in others that you also possess? It always interests me when we discuss this in the You and Money Course, because I see how quick we are to admit to the first saying, and how reluctant we are to own up to the second.

You possess the possibility for a host of attributes or characteristics that you consider to be special and admirable. When you see them in others, your heart lights. When you, yourself, act in accordance with these qualities, you feel a sense of well-being, wholeness, and completeness. You are acting with integrity. The qualities that you are demonstrating are the standards that are most important to you; the standards that, finally, express who you are.

THE INTEGRITY FACTOR

Many people cringe when we put the word "integrity" next to the word "money." This combination has stirred up intense emotions at You and Money Courses.

> MARLENE: Integrity? Hardly anyone really has it anymore. Just look at what you read in the papers. It's everyone for herself out there!

> ALBERT: Integrity is all relative. Sometimes you have to bend the rules. It's all about knowing when and when not to cross the line.

> MEL: Now we start talking about what I should and shouldn't be doing with my money! This is going to be a lecture on morals, isn't it?

In the You and Money Course, this is the point where people get a pinched look on their faces. For many of us, the word "integrity" is laden with heaviness. We may have been taught that integrity is a stiff, unreal sort of perfection. Many of us have come to believe that we don't have it ourselves, so what's the use in seeking it in our experience of life or other people? Even talking about integrity can bring up feelings of guilt, remorse, or anger. It's associated with decency, honor, principles, and virtue—all hard to live up to.

The most useful definition I know for integrity is simply "whole and complete." Integrity, then, is your original condition—who you really are in your heart.

We see our heroes as possessing integrity and honorable characteristics. That's what separates them from brutes or bullies. Their core qualities come through when the going gets rough. In medieval times descriptions of heroic traits, such as "loyalty, courage, honor," were emblazoned on banners, standards, and coats of arms to remind the hero what he stood for. Any action that transgressed these "standards" was considered to be barbarism and devoid of aim or purpose.

A CAVEAT

Are you willing to discover your Standards of Integrity? They could become your personal rallying point. Frustration, anxiety, and discouragement can be signals that we are not living according to our Standards. Inspiration and energy come from living up to our Standards.

Before we start, I want to warn you. There is a downside to knowing what qualities you value most in life. When you know your Standards of Integrity, you have to give up what I call "our cheating little ways" with money—things like cheating on your income-tax returns, or pocketing the difference when a waitress undercharges you, putting in a couple dollars too little when you and your friends are splitting a check. When you know your Standards of Integrity, it will be very painful to do these things. You'll find that if you do, you'll be acutely uncomfortable.

The more conscious you become of your true nature and your Standards of Integrity, for instance, the more difficult it is to snatch a newspaper from an open stand and not pay for it, or keep the extra $5 in change given to you by mistake. The reverberations from acts that you may formerly have thought of as insignificant take on new meaning. These "petty" acts result in a reduction of energy overall, which is reflected in your personal relationships, health, and creativity.

Are you willing to trade your unconsciousness and your cheating little ways with money for clarity and ease with money's energy? If so, let's proceed.

Exercise: Your Standards of Integrity

Take out your notebook or journal and have at least four clean pieces of paper handy. This process requires you to be quiet and contemplative, going deep within yourself for the greatest accuracy. In doing so you are giving yourself the gift of discovering what empowers you. You will see the pattern of your potential.

You will need about forty minutes for this process. Doing it all at once is fine, or you can divide the time over two sessions of about twenty minutes each. Make sure you are not distracted during your work periods.

First, take out a clean piece of paper.

1. On the left side of the page list all the people who have qualities you admire. Write their names, using the checklist below to spur your memory. Take your time and reach back into your past. The list of possibilities include:

a. Your family, such as your mother, father, sister, brother, aunt, uncle, grandfather, grandmother
b. School, such as teachers, principals, janitors, and classmates
c. Religious teachers and leaders, ministers, priests, Sunday school teachers
d. Friends from school, work, home, social clubs, or any other source
e. People in the healing professions, such as doctors, therapists, alternative-medicine professionals
f. Sports figures, whether from professional or amateur sports and the Olympics
g. World leaders, spiritual or political
h. People in the arts and entertainment industry, such as actors, directors, singers, dancers, artists, musicians, and composers
i. Biblical figures, people important to your religion
j. Mythological characters, from Greek, Native American, East Indian, African, Egyptian, or other cultures' myths
k. Anyone you have ever read about, whether real or fictional

2. Survey your list. Look at each name, starting with the first and working down. On the right side of the paper, record the

qualities or traits you admire about the person. A quality is something that inspires you, such as loyal, intelligent, adventurous, courageous, creative, truthful, and so on. Go to the next person on the list. If that person shares qualities with the first, simply put a check mark next to that attribute. List any additional traits not found in the first person. As you proceed you will develop a list of qualities, with check marks that indicate when that quality was noted more than once.

Mother	Loyal ✓✓
Dad	Courageous ✓✓✓
Aunt Gloria	Truthful ✓✓
Uncle Arnold	Compassionate ✓✓
Father O'Rourke (priest)	Intelligent ✓
Mother Teresa	Kind

Bear in mind that your lists can be as long or short as you like. However, give yourself enough time to compose an inventory that is as complete as possible. Remember, this process is vital to the rest of your work.

3. Now we are going to revisit your list of qualities. Take out a clean piece of paper. Starting from the top, look at each trait. Spend a few moments contemplating each attribute. Ask yourself:

• Does reading this word, aloud or to myself, warm my heart, if only for a moment?
• Do I like being in the presence of people who have this quality?

You could think of your heart area as a little lantern that lights up when it encounters certain traits. If that warmth, light, or sense of well-being is present, write that word on this new piece of paper.

Repeat this process until you have contemplated each word on your original list. You may find you have transferred all or just a few of them. Quantity is not important. What matters is that you are willing to see what touches your heart. If one or two other traits occur to you as you do this, write them down as well.

4. Take the new list and place it in front of you. Each trait has significance and meaning for you. That is because you possess the receptor site for it in your heart. If you didn't know what each quality meant, it would not have the power to evoke a response from you. To put this another way: If you see these qualities in others, and if your heart resonates with them, then they exist inside of you. If not, you would not be able to see them in others.

5. Take this list and print it on a three-by-five-inch card. At the top of this list, write: "These are my Standards of Integrity." At the bottom of the list, write: "I know these are mine, because I see them in others." Keep this card with you and look at it often. Many people have found it useful to laminate their lists. As one woman told me, "I'm protecting it against blood, sweat, and tears."

What you have before you—the list of your Standards of Integrity—is the blueprint for your personal power. You possess the qualities you listed. They are part of your nature. You can't get rid of them, no matter what you do.

What do you feel as you read the words you wrote on this list? You might want to share your reactions with a friend. When couples do this exercise together, the discussion can lead to profound insights and understandings. If you do this exercise in a group, you might have each person stand and read his or her Standards out loud. For some people, this can be an emotional moment, as they begin to realize that they really do possess these qualities. While they read these Standards out loud, you will notice that they are describing themselves! They are listing precisely the traits you have seen in them. You will have a window into their heart.

Take your integrity card with you and read it at least once a day for one week. Become familiar with your Standards. Get used to the possibility that they really *do* describe your authentic nature. After a week, ask yourself if you have noticed any changes in your relationships with others or your relationship with money. You may see a subtle shift in your behavior, mood, and conversations.

Record your observations about yourself in your notebook. When you are aware of your Standards of Integrity, is it easier to communicate with others? Do you think before you speak?

Do you let them "in" a little closer? Observe yourself. If you do, you will be practicing a skill that is essential to the hero's journey.

Try this experiment: Spend a week consciously trying to demonstrate your Standards of Integrity, and make notes about your experience. Notice specific cases where you actually do show those qualities or attributes. How do you feel at those times? What is your experience of yourself? Pay close attention to these inner messages.

COMING FULL CIRCLE WITH INTEGRITY

Once you have a clear picture of the traits that identify your true nature, you'll immediately become conscious of where you fall short. As you think about the qualities you most admire, and therefore possess yourself, you'll be repeatedly drawn to look at the places where you're not demonstrating them.

Who you really are, at your core, is compelled to look at areas in which your integrity is not complete. Incompletions pull life's energy to them. After all, it takes a lot of energy to push down even low-level anxiety or dread. This energy leak only makes it harder to get your goals and dreams with ease.

As you connect with and express your genuine values, your true nature, as you become conscious of who you truly are, you can no longer remain in the dark about your self-limiting ways. It becomes almost impossible to avoid taking the actions that will transform your relationship with the energy of money. This happens to everyone.

> MAXINE: I really value loyalty, but when I applied it to myself, I saw all the times I've been disloyal lately. This isn't fun. Am I supposed to feel good about this? I really feel guilty.

> JORDAN: I know I haven't been acting courageous and trustworthy at my job, and these are two of my top Standards. In fact, my gut feels tight right now just thinking about it.

These people are describing what I have come to call the *Impetus Toward Integrity,* a phenomenon that can help you identify and seal some of the leaks that drain money's energy. To see how it works, look at the diagram below, a circle with a piece missing. You recognize it as a circle because as humans, we have a strong natural ability to see the whole, even when a part is missing.

Do you notice that your eyes keep returning to the gap in the circle? That's another part of our wiring. Your eyes are drawn there by the tension of the incompletion. The eye and the mind need to restore the figure to its "whole"—known in the psychology of perception as a gestalt.

If you keep in mind that your integrity is your own wholeness, it's easy to understand why once you see it, you also see places where it might need to be patched or filled in. Until you restore that wholeness, you remain in a state of tension.

For example, if one of your Standards of Integrity is being trustworthy, every time you don't follow through on the promises you make to yourself and others, you've sprung an energy leak. Until you keep the promise, your attention—and all the energy of guilt or remorse or rationalization—is drawn to it, no matter how much you'd like to focus on your goals and dreams.

You know in your heart that when you break a promise, you initiate a series of events that drain your power and energy. But the reverse is also true: when you keep your word, you gain strength and energy to realize your dreams. This is the process that comes into play each time you intentionally act in accordance with your Standards of Integrity.

If you feel uneasy about how far you've strayed from your Standards, don't be dismayed. It means that the qualities you long for—and feel you've fallen short of—are in your heart. If you're uncomfortable about your own behavior, it's a validation of who you are, not a condemnation! The discomfort means you're aware of your integrity, and it's urging you to attain wholeness. No one likes to see a gap between their Standards and their actions. But if you think that feelings of doubt, guilt, frustration, or anger are about to overtake you, allow yourself a deep breath and some compassion as you continue on your journey. Little by little, and step by step, we'll move you closer to expressing who you really are.

EXTRA-CREDIT WORK

This part is for you if, like many of us, you're a "high achiever" and want to make sure you get more than your money's and time's worth out of this work. This exercise takes Principle 2 a bit further by exercising your natural Impetus Toward Integrity. I promise that if you do this, you will connect with the hero within in a powerful, indelible way. You will equip yourself to attain your goals and dreams with ease.

Your assignment, should you choose to accept it, is this: Within the next forty-eight hours, identify one specific place in your life in which one or more of your Standards of Integrity aren't present in your relationship with money. Take action and correct the situation. Have compassion for yourself and choose something that is attainable. For example, perhaps there's someone to whom you owe money and whom you've been avoiding. Maybe even the thought of his or her name makes you cringe a little inside. Take a look at what you owe and be willing to take the authentic step of paying it back or setting up a payment schedule.

One of my clients, a public health professional, is a striking demonstration of what happens when you decide to act within your integrity. This woman was making a good living with her job, and she was also making about $600 a month selling marijuana. As she worked with her personal Standards, she saw that selling drugs was obviously out of alignment with her Standards—so she stopped.

"Oh, this is great," she told me. "I take a course on money and the first thing I do is cut my income." But five years later, I got a letter from her telling me what had resulted from closing an energy leak in her life. She's now the head of a major program in her community, earning at least three times what she was making before—more than making up for her lost drug income. And more important, she can sleep at night, without fear of what will happen to her.

You may be telling yourself that you'd never sell drugs, and anyway it doesn't take brains to see that a person's financial and professional life would take a turn for the better when she stopped her illegal activities. But I'm sure you can identify at least one place in your life where it feels risky to put your behavior in line with your Standards of Integrity because so much money seems to be at stake:

> ALICIA: Yes, it would be just great to stop taking the deduction I've been claiming on my taxes for a storage closet I'm calling my home office—but I need to cut my tax bill somehow, and who's it hurting?

> TOM: Sure, it would be wonderful to stop paying people under the table to care for my children and help me out in my business. But I live in a low-income rural area. We're just able to make ends meet. How can I possibly pay Social Security or insurance or a higher fee? And why should my wife and kids and my tiny business suffer because of my so-called "standards"?

When we talk about our Standards of Integrity, we often wind up voicing a lot of our own resignation: This is the way things are, and they're never going to change. "Everybody cheats," we tell ourselves, "so why should I be the Pollyanna who pays full price?" And sometimes, if we can remain cynical enough or skeptical enough, we don't have to ask ourselves the hard questions like "Isn't there something I'm here to contribute?"

But what if life really *is* a hologram? The question for those of us on the hero's journey might be: If I'm compromising my Standards of Integrity regarding money as a reaction to fear:

1. Where else is fear running the show?
2. Where else might I be compromising my Standards (look at your relationships, creativity, physical stamina)?
3. If I clean things up with money, where might I feel relief in other areas of my life?
4. What would my life be like if I were no longer afraid of being caught, found out, or confronted by anyone?
5. Would it be all right with me if life got easier?

VIRTUE AND MONEY

The virtuous life is well within your grasp. After all, the Standards you want to live up to, and the rules you're following, are absolutely personal. You set these Standards for yourself and are only following your own rules. I know this may seem like a tough assignment, but I think you may find that, as the actress Tallulah Bankhead once said, "There may be less to this than meets the eye."

Part of being a hero is to be willing to use your Standards of Integrity as a truing mechanism in any given situation, to see if there's a gap between who you really are and your behavior. It's not always comfortable, especially when you look at your relationship with money. Sometimes in order to look at our own Standards of Integrity, we have to pass through that ring of who we're afraid we are. But as we gain in the ability to make these distinctions, we see that the rewards of demonstrating our Standards far outweigh the cost of remaining unconscious. Life becomes easier.

There are two ways to use your Standards of Integrity. First, you can let them guide you to seal energy leaks by taking care of unfinished business or taking action to clean up behavior that does not reflect who you are.

The second way to apply your Standards of Integrity is by practicing virtue. Virtue isn't some abstract, hard-to-achieve state of being. Virtue is the focused use of energy to achieve results that are within your Standards of Integrity. It's the natural result of actively demonstrating your Standards of Integrity in physical reality. It's being proactive in the sense that you're not cleaning up any messes from the past; you are actively demonstrating your Standards in the moment. It's tremendously empowering when you can say, "Today I really practiced compassion with my co-worker."

Virtue is also a perfect antidote to insomnia: remember the old saying about "sleeping the sleep of the just"? Virtuous action usually produces a general state of well-being. You are expressing who you really are in your heart without reservation or qualification.

The virtuous life begins when you ask yourself the question "How would an honest, intelligent, creative [fill in the qualities that appeal to you] person handle this situation?" This question directs your attention away from yourself and toward making a real contribution to others—and often it changes the whole energy dynamic of an interaction.

ARNOLD: I admire people who are kind. Yesterday I had a talk with one of my salespeople. He hasn't brought in one client to our computer-training company in two weeks. Normally, I'd have had his head on a plate within ten minutes. This time I asked myself: "How would a kind person handle this situation?" Just asking that question gave me some ideas. I began by letting him know that I knew he wanted to be successful, and that this period of nonproductivity was probably hard on him. The result? We had a good session on what to do next. I felt great. This morning he called me. He'd just landed a contract for us.

"I felt great." These three high-energy words epitomize the experience that comes from putting what is in your heart into practice. Whether you experience success or failure in your external circumstances, when you demonstrate your Standards of Integrity, you know that you've brought everything in your power to the situation, and there's no energy spent on regret.

You'll be amazed at how much energy you free up when you look, see, tell the truth, and take Authentic Action in line with your Standards of Integrity. At the beginning it's not easy. Monkey Mind will tell you not to do it. But when you do, you'll feel a satisfying burst of energy that helps you pursue what you really want in life.

When you act with integrity you increase your capacity to bring goals and dreams from the metaphysical into the physical. You are able to transform your heart's desires into completed goals efficiently and effectively. You do not waste energy. There's no extra weight to drag along on your hero's journey.

Your true power, the personal power that comes from virtue, is the wellspring from which your success will emerge. Despite your best intentions, you will periodically find yourself acting outside your Standards in the heat of the moment, when you are angry or anxious. What then? Go back and clean it up, make amends. Move on.

YOUR LIFE'S INTENTIONS

Take out the list you made of your Standards of Integrity and spend about five minutes thinking about them. They are a reflection of your heroic nature. You possess all the strengths—some in full bloom, some in seed form—that you need to work with the energy of money to bring your dreams into reality. The particular combination of qualities you find within yourself will be uniquely suited for the tasks that arise on your journey.

Now the question becomes: Where do you want to go? How do you discover your goal or destination? How do you discern your most exciting dreams? The answer is in your Life's Intentions.

A Life's Intention, as I use the term here, is a direction, aim, or purpose that comes from deep within you. It's the living spirit behind your goals and dreams, a shunt that directs and carries energy into the physical realm. Albert Einstein was describing the energy of Life's Intentions when he said, "All means prove but a blunt instrument, if they have not behind them a living spirit. But if the longing for the achievement of the goal is powerfully alive within us, then we shall not lack the strength to find the means for reaching the goal and for translating it into deeds."

Your Life's Intentions give a clear, pure focus to energy. They are so alive with your passion that you never forget them once you see them. Our culture is full of examples of the power of Life's Intentions. We see them when we watch Olympic athletes striving for excellence. I saw it in the movie *Rudy*. The film's hero wants very much to be a football player for Notre Dame, even though he has few athletic gifts. So great is his desire that he insists on spending time with the team, carrying towels and playing on the practice squad. The football players run all over him, but he keeps getting up. And in the last game of the season, he gets to suit up with everyone else. Inspired by his courage and persistence, his team lets him play in the game and then carries him off the field in triumph.

You could say that people who have Life's Intentions like that are lucky. They know what they want, and they have a sense of purpose. You have Life's Intentions, too, and by doing the exercise in this chapter, you'll give yourself the gift of discovering exactly what they are.

Your Life's Intentions, like your Standards of Integrity, live in the metaphysical domain. They are more highly organized than ideas or wishes, closer to the pull of physical reality. Because they represent ways of being, they usually start with the words "to be."

Some examples of Life's Intentions are . . . to be:

- a successful entrepreneur
- a well-respected professional
- financially successful
- creative
- well educated
- an adventurer
- a good provider
- a generous, charitable human being
- physically fit and healthy
- artistic
- a contributor to my community
- a great mother (father, brother, sister, etc.)
- a great entertainer (host, hostess)
- a good friend
- surrounded by love and beauty
- an author (or poet or playwright, etc.)

We all have a different blend of Life's Intentions that reflect the unique contributions we are here to make. As far as I can tell, there is no correlation between your Standards of Integrity and your Life's Intentions. You cannot predict one from the other. However, taken together, your Life's Intentions and your Standards of Integrity provide the guides that allow you to find and express who you really are.

You'll realize both mental and physical vigor as you begin to see and work with your Life's Intentions. Intention and intensity share a Latin root, *intendo,* which means "to stretch forward." Our Life's Intentions rouse us forward on our hero's journey, calling us to grow and develop.

Swami Yogananda, a teacher of compassion and vision, explained the principle in this way: "The world is nothing but an objectivized dream. Whatever your powerful mind believes very intensely instantly comes to pass."

It is easy to bring intensity to our Life's Intentions, because they bring us joy and meaning. If you are still worried that you don't know your Life's Intentions and doubt that you ever will, take heart. They are already there, and you are about to discover them.

Exercise: Your Life's Intentions—A Treasure Hunt

Your Life's Intentions are your greatest personal treasure. You can discover a few or hundreds of Life's Intentions. It's up to you. But no matter how many you list, you will have a rich experience of yourself when you see them.

You will need your notebook and about forty minutes for this exercise. You can do it all at once, or in parts. Just make sure each segment is at least twenty minutes long, and that you can work in a quiet, undisturbed place.

1. First you are going to empty your mind. Pretend that you have found a magic lamp. As you rub it, a genie appears and offers to give you anything you want. All the money, time, and talent that you need is yours for the asking.

On a clean piece of paper list all the things that you have always wanted to do or have in life. Write down whatever comes to mind. You have all the freedom in the world. You will not be held to this list. It can be pure fantasy, not necessarily based on the reality of your current circumstances. This is just to get out of your mind and onto a piece of paper everything that has captured your interest over the years. Write it down, even if what you want to have or do seems outrageous. In fact, the more audacious you are, the better. Just make sure it is something you really want. The list may look like this:

- Having a new car
- Writing a best-selling novel
- Owning a home
- Directing a motion picture
- Learning how to scuba dive
- Owning my own sailboat in the Bahamas
- Going on a picture-taking safari to Africa
- Swimming with the dolphins
- Having a new wardrobe
- Taking my kids to Disney World
- Raising a million dollars for the community food locker
- Running a marathon
- Going on a trip around the world
- Having enough money for my daughter's education
- Taking art lessons and painting a picture

- Eating at the best restaurants in Paris, New York, and San Francisco
- Becoming a pediatric physician
- Making a major healing discovery
- Becoming an astronaut

2. Look at each item. Ask yourself: Why do I want this? What desire will it satisfy? When you discover the underlying reason for your choice, write it down on a separate piece of paper. Put it in these answers in the form of "to be . . ." For example, you may want to take your kids to Disney World because it would satisfy your desire to be a good parent. Write "to be a good parent." Similarly, writing a best-selling novel would make it possible for you to be a well-respected author, so write "to be a well-respected author."

You may discover that the reason you want to become a pediatric physician is "to be a healer of children." Or traveling to Africa or around the world might satisfy your desire "to be an adventurer."

Remember, putting items on your list doesn't commit you to actually doing these things. It's a way to get to know the desires that influence each of your choices. When you complete this phase of the process, you will have a list of your Life's Intentions. Put the list aside for the moment and go on.

3. For the next phase of this exercise, imagine a group of your friends, family members, and co-workers at a party honoring you on your eighty-fifth birthday. Everyone is there, still alive and in good health. So are you. A group of these people have prepared an acknowledgment of you, describing all you have done in your life. They are about to read what they have written. You will be taking notes on what they say, so have your pen and notebook ready.

4. Write the list of who is there at this party to honor you. Put their names down: husband, wife, children, teachers, colleagues, friends, parents, co-workers, bosses, minister (rabbi, priest), students, neighbors, committee members, aunts, uncles, cousins.

Picture each person getting up and speaking about you. What do you hope, in your heart of hearts, that they would say about you? Boil what they say down to two or three sentences.

This is what two people, Alex and Mary, reported in a recent workshop:

> ALEX: The first person to stand up is my best buddy Dave. He starts to roast me, but soon he settles down and gets to the heart of things. He says I have always been a good friend. He compliments my sense of humor and says I always watch out for other people to see that they're okay.

> MARY: My sister says that I am a great mom and that I was always taking her and everyone else on adventures. She remembers the time I took a bunch of friends petroglyph hunting in Hawaii.

5. Distill to an essence what the people at your gathering say about you, preceded by the words "to be." For example, Alex wrote the following statement: "To be a good friend, to be humorous, to be kindhearted." Mary wrote: "To be a great mom and to be an adventurer." You may have to use your creativity to turn the words of your imaginary gathering into "to be" statements. Stick with it. Add these phrases to the list you began earlier.

6. At the conclusion of this process, you will have a list of "to be" statements.

Look at them. This is the fun part. Which ones do you really want to be true of you? Circle them. Never mind if you don't feel you have fulfilled any of them lately, or ever, for that matter. Do you want "to be an artist" or "to be a healer"? Give yourself the gift of choosing what sings to your heart. Transfer everything you have circled to the list of intentions you created in the first part of this exercise.

You now have a preliminary catalogue of your Life's Intentions. I ask that you live with it for at least one week. During this time, go back to the list and notice how you feel when you read it. After a week, you may add or subtract any item you wish. After all, this is *your* list!

It's useful to share these Life's Intentions with another person. If you do this in a group, have each member stand and read his or her list, much as you did with the Standards of

Integrity process. The group offers support and will help you clarify items as necessary.

You may find that doing this work is both emotionally satisfying and challenging. Many people feel the same way. You are taking a different view of yourself and your life. As with the Standards of Integrity process, you will likely notice a bittersweet reaction when you encounter the Life's Intentions that you have not yet manifested in your life. This discomfort is a signal that you are on the right path. Your work in this book is specifically designed to assist you in bringing your Life's Intentions from the metaphysical into the physical.

Take yourself and your Life's Intentions seriously. They are your reasons for being on the hero's journey. If it is difficult to see this in yourself, ask your friends or loved ones to help. They may see these Life's Intentions in you long before you are able to see them.

Your Standards of Integrity and your Life's Intentions are the reflections of your inner self, and they offer you a clear map to the kinds of actions and achievements that will bring you the most joy. Take out the card on which you printed your Standards of Integrity and print your Life's Intentions on the back. You may want to get this card laminated. Take it with you and look at it daily. As you connect with your Life's Intentions and your Standards of Integrity, you connect with the power to move you through your hero's journey.

When you let yourself be pulled by virtue, and by the juice of Life's Intentions that hold your deepest desires, you draw energy from your core and find an endless source of comfort and courage. This will ease your path as you encounter the dark side of your relationship with money and learn the lessons that will empower your hero's journey.

PRINCIPLE 3

GOALS FOCUS YOUR
MONEY ENERGY

You were designed to create and attain goals. The purpose of this chapter is to rehabilitate your innate capacity to create goals that reflect your true nature and Life's Intentions. I say *re*-habilitate, because when you were young you knew how to create goals that were exciting and fun. As you "matured," you probably put this creative capacity on the back burner until *someday* or *one day* when life finally cleared up long enough for you to catch your breath and begin dreaming again. Yet you already have every skill and ability you need to energize your dreams and make them real.

This chapter will give you ways to infuse your goals with the energies of money, time, creativity, physical vitality, enjoyment, and support. As you do this, your dream begins to take shape, to become solid, to materialize. And as you develop your relationship with the energy of money, you'll see ever more clearly how it relates to other energies.

The goals we'll identify here will not conform to what you usually think about goals. Goals that reflect your nature come from your heart and nurture your spirit. They're shaped from the inside, not imposed by outside circumstances. Most of what you now consider to be goals are probably tasks or "to do's." They are important, but they don't carry a big enjoyment factor.

On this leg of the journey, you will discover goals that have real juice for you—and create a map to the treasure that this goal represents. First let's look at why the word "goals" sends such shivers up and down our spines and makes it difficult for us to even consider creating some, let alone attaining them.

WHAT IS A GOAL?

Reaching many of our conventional goals, such as making a business plan, losing ten pounds, or crafting a budget, is usually a struggle. Sure, we're proud of our accomplishments. But, looking back, what do we remember—the delight of reaching the goal, or the effort it took to get there? In fact, these are not goals but tasks or to do's. They are necessary, but not fun. This is why the mere mention of the word "goal" often elicits groans, and comments like this:

> CARL: Just thinking about making goals leaves me cold. I don't know how to do it. Besides, let's say I finally pick one. How do I know it's the best goal for me? How do I know I'm not just fooling myself?

> LYNNE: I guess you could call me a goal junkie. I set goals every week. I'm in sales, so my goals have to do with how many cold calls I've got to make. I've heard that successful people have goals, and I certainly want to be successful. How do I feel when I make my goals every week? Relieved. For about fifteen minutes. Why don't I get a real bounce from them? I don't know.

> RHONDA: I don't believe in goals. At least not formal ones. I believe in trusting the universe instead. If something I want is meant to happen, it'll just show up. Take money, for instance. I don't have much, but it shows up when I need it. So there's no need to set a goal for what I want.

The problem with most "goals" is that they're not connected to what we really want from life. And much of the time we think we're too busy to find out what we want. If a genie were to slip out of a bottle and ask us our heart's desire, we might be stumped for an answer. Most of us know what we *should* want, and we may have memories of what we used to want. We also have convincing reasons for why we cannot pursue what we want right now. Hidden in our souls, though, are the dreams that express our life's purpose and the intentions that lie at our core.

For the moment I'd like you to set aside everything you think you know about goals. They're not foreign, they're not business-school-designed forms of torture, and they're not drudgery. Remember that in this work we use Webster's definition of a goal: "an area or object toward which *play* is directed in order to score." Keep this in mind as we do the work in this chapter. I want to emphasize the word "play." It's the key to the process.

GETTING THE FUN BACK: GOALS VS. TASKS

When we were young it was simple to see the goals in our lives. Just close your eyes and think about one of the first things you can remember wishing for as a child. What did you want for your birthday or the holidays when you were eight or nine? Can you see it in your mind's eye right now? For me, it was a red bicycle. I knew that when I got it I'd pin playing cards to the spokes with clothespins so they would make a loud shuffling sound as I rode around. I can still feel the sense of excitement I had about getting that red bike. Try to recall the excitement of contemplating what you wanted so badly as a child.

We're happiest when we're creating what we truly want in life, and going out to get it—authentically, compassionately, and consciously. True goals, unlike the onerous items we put on lists and gear ourselves up to accomplish, are actually meant to bring out a childlike excitement in us.

How did we lose touch with the joy in this process? Maybe during your teens you decided to "grow up" or "chill out." Maybe you didn't get what you wanted and gave up. Maybe you found that it wasn't cool to get so excited about life's possibilities. A lot of us hit adulthood and decided to shelve our goals and dreams, trading them for lowered expectations and heightened cynicism. But you still have dreams in your heart, and you have the ability to make them come true. It's one of the gifts that come with being human. The question you need to answer now is: What are your authentic dreams?

What's the "red bike" that fills you with anticipation and excitement today? Think about the life you want the most, and the goals that might take you there. Can you imagine reaching them with a playful spirit? If you're like most adults you're probably rolling your eyes. As much as I insist that play's the key, it probably doesn't compute with your personal paradigm about goals. You may feel certain that you'll only reach them with fortitude, strength, perseverance, and a set jaw.

Let's stretch that belief just a little. Imagine a rating scale that goes from 1 to 10. A score of 1 means "I don't want this" and 10 means "I want it very, very much." The goals I'm talking about are the 8s, 9s, and 10s on the scale, the ones that truly excite you. Those are the kinds of goals that will transform your life.

If you're not excited about your goals in life, it might be that they are not goals. They could be tasks that should or ought to be done. Some common tasks that people confuse with goals are:

1. Getting rid of credit-card debt
2. Creating a will or revocable living trust
3. Opening a retirement account
4. Hiring a money manager
5. Fixing the roofing, plumbing, or heating at home
6. Filing forms or documents on time
7. Buying health insurance

These are not goals. They are tasks that will clear the way for you to play for your goals. They just don't have the same energy as that trip to the Caribbean, the black belt in karate, the pilot's license, the picture you want to paint, or that gift you've been wanting to give your mom and dad. Not even close. Notice how different tasks feel from the goals I just listed. In your heart you'll recognize the call that true goals sound—even if your brain still thinks goals have to be tough or unappealing to be worthwhile.

The tasks on the numbered list above are items of unfinished money business. When you complete them you give yourself breathing room that engenders success and peace of mind.

One key for determining whether you have a task or a goal before you is to ask yourself: "Will I be *relieved* when it is done?" If the answer is yes, then it is a task, not a goal. When you finish a task, you feel relief. People who are driven in life have learned to strive for relief, mistaking it for joy. When you complete a goal, you feel joy.

THE WHIM FACTOR

A second question to ask about your goals is: What's the Whim Factor? If you have an itemized list of goals that you want right now—especially if they're the newest/flashiest/fastest model of some product—take a moment to consider the difference between a goal and a whim. Whims are based on impulse and immediate gratification. This spontaneity brings spice to life, but it can easily become habit-forming.

One of the symptoms of Monkey Mind is the unwillingness to suspend reward. Goals exist in a definite span of time, and they often require you to wait for results while you focus your energy on your target. Your hero's journey is enhanced by your ability to create and sustain interest in a genuine goal that takes time to achieve. This will nurture your spirit.

Identifying your true time-based goals brings clarity and power to your life. You don't give in to impulses that have no lasting meaning. I have talked with thousands of people who have the newest VCRs, the latest exercise equipment, and the most advanced cappuccino machines—bought on whims and gathering dust. On the other hand, purchases that have been planned for are generally cherished and enjoyed.

The first types of goals—the ones with a high Whim Factor—are Type One goals. They lack meaning, and you may find that it's difficult to say why you picked them over others. They feel frivolous or trivial. Type Two goals, however, are attached to your Life's Intentions. These Intentions anchor your goals and provide conduits for energy that bring these goals into physical reality. Type Two goals allow for maximum creativity and fulfillment. You develop meaningful goals by differentiating them from tasks and anchoring them to one or more of your Life's Intentions.

CREATING POWERFUL GOALS

Here are some guidelines for creating powerful goals. A goal is a projection of your Life's Intention into physical reality. It is a promise you make yourself. Powerful goals have five qualities, represented by the acronym SMART. *Each* quality must be present for an item to qualify as a goal.

S is for specific. Is your goal explicit and precise? For example, "I want to be happy" is not a goal. It is not specific. "I want to learn scuba diving by next summer" or "I want to buy a house" is specific. Monkey Mind wants you to keep your goal fuzzy. Being vague about what you want keeps you in a state of suspended animation. *Your power lies in clarity.*

M is for measurable. How will I know that I have learned scuba diving? One way is by getting my certificate. "I want to get my scuba-diving certificate" is measurable. I will either have it or not. Similarly, "I want a two-bedroom home with a swimming pool" leaves no wiggle room. *Pin down your goals.*

A is for attainable. A goal needs to be a stretch for you but not impossible. For example, to say that you are going to save $600 a year when you are already saving $50 a month is not a stretch. It's predictable. At the same time, "pie-in-the-sky" goals are a setup for failure. One man I worked with wanted to make $100,000 a year, a specific, measurable goal. But he told me, when I asked him, that he was currently making $30,000. I don't say that luck doesn't happen, or that you can't win the lottery, but the great thing about goals is that they're not dependent on luck or chance.

Your goal is a promise that you make to yourself about something you are really going to do. When the man thought about this, he decided that an attainable goal for him was to earn $40,000 by the end of the year in his consulting business. He could actually plan for that, and he did it.

Many people create unattainable goals. They then become discouraged or righteously indignant about the entire process of setting goals. *Make the goal worth playing for, yet attainable.*

R is for relevant. This is where we take care of the Whim Factor. Take out your Life's Intentions. To which intentions does your goal relate? In other words, is it relevant to who you are and what you want to be? One of my Life's Intentions is "to be an adventurer." Another one is "to be physically fit." And when I attach my goal of white-water rafting down the Colorado River to that intention, I give my goal the juice of my Life's Intentions. A goal of owning your own home might satisfy the Life's Intention "to be financially successful." Write the Life's Intention(s) satisfied by your goal next to it.

Next, does proceeding with this goal demonstrate one or more of your Standards of Integrity? For example, one of my standards is "courageous." If I learn to scuba dive, whether or not I am afraid, I demonstrate courage. If I actually save the money to make a down payment on the house I want, I might be demonstrating the Standard of Integrity of being trustworthy.

In going for any goal, ask yourself if it is consistent with your Standards of Integrity. Is the goal outside your integrity in any way? Does it ask you to lie or cheat? Are you being irresponsible in trying to attain it now? Check this out. When you maintain your Standards of Integrity, you propel yourself forward to meet your goals. The way is clear and easy. Acting outside of these standards usually results in struggle and a definite lack of enjoyment.

Finally, what number do you give your goal on the 1-to-10 "How much do I want it?" scale? Is it a 10, a must-have? Or a yawning 1? Assign your goal a number right now. If you chose 8 or above, go for it. If the number you picked is below 8—I'm sorry, you need to cross it off the list. Why? Because you don't really want it. Allow yourself to pick a goal that represents something you want, something that brings you joy.

Screen your goal to be sure it's relevant in these three ways. It may seem laborious at first, but remember that you are learning to create integrity- and joy-based goals. They will have the living spirit that sustains you on your path.

T is for time-based. You must anchor your goal in time by giving it a date by which it'll be accomplished. As you do this you are making a promise to yourself and demonstrating that you are earnest about getting it. This is a powerful step to take. At the same time, it is a step that many of us avoid. We prefer to say "Next summer sometime," or "I'll do it next year." This takes the teeth out of your goal. In sales terms, it is like doing all the work to make a sale and not closing the deal. A definite date closes the deal you make with yourself. In this way, you are taking yourself and your goals seriously.

I know Monkey Mind is screaming, "Wait! I don't know! It's impossible to figure out how long this will take. Don't be unreasonable!" But just pick a date anyway, a time within one year when you are actually going to accomplish your goal. If it's hard for you, ask a friend or loved one to sit with you as you do it. Sometimes, creating goals for the first time makes us feel vulnerable, because we're opening ourselves up to the possibility of bringing more joy into our lives. Exciting as that is, it's also frightening. Feel the fear, and the excitement, and *let your goal be specific, anchored in time*.

Exercising three times a week for one year is not a goal. Neither is "reading five pages of inspirational writing." A goal is not an open-ended process. You complete it, rejoice, and go on to the next one. As a matter of fact, when you reach a goal it disappears! It is no longer a goal. It has been actualized.

A GOAL IS A YES, NOT A NO

There's one more filter to use as you look at the goals in your life. Ask yourself: Is my goal a positive or a negative?

Losing or stopping something is not a goal. You may want to lose twelve pounds, or to stop smoking. Those are laudable ambitions, but they are not goals. They're tasks. How do you know? You get no excitement from doing them. You would not wake up one morning and say "I just love detoxifying from nicotine!" Similarly, you could lose twelve pounds in many ways. One way is by being ill and unable to eat.

If you're a consultant and have huge accounts receivable, then collecting these overdue accounts is a good thing. But it's not a goal; it's a task. It's not fun to do. What you experience when you've done it is relief, not joy. You are relieved that you got the money, and perhaps a bit regretful that it took so long to get it. That kind of relief, coupled with regret that you didn't do it sooner, are the hallmarks of "to do's."

Or you might make an appointment with a certified financial planner. Again, a great "to do," but not a goal. You recognize that you ought to do it, that it would be good for you, but it doesn't exactly make your heart sing.

It is possible, however, that goals are hidden beneath those tasks. This is how you discover them:

1. Look at what you really want for your body. What are your Life's Intentions? For example, you may find that one intention behind wanting to stop smoking is "to be physically fit." The intentions behind getting current with your accounts receivable and seeing a financial planner might be "to be financially successful."

2. Look at one goal you could have that would demonstrate that you are physically fit. Something you want to do on a level of 8 or above. You may discover that you have always wanted to hike in New Zealand, run a 10K, go white-water rafting on the Colorado

River, or bike from inn to inn on a trip to Vermont. In some cases you may have put off your dream until you lost that weight or stopped smoking. Yet this strategy has gotten you nowhere.

Your goal for the accounts receivable might be to buy the new office furniture you've been wanting forever, and doing it with ease. Seeing a financial planner might make it possible for you to take that three-month vacation in Europe you've been putting off.

3. Are you willing to have a goal that demonstrates the intention to be physically fit? If you say yes, you are on your way to expanding your personal paradigm. For example, if you choose to bike from inn to inn, you will need to exercise in order to prepare. Exercise will help you lose weight, although not as much weight as you think, if you are adding muscle. I have a friend who says she doesn't care how much she weighs as long as she looks like Tina Turner.

The exercise will most certainly support you in a task like stopping smoking. But it is the goal itself within the task that will inspire you. New abilities and experiences become available when you have a body that is physically fit, and when you are financially successful.

Now that you know what a goal is, and what makes a goal powerful, let's bring what you know into physical reality and create some.

Exercises for Creating Your Goals

The following is your handbook for creating powerful, meaningful goals. It will let you work with the ideas you've just considered. Like a magician's notebook, it's precisely crafted to help you energize your dreams more quickly than you've ever imagined.

In the exercises that follow, you'll come up with a list of goals that have power for you and that are connected to your deepest Life's Intentions. Then you'll choose a handful of goals that you want to reach in the coming year, and create a Treasure Map for the one you'd like to start playing toward first.

Please give yourself fully to the exercises below. They work. You're ready for them. They are an important aspect of your hero's journey. If possible, do this next work with at least one other person. Support is crucial here.

PART ONE: HOW DO YOU FEEL ABOUT GOALS?

You will need your notebook, a pen or pencil, and about twenty uninterrupted minutes.

On a new page in your notebook, write the word "goal." Take two minutes and write down every thought or feeling that occurs to you when you see that word. Be honest. Write it all down, even if it does not seem to make any sense. You can write whole phrases or single words. If you notice a body sensation, write that down as well. What do you notice? The following examples may spark your examination.

> JESSIE: At first my mind went blank. Then came words like "play," "inspiring," and "free." But as I listed those words, I found my chest tightening up, and a sense of sadness came over me.

> MARK: "Productive," "useful," "purposeful," "on target" came to mind. All that's okay, but where's the fun?

> ROGER: I didn't want to do this exercise. I thought, "This will be too hard, and besides, I don't deserve to have the goals I really want."

> ESTHER: I got annoyed at the thought of looking at the word "goal." Why should I have goals? They won't come true anyway.

> BOB: As I did this exercise I saw that I like to create goals. But once I do, they seem to go flat. Maybe I'm just an idea person.

You may have a reaction to the word "goal" that's unlike any of the above. That's fine. Just look at what you wrote. Would you have written the same thing when you were ten years old? Would your mood have been the same?

Next, on the same piece of paper make a list of at least ten goals you have that would take time or money to accomplish. Can you even think of ten? Does it seem like a burden to do this? That's okay. You're on track. Just keep going!

Read these goals to another person. How do you feel? Would you really want to post this paper when you could see it every day? Would you be just as happy tearing it up and using it for hamster litter? Be honest. There may be some that are great, but some you just dread. How does this all compare to the way you might have experienced the exercise when you were ten years old?

Many people are surprised at how onerous it is even to think about goals. They find themselves feeling heavy, and even achy. It's important to notice if you have these feelings. Stick with it. Relief is in sight. If you want, tear up this list and throw it away! You're going to go beyond those thoughts and feelings to discover the joy of true goals.

PART TWO: OPENING THE DOOR TO YOUR DREAMS

You will need your notebook and pen, and a small tape recorder. To help you in the process of creating some goals, record what follows on a cassette and then play it back to yourself. If you prefer, have someone read it to you. This exercise will take about twenty minutes. You may repeat it as many times as you like.

Record and then listen to the following guided meditation. Pause for two seconds where you see the three dots.

> Sit back and relax. Have both feet on the floor, hands resting gently in your lap. Close your eyes when you are ready. Take a deep breath. Feel for any tense spots in your body. Locate them, and breathe into these points of tension. As you breathe out, let that bit of tension go . . .
>
> Recall a time when you were eight or ten years old and wanted something. Was it something you wanted to do? To be? What was it? If it was an object such as a bike, what color was it? If it was to have a special job or life's work, what was it? Did you want to travel?

Become a professional athlete? A musician? A painter? Let yourself remember what it was like to want what you wanted. Notice how your body feels as it remembers how it was for you to know you really wanted things . . .

Take another deep breath. Exhale gently . . .

Bring your awareness back to the present. You are sitting in a seat of power. It looks and feels just like a seat of power would . . . however you might picture that in your mind's eye. It might be a huge throne in a royal palace or a comfortable leather executive's chair in a spectacular penthouse office . . .

In this seat, anything you truly want to have, do, or be can be made real . . . All you need to do is let yourself know what it is. Let yourself pick what your heart really wants . . . What brings you joy? Education, travel, creative projects, the perfect job and more are yours . . .You have only to ask for what you want and you will receive it . . .

Let yourself see, feel, or hear what it is you really want . . . What is it that makes you glad or excited? . . . Find the words for what you want and say them to yourself . . .

Whether you have become aware of some goals or not, something wonderful has happened. Sitting in this seat of power you have begun to energize your imagination. You have opened the door to discovering your goals. If you do not yet know what they are, you may surprise yourself by daydreaming or having a dream when you go to sleep at night that will reveal something to you about your goals. Whenever this happens, write the dream or daydream down so you will remember it. You will also see that you have always known somewhere in your heart what these dreams are.

When you are ready, open your eyes. Write down whatever goals presented themselves to you.

Make a list now of all the goals you can think of that would be worth having. Note them no matter how much you think they might cost or how much time they might take to get. Just look inside. You may hear Monkey Mind saying, "But how will I get it? This is too difficult. I don't have time or the money. I have no direction." Stand back for a moment. Ask yourself, "Which am I more interested in, dancing with my doubts, or dancing with my goals and dreams?" Choose the dreams to dance with, regardless of how Monkey Mind chatters.

Let the goals come from the top of your head and the bottom of your heart. List whatever comes up, no matter how silly or frivolous it sounds. This is no time to censor yourself. You have probably done that for too long already. Keep going until you have at least ten to fifteen items on your list. Feel free to repeat the closed-eye meditation as often as you like. Each time will open you more to this process of digging for goals.

Here's a partial list of the types of goals people in the You and Money Course have chosen over the years.

- Replant my garden
- Sponsor a local child for educational travel
- Take my children to Yellowstone Park
- Go white-water rafting on the Colorado River
- Write a storybook for children six to eight years old
- Open a restaurant
- Buy a new home
- Be a benefactor for the Red Cross
- Buy a computer
- Get an airplane pilot's license
- Redecorate my home
- Go to Tahiti with my honey
- Have an investment portfolio of $2,000
- Write a screenplay
- Have my first art exhibit
- Enroll in a Ph.D. program
- Reach the Golden Circle award for real estate sales

How did you feel as you got in touch with some goals? Excited? Scared? Vulnerable? Were you bursting with creativity or dried up like an old desert watering hole? If it's the latter, keep going. There *is* water there. How many passes did it take before you came up with a list? Did Monkey Mind come up with some new objections? Now is the time to talk about this with someone you know. You have started a process that will continue long after this particular exercise.

Part Three: Refine Your List

To master the art of creating meaningful goals, you must learn to see what you truly want. This involves the discipline of laying aside, at least for a moment, whatever is not what you want. Thus you cultivate the ability to generate energy by letting go of insignificant elements that dissipate it.

Returning to your list of goals, choose one that you are willing to have by one year from today. When you choose a goal, you embrace it as a possibility. This is often difficult, given the nature of Monkey Mind. For a moment, become unreasonable. Look at what you want to be, do, or have within this year. Pick one goal. In that simple act lies more courage than almost anything else you could do.

If you have chosen a goal, congratulate yourself! You are stepping beyond your structure of knowing. You are reinvigorating an ability you have had all your life—the ability to choose what you want. If you have not yet chosen a goal . . . breathe! You may, as many others have done, come up with a choice later, when you least expect it. You might even dream about the choice. Just acknowledge yourself for coming this far! You're doing well.

Part Four: Be Sure That Your Goal Is Powerful

Look at the goal you have chosen. Now turn back to the section that describes how to have powerful goals, and walk your goal through all the filters we've put in place. We want to ensure that it's a goal and not a task. Then, step by step, ask yourself if you have crafted a SMART goal. Is it Specific? Measurable? Attainable? Relevant? Time-based? Measure your goal against each of the questions you find. Most of all, ask yourself: Will attaining this goal bring me joy?

If your goal is true, SMART, and joy based, then continue on. If you need to refine your goal, or choose a new one, go back to Part One. Be gentle with yourself as you focus on your dreams.

THE TREASURE MAP: A PHYSICAL PICTURE OF YOUR GOAL

One of the most powerful ways I know to focus your energy on your goal is called Treasure Mapping. Writer Napoleon Hill discovered that people who are successful write their goals down. In Treasure Mapping, you go one step further. You create a graphic, colorful representation of your heart's desire. A Treasure Map is your best effort to create a comprehensive, mental visualization of how your life will look when you have attained your goal.

Treasure Mapping begins the process of taking your goal from the idea stage into physical reality. It acts as an energy magnet or goal generator, boosting your power. The very act of creating a Treasure Map puts you on the path to success.

The urge to create visual representations of what we want is in our blood. Ancient pictographs or petroglyphs by prehistoric humans are thought to have been an artistic way to bring forth "bison energy." Today you can also experience this process. Look at a picture of a car you want. Find a travel brochure with the mountains or beaches you love. Do you feel the excitement? Can you put yourself in the picture?

When you consciously energize your goals in this way, you awaken an ability that may have been dormant within you for much of your life. In creating a Treasure Map, you call forth the spirit of what you are pursuing. This is a simple process, although it might not immediately seem so. You may have many years of inertia to clear away. Perhaps you have told yourself that it's silly to be guided by your dreams. The act of creating Treasure Maps for your goals is an act of vulnerability that contradicts Monkey Mind's chidings, which may include:

- "You're acting like a kid playing 'let's pretend.' "
- "This will never work."
- "You'd better make sure nobody sees what you are doing."
- "Getting what you want is way too complicated!"
- "Are you sure you want to make such a big deal out of this?"

Over the past sixteen years I have consulted with people on approximately 16,000 Treasure Maps. During the You and Money Course, each person comes up with a number of goals and makes

Treasure Maps for each one. I often have seen and heard about many miracles associated with them:

ALAN: I Treasure Mapped a Victorian-looking home, white with blue trim. I cut out a magazine picture of a house and put a picture of myself—holding a SOLD sign—in front. It was dated eight months into the future. I had no idea how I was going to come up with a big down payment. Four months later I was riding my bike when I saw a house with a FOR SALE sign. The owner had to move because of a promotion at work. He was willing to carry the paper with a small down payment. I bought the house. It was almost an exact copy of my Treasure Map picture.

CHRISTIE: Two months after I did a Treasure Map about wanting to make money while traveling around the world, I met a cousin at a family reunion. He was going to travel the South Pacific, teaching scuba diving. I remembered my Treasure Map. I'd already gotten my scuba-diving certificate, and I decided then and there to get my instructor's license. Why pass up something that might make my dream come true? I wrote my cousin in Tahiti. He'd landed a great job with a cruise line teaching resort diving courses. They needed another instructor. I flew down and got the job.

JACK: I sell medical equipment and Treasure Mapped a goal of making a net income of $10,000 a month for three consecutive months. I looked at my Treasure Map every morning. It was like a beacon. I wound up clearing $12,000 a month!

LOUISE: My Treasure Map was to double my gross by the end of the year. I help cities with their designs for traffic flow. I got very clear about my Life's Intention and my goal, and I expressed myself so clearly to contractors that two weeks later I landed a $27,000 contract—and I actually doubled my gross in three months, with six months remaining before the end of the year.

These are just a few of hundreds of stories I've heard from people who've used the Treasure Mapping process. Others traveling this path have:

• Published books and screenplays
• Been recognized as Successful Entrepreneur of the Year

• Completed an award-winning architectural project in record time, with ease
• Trekked the Himalayas, with the time and money to do it thoroughly
• Had success at their first art exhibits
• Become a well-respected and highly paid business consultant
• Created a new wardrobe with a well-conditioned body to fit into it
• Developed a successful software package for electronic books.

If you look, you'll find that every goal you create involves the energy of money in some way. Your Treasure Map will help you focus all six forms of energy toward your goal. All manner of unforeseen incidents will begin to come your way. You will become more aware of already existing windows of opportunity. Perhaps conscious intention really does create the probability that something will happen, as quantum physicists believe. Whatever the case, the Treasure Map helps you prepare for your success. With the intentional focus that a Treasure Map represents, you will likely realize your goal in full.

Treasure Map Exercise: Mapping Your Goal

Are you willing to have what you want—even if it means doing something new or different? If you answer yes, use the following guidelines. I've developed them carefully and thoroughly after years of working with people on their dreams. You are about to step outside your personal paradigm about goals. Start right now by taking your dreams seriously and do exactly what successful people before you have done. Be precise about *every detail* of your map and get ready for miracles!
You will need:

• Scissors and two glue sticks
• One piece of poster board, around 18" by 24". White is the best color to use.
• Colored construction paper: about five pieces
• Magazines, brochures, and catalogues with colorful pictures. Having publications that depict the general subject area

of your goal is best. For example, get architectural or home magazines for home, travel magazines or brochures for vacations, and business magazines for career goals.

• Magazines or brochures with catchy or inspirational phrases that can be cut out and pasted to your map.

• Calendars with dates at least 1" high that can be cut out.

• A recent photograph of yourself and whoever will share this goal with you. Please note: Make sure you get permission before placing anyone but yourself on your Treasure Map.

• Your notebook.

In the You and Money Course, making Treasure Maps is a group process. We work together, give feedback, and share ideas. The sheer energy and synergy of the group help overcome the inertia of your old beliefs.

Consider making your map with at least one or two friends. After all, everyone who has a dream or a goal can use some company as they begin their journey toward it. And everyone can benefit from having a Treasure Map. As you help each other, you can find pictures and words to share. Support each other to venture outside your old beliefs. Entertain and include novel ways to represent your goal. In fact, the most powerful way to make a Treasure Map is to be present while your friends make it for you! You pick a few of the pictures, but you give them permission to find most of them and construct the map. One You and Money participant reported the following:

> SUSAN: My heart almost stopped when you asked us not to work on our own Treasure Maps! I didn't think I could just let other people make it for me. I thought they'd miss the essence of my goal, which is to take a trip to the Bahamas with my husband for our fourteenth anniversary. Well, after I got over the shock, I relaxed. Surrendered, really. They came up with some of the most beautiful pictures and feeling words. I wouldn't ever have imagined such an exquisite, gorgeous map for myself!

The process of creating a Treasure Map can bring up some of the mental obstacles that have distracted you in the past from getting your goal. These may be the very ones you have been waiting to disappear before you set out on your journey. In this way, it's like a small laboratory in which you get to hear Monkey Mind's medley of your favorite excuses. As you continue to work, regardless of your mind chatter, you diminish their potency. It will be useful to pause from time to time and note the conversations and feelings that arise while you create your map.

Here is how to go about putting your Treasure Map together:

1. Create a phrase that describes your goal. Put it in the present tense. For example, instead of saying, "I will be on a beach in Hawaii with my children, April 14, ____ [year]," write "I am at a beach with my children, April 14, ____ [year]."

2. Take out your photograph(s) and glue them on your Treasure Map. Place them anywhere you like. This is the first big step in putting yourself (and anyone else you have chosen, with their permission) on the journey toward your goal.

3. Look through your magazines and form the goal phrase from words you cut out. Do *not* write these words or print them from your computer. As you look for the words in these magazines, you are broadening your options. You may find an even better way to express your goal. Glue this goal on your Treasure Map, preferably somewhere toward the top. If you wish, cut out a piece of construction paper and use it as a colorful backdrop for the new phrase that describes your goal.

4. Find colorful pictures that represent your goal. Use the magazines, brochures, and catalogues that you have collected. Do *not* draw anything on your Treasure Map. Your drawings are influenced by the very beliefs that you are moving beyond. Whether it is a car, a home, a new job, a trip around the world or an academic degree, find pictures that make your goal crystal clear.

5. As you place the pictures and glue them down, make sure you fill your entire Treasure Map. You want it to explode with color as it embodies your goal. Do you want a car? Get a picture of it from a magazine. You can even place another picture of yourself inside it. How about opening a business? You may want a picture of yourself sitting at a desk, or standing in front of your store, equipment, ranch, etc. Let your imagination flow.

One woman wanted to begin a career as a motion picture photographer. We found the type of camera she would be using and had her picture taken with it. A man who wanted to open a homeless shelter got a sign, printed it with the shelter's logo, and got his picture taken standing in front of it.

6. As you work on your Treasure Map, remember to breathe. You are doing what you have been born to do. You are bringing a dream into reality. You are showing that you respect yourself and take your goals seriously. Honor your goals. They come from your heart.

When you notice thoughts or feelings becoming strong, take out your notebook and write about them. What are you saying to yourself? What emotions are coming up? Have these stopped you in the past? If so, when? You are re-creating your ability to picture and claim your goals. You will encounter your old obstacles along the way. This is a natural process.

7. Clip words and phrases that reflect how you will feel when you attain your goal. Make sure that you choose feeling words that describe feelings. They must have an emotional charge for you. Words such as "important" and "successful," and phrases such as "the best just gets better," are motivational, not emotional. You can put them on your Treasure Map, but they are not feeling words.

Here are some examples of feeling words: admiring, adoring, amused, appreciative, blissful, boisterous, bold, brave, calm, certain, cheerful, comfortable, confident, courageous, daring, determined, eager, ecstatic, enchanted, encouraged, energetic, energized, enthralled, enthusiastic, excited, exhilarated, exuberant, fascinated, free, glad, grateful, gratified, great, happy, hopeful, intrigued, joyful, joyous, loving, moved, optimistic, passionate, patient, playful, relaxed, satisfied, secure, sensitive, strong, tender, thankful, thrilled, valiant, vibrant, warm, wonderful, zany, zealous, zestful.

You might use colorful construction paper as a backing for the words. This helps make them distinct on the map.

As you go through magazines and brochures, you may be surprised to discover how *few* feeling words we use. We rely upon concepts. "Go for the gold!" "Be a winner." "You deserve the best." These expressions are not reflections of the heart-centered emotion we're looking for. Hunting for feelings and placing them on your map puts you into the immediate experience of the goal. The immediacy of feeling words will draw you down your path. If you glance at an ancient pictograph, you can sense the feelings of its creator. The experience is vivid, even after thousands of years.

8. Include, in clearly visible type cut from a printed page, brochure, or calendar, the exact month, day, and year you will attain your goal. The date is where the rubber meets the road. This anchors the goal in physical reality. Make it bigger than you think you should. Then it will be just right.

9. Add to the map at least one of the intentions that support the goal. It, too, should be in a phrase made up of words clipped from magazines. Have them, as much as possible, begin with the words "to be." For example: "to be financially successful"; "to be an exhibited artist"; "to be physically fit." Once again, you might use some colorful construction paper as a backdrop. This sets the words off from the rest of the map.

You have just completed an important project. It is time to share your experience with others. What were your thoughts and feelings during the process? Here are some questions to ask yourself:

1. Did any Monkey Mind conversations emerge? Did you write them down? If not, take a moment here and note them. What was it like to work through these without waiting for them to go away?

2. What was it like to hunt for feeling words? Has this process broadened the types of words you can use to express your emotional states in general?

3. Is your Treasure Map colorful and graphic? What do you perceive as you look at it? Now is the time to add any parts that are missing.

Show this Treasure Map to at least two people who have not helped you with it. See if they can tell what the goal is without your explaining it. If they are confused, look for what is missing from the map. People should be able to tell at a glance what it is about. You want to come away from your Treasure Map feeling that the total image you have created is printed indelibly in your mind.

Place the map where you can easily see it. Look at the map once a day for thirty days. Read the goal, intentions, and feeling words. The process has begun.

KEEP GOING

If you have completed the process outlined above for one goal, congratulations! Continue with the process until you have identified two goals that you are willing to have within one year from now. I encourage you to choose at least one goal that expresses your Life's Intention to be financially successful. Remember that you needn't think in extravagant terms. You can start out small—say, by saving $50 a month toward creating an investment portfolio. And if that sounds too uninspiring, find something that truly excites and challenges you. Let your goals be big enough to stretch you, realistic enough to let you demonstrate success.

If you continue on this path, and follow the coaching you'll find in the next chapter, I promise you miracles! Remember, you are successful if you can take a dream, articulate it as a goal, and know that you will keep your promise to yourself to attain or even surpass it.

PART II

Identifying the Inner Blocks to Progress

DRIVEN BEHAVIOR WASTES MONEY ENERGY

You have your Standards of Integrity, Life's Intentions, and some goals to manifest in the physical realm. What now?

The minute you become clear about where you're going, you may start to see where you've slowed yourself down in the past. The next three chapters are about identifying inner blocks to progress. You will learn how to deal with your dragons, so that you can keep moving forward. What do you do when you step out on your path and encounter your old ways of proceeding? How do you go beyond your self-created patterns? Do you throw more energy at it in the forms of physical vitality, time, and money?

Notice if you're feeling a little concerned or impatient as you read those words. Many of us are used to just "going for it" full tilt and trying to power ourselves down the road. If something doesn't work, we may even try to do more of whatever we're doing—just a little bit harder. As much as you might want to run full speed down your hero's path, that's not always your next best course of action. Now that you're able to free up more energy, you need to know how to use it wisely.

In the next few chapters I simply ask you to observe your behavior. Take some time to ask yourself if what you are doing is in alignment with your Standards of Integrity and your Life's Intentions. We all engage in driven behavior and have other mental blocks to progress.

You know your own particular tendencies. What you need to do about driven behavior is to notice when you are engaged in it, tell the truth, and shift your attention to your Standards of Integrity, your Life's Intentions, and achieving your goals. That will keep you on your hero's journey and stop the Monkey Mind.

FACING FEAR

Fear is a natural response to a perception about the future. Sometimes our Monkey Minds paint dreadful pictures about what *could* happen, and we react to it as though it really *will* happen.

I once heard someone say that fear stands for False Evidence Appearing Real. It reminds me of a saying attributed to Mark Twain: "I am an old man, and I've lived through many trials and tribulations, most of which never really happened."

If your goals are attempts to get away from fear, you waste a lot of energy trying to get something you don't really want. You expend effort in an attempt to handle your discomfort. Trying to achieve a goal to get away from your fear is qualitatively different from going for something you really enjoy. You use your energy in ways that exhaust you. There's no satisfaction, maybe just momentary relief before the next surge of anxiety.

If you can identify with what I'm describing, then I know you're tired of doing things in the old ways that you're used to. Instead, you want to use your energy to accomplish goals that will contribute to you and those you love. That's what your hero's journey is all about.

This chapter will have you look at when and how you run from fear, so that you can channel the energy of money toward what you want. For this reason, each section concludes with a series of questions. As you answer them, you'll see more clearly what has real value for you.

Bring your Standards of Integrity and your Life's Intentions with you as you read this chapter. If you haven't yet discovered what they are, please return to Principle 2 and complete the exercises there. You'll use them to remind you of who you really are.

Sometimes we will do whatever it takes to get away from the feeling of fear. Enter, driven behavior.

DRIVEN BEHAVIOR: *DON'T* JUST DO IT!

You may not be aware of it, but "Just Do It" is a slogan that greets you first thing every morning as you snatch ten minutes for the newspaper and your first cup of coffee. It is there in almost every ad you read or commercial you listen to as you head for work. It walks with you during the day while you check off items on your "to do" list, and it waits for you as you take your tired body and mind to the bookstore to buy the latest primer on peak performance. The ubiquitous phrase is always completed with an exclamation mark: Just do it!

Think about it. For most of us life is all about "peak performance," doing more, and doing it better and faster. A recent billboard ad for a health club shows a woman hitting a punching bag next to three-foot-tall letters that read: "You can rest when you're dead."

We have our lists, our goals, our plans—and to accompany them, we have endless activity. We're sleep-deprived, exhausted, busier than ever before, and yet our dreams still seem distant.

That's because we can't reach them by just any kind of action. Many of us are caught up in a cycle of driven behavior: activity in the physical domain that is not anchored to our Life's Intentions in the metaphysical domain. Driven behavior is a lot like flies buzzing in fast circles on a hot day: it produces a lot of noise and activity but leaves behind nothing of substance. There's no connection at all to our purpose, direction, aim, or dreams—and all the driven behavior in the world can't take us any closer to them.

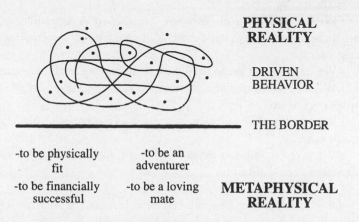

PHYSICAL
REALITY

DRIVEN
BEHAVIOR

THE BORDER

-to be physically   -to be an
       fit   adventurer

-to be financially   -to be a loving   METAPHYSICAL
   successful   mate   REALITY

Driven behavior commands our attention because it feels extremely urgent. In fact, there's a sense, when we're caught up in it, that it's a matter of survival, as though we're sharks fated to either keep moving or die. This kind of behavior is all about trying to avoid fear, whether it's fear that we don't have enough money or enough time, don't know enough, or don't have enough talent.

Running from this fear locks us into patterns of behavior that we don't think about much. We're under too much stress to stop what we're doing and ask if it's working for us, or if it's what we really want. We think we don't have time to get off the fast track and change. Our racing thoughts blind us from seeing what has real meaning for us. Instead, we're distracted by what we must have, be, or do just to survive. "I'll rest and figure out what I really want someday," we tell ourselves, "just as soon as I get past this crisis." Gut it out, we say. "You can rest when you're dead."

In *The Tibetan Book of Living and Dying*, Sogyal Rinpoche writes that our driven behavior is a type of active laziness that "consists of cramming our lives with compulsive activity, so that there is no time at all to confront the real issues. Our lives seem to live us, to possess their own bizarre momentum, to carry us away. In the end we feel we have no control or choice over them."

The cost of living our lives filled with driven behavior is high:

• We take on too much overhead—big offices, secretaries, support personnel, phones—because we need to look successful. And we spend most of our energy worrying and just trying to keep the business afloat.

• We accept too much business because we're scared to turn anything away, and we have difficulty making good on promises to customers.

• We let ourselves get so tired we end up making costly mistakes.

• We cut corners to give ourselves a break, and the quality of our work goes down.

• We take unnecessary or unwise risks in the hopes of making a quick profit.

• We take on way too much work but refuse to hire help, even though we could afford to.

All of us fall prey to driven behavior at one time or another. It's a natural consequence of listening to Monkey Mind's chatter. So for most of us the question is not whether we're driven but in *what ways* we are driven by our worries, doubts, and fears. As psychological and spiritual counselor and meditation teacher Sylvia Boorstein says in the title of one of her books, "Don't just do something, sit there!"

Our goal here is to uncover where your own driven behavior has kept you from focusing energy effectively. We want to find out where behavior of this kind has dissipated your energy, and perhaps even left you depleted. The clearer this becomes, the more quickly you can make authentic choices—ones that are deeply rooted in your intentions and dreams. Authentic choices yield results. *Your experience of an abundant life is the sum of your authentic choices minus the sum of your driven behavior.*

IS IT AUTHENTIC, OR AM I DRIVEN?

How do we distinguish between an authentic choice and one driven by fears and Monkey Mind? First, use the joy filter. Because an authentic choice reflects your Life's Intentions, it brings you a sense of joy. When you have made an authentic choice, it just seems right, and it's deeply satisfying. You know you are moving closer to your goals and expressing your true nature in ways that are constructive and creative. You are doing and having what you really want, without guilt, exhaustion, resentment, or a sudden loss of interest once you hold it in your hand.

Driven behavior, on the other hand, has three distinguishing characteristics, which we will look at in detail: repetition, limited satisfaction, and perfectionism.

SYMPTOM #1: REPETITION—PLAY IT AGAIN, SAM

The repetition of driven behavior looks like this: You do or think something over and over, even if it causes you trouble or needless effort. Even when you get frustrated, angry, or sad about it, you continue the behavior or thought. As Rita Mae Brown put it, "Insanity is doing the same thing, over and over again, expecting different results."

Here's how repetition looked in the lives of a few You and Money participants:

FRANK: I always wait until the last minute to pay my bills. I have the money, but that doesn't matter. Last month I waited too long and they cut off my phone. It embarrassed the hell out of me. Some of my clients called and got that recording about me being "no longer in service." This is the third time it's happened.

JANE: I know I can't afford it, but I have to have cable television with all the channels. I don't have much time to watch TV, but when I think about not being able to see what I want, when I want it, I get frustrated.

Look now at your own life. What thoughts or behaviors are you repeating, even though you know they don't serve you? Write down what you discover in your notebook. Do you overspend regularly, or accumulate parking tickets? What is it that you promise yourself never to do again, only to catch yourself doing it yet another time? Look at what you do or think around Christmas, Hanukkah, Kwanzaa, birthdays, or other regular events. Do you find yourself buying presents you really cannot afford? Are you driven to explain yourself?

I know this isn't easy, but tell the truth to yourself. Take notes on how you feel as you look at your repetitive behavior. Are you embarrassed, humiliated, annoyed, bored, or overwhelmed? Remember, this is part of the hero's journey. We are facing the dark side here, with open eyes. You may want to pause to look again at your Standards of Integrity and Life's Intentions. They are what matter here! This other stuff is what's been in the way of expressing who you really are.

The Rut Syndrome

Repetition may play itself out in what I call the "Rut Syndrome." A rut is a habit or pattern that blocks your progress on a particular path. Although repetitious, it may be so automatic as to escape your awareness. When you are in a rut your vision is blocked. You feel uncomfortable, frustrated, or resigned.

Assess the following true scenarios. In each case the person relies on old, familiar ways of coping, even when these coping mechanisms cut off the path to achieving his or her goals and dreams. Note, too, that the excuses for staying put usually seem very "reasonable."

RAY: I know I'm in a rut, but at least it's familiar. It's not like stepping out into the unknown. There's nothing worse than that. I'm forty-seven and I work for the state. For three years, I've been trying to decide whether to leave this job and run my own consultant and seminar business. I know lots about executive development, and it's something I've always wanted to do. But I'm seven years from retirement and I'm making pretty good money. Besides, I know I can put up with seven years of anything.

FRANK: I hate to stay in one job for more than about a year. Last year I sold computers at a retail outlet. I was the best salesperson there. I know how to talk to customers. Sooner or later, the manager starts to bug me. It's always the same. So what if I'm a few minutes late or take a longer lunch hour? I'm still the best producer in the place! The manager keeps bugging me and I'm gone. And fast! That's what happened last month. Now I'm working for another store. But it won't be long before this gets on my nerves.

To look at the Rut Syndrome and how it may be a factor in your life, answer the following questions in your notebook:

• What specific ruts am I in right now? Look in your financial, career, personal, and social lives, as well as at your physical well-being.
• What reasons do I use for staying this way?
• What has it cost me to maintain this rut? What is it continuing to cost me? Look first in the area of money. Can you calculate the specific cost of remaining in the rut? Go on to areas like money, time, dreams, well-being, and creativity.

Take a few deep breaths! I know this is difficult reading, but if you're even contemplating these questions, you're doing a great deal to free up your relationship with the energy of money.

SYMPTOM #2: LIMITED SATISFACTION: "I'M TOO TIRED/WORRIED/DISTRACTED TO ENJOY IT"

Driven behavior is particularly joyless. Often there's a bit of the martyr in the way we feel compelled to fill every waking hour with

an item on our to-do lists. We run ourselves ragged, leaving no possibility for enjoyment or creativity to come through and bring fresh-
ness and life to our routines. Yet we decline offers of support from
others, because we tell ourselves we're responsible adults and ought
to be able to handle everything ourselves. Besides, the other guy
will screw things up. When it comes time to enjoy the fruits of our
labors, we're too numb, distracted, and worn out to care, much less
be fully present. Our mantra becomes "Just get me through this."
Ultimately we find that the satisfaction in doing things is either
fleeting or nonexistent.

> SYLVIA: I'm so glad my daughter's wedding is finally over. I
> worried about the plans for the reception, even though we hired
> someone to take care of everything. I worried about the money,
> even though I knew we were getting a good price from the
> caterer. And on the day itself, I just waited and watched for
> something to go wrong. I'm just not used to leaving someone
> else in charge. I was a pool of nervous exhaustion by the end of
> the day—even though everything was fine.

> FRED: I remember standing with my diploma in hand
> during graduation last summer. My parents and friends were in
> the audience cheering, and there I was with my B.A., ready to
> go on for my teaching credential. I know I should have felt
> proud, but this question kept going around in my head: Is this
> all there is? I thought: "I've graduated. So what! Now I've got to
> bust my butt to get the credential. Then it's off to work. I
> couldn't just stop and appreciate anything."

Return to your notebook and jot down the times you were too hur-
ried, worried, or distracted to enjoy the satisfaction of a job well done.
Is your pleasure short-lived? Are you usually focused on the next
task? Do you approach celebrations, vacations, or family outings with
the thought "Just let me make it through this"? As you think about
these experiences, be specific. Recall names, dates, and places.

SYMPTOM #3: PERFECTIONISM—"JUST ONE MORE FINISHING TOUCH . . ."

In the world of driven behavior, there's Superman/Wonder
Woman—and then there's us. Superman/Wonder Woman set the

standard we think we have to reach, and in our heart of hearts, we know we're just not good enough to measure up. We're afraid of trying because we're worried that we're inferior or untalented, or not as competent as we'd like to be. So we don't complete projects; we keep on polishing them. If we don't finish, no one can judge us. We can always say, "But I'm not finished yet!"

Perfectionists almost never feel that they've done anything well enough. They don't feel they've done enough to justify a rest, or some acknowledgment.

JACLYN: I didn't enter my photo in the local competition. I didn't think it was good enough. My friends all encouraged me to do it, but I wasn't 100 percent satisfied with it. Last week I saw the photo that took first place. Mine was just as good. I've always wanted to be a professional photographer. But what if I'm not good enough? Besides, I hear there's no money in it.

JORGE: All right! I have two days to do what I want. I could finish the cabinet I started six months ago. It's almost finished. Or the dollhouse I promised my daughter last year. Just needs a final paint job. And I've been meaning to continue with that new accounting software. So many great projects, so little time!

Consider the following questions as you write about how perfectionism shows up in your life:

• After you start something, do you quit just before it is almost finished?
• When you work on a project, do you hold on to it even when you know you have done all you can?
• Is there an unfinished final report, thesis, or dissertation that stands between you and getting that degree or certification for which you have studied long and hard?
• Do you keep putting off a promotion interview because you are worried you have not prepared well enough?

We soothe or congratulate ourselves by saying that we're perfectionists. But it is most often a ruse. Perfectionism is the just the inability to arrive at closure. It masquerades as virtue, but it's really most often an excuse for not producing the result.

Think about this for a moment. Have you ever used being a "perfectionist" as the reason for not keeping your word or finishing a project? Do you see the term "perfectionism" as a virtue instead of an excuse? Have you ever heard someone use it to explain why he or she got a project done early?

Whatever the cause of perfectionism, it keeps our energy tied up in almost-finished projects, never allowing us to claim the rewards of completion—or to come in touch with the glowing energy of satisfaction.

DRIVEN, OR IN THE DRIVER'S SEAT?

When you are driven, your thinking can border on being obsessional, and your behavior on being compulsive. Obsessions are recurring thought patterns that get in the way of doing things with ease, and they're energy sponges. Suppose you worry about finding the job you want. The worry by itself is not an obsession until it becomes almost the only thing you think or talk about. An obsessive thought takes up all your energy, and it doesn't necessarily motivate you to solve the problem. In fact, obsessive thoughts can immobilize you. Or they can compel you toward inappropriate actions as you try to alleviate the anxiety they keep in front of you.

Compulsions are a little different from obsessive worries. These are acts you must perform again and again to maintain some level of comfort or security, even when these behaviors themselves are tedious or painful. For example, you might insist that Christmas dinner has to be prepared a specific way, year after year, without any deviations. Or you might feel you must have large amounts of cash or carry credit cards in your purse or wallet, "just in case." You might have the urge to go to the racetrack every week because you "just know" you are going to win this time.

Obsessions and compulsions act like blinders on a horse. They keep your attention narrowly focused on one fear you must avoid, or one aspect of life you must control. You have little chance to enjoy the present moment as it unfolds. Sorting out these driven behaviors starts with telling the truth about what you think you must have in order to feel secure. "Must have" thoughts sound like this:

• But I really do need a new car every three years.
• I work hard. I deserve to eat at the best restaurants.
• We know the children are gone, but we have to keep this big house. What if they want to come back for a visit in a few years?
• I must have that speedboat. I don't care what it takes.
• I always go to the local bar to blow off steam on Fridays.

One thing you are sure to discover when you start looking at your "must have" conversations is an endless stream of internal arguments, perfectly good reasons, rules, and stories for what you need. All this will be very convincing.

ADDICTIONS

Many experts say that parallels exist between driven and addictive behavior. Addictive behavior, like driven behavior, can be measured by the extent to which it interferes with our lives, and leads us further from our authentic choices and goals.

Addiction may become intertwined with driven behavior this way. Driven behavior overheats your mind. You can't stop thinking about what you must have, or doing what you feel you must to feel free from anxiety or dread. For relief you may "self-medicate" yourself with activities or substances that divert you: eating, shopping, gambling, work, sex, drugs, alcohol. And soon enough, you may *need* these activities or substances—becoming dependent on them, then addicted.

The addiction, in turn, interferes with how you function. You become more stressed, and need more of the addictive behavior or substance to handle it. Soon the addictive spiral begins. The "medicine" that dulled your symptoms has become the problem rather than the solution.

The first sign of an addiction is that you get withdrawal symptoms when you try to stop using the substance or engaging in the behavior in question. You undoubtedly already know about this where drugs or alcohol are concerned. But what about the emotional withdrawal reaction that goes along with things having to do with money?

As we venture into the territory of compulsion, consider not only what you do but also what happens when you try to stop one of these forms of driven behavior.

SPENDAHOLISM–OBEYING THE CALL OF THE SIRENS

The Sirens were mythological women with beautiful and compelling voices who lured Greek sailors to dive from their ships onto jagged rocks. As we deal with the energy of money, our "Sirens" are the voices, inside and out, that entice us with visions of things we "must have." We may be clear about our main course–say, to save enough for a down payment on a house, or to pay for our kids' college education–but the Sirens offer instant gratification, fun, freedom, soothing rewards for our hard work. And when we follow them, our best intentions wind up on the rocks.

> CHRISTINA: I wander around shopping malls a lot. Their bright lights are especially great in the winter when it gets foggy outside. Inside the mall, the color, glitter, and wonderful smells boost my mood. I can easily drop $20 on yogurt and assorted "knickknacks" in the first fifteen minutes I'm there. And I usually stay a couple of hours.

> DENISE: My friends call me "Bookwoman." I don't spend much on clothes or eating out. But if you put me in a bookstore, any bookstore, and let me loose for less than an hour, I'll crawl to the cashier's counter, my arms filled with books. I want to have them with me in my home, just in case I do have the time.

> MARK: My wife and I fight a lot about money. She says I spend too much on my toys, but I'm old enough to decide what I want. I work hard. So what if the stuff sits in boxes for weeks before I unpack it. Last week I bought some great software for my PC, which I still need to load up. The week before, it was a portable CD player. There's a relaxation machine I bought six months ago that I haven't learned to use. I do have to admit, every time I see one of those slick new catalogues in the mail, I know I'm a goner.

When you are caught in this pattern of behavior, the thought of not having what you want at the moment you want it can make you frustrated or anxious. You feel deprived and experience moments of sadness. Do you give in to the Spendaholic Sirens? Check on this by answering the following questions in your notebook. Tell the truth.

• When I get it in my mind that I want something, like new clothes, books, toys, or collectibles, do I usually find some way to buy it, even though it might get me in financial trouble?

• If I don't get what I want, when I want it, do I feel sad, angry, or bored?

• Does the thought of being on a budget send shivers down my spine?

• Have I created a budget, only to fail at following it, over and over again?

• Do I ever get home and discover that I don't really want what I have bought, yet never take it back?

• What has doing it this way cost me? Look first at monetary costs. Then think about what this kind of driven behavior costs you in time, relationships, physical well-being, and peace of mind.

BINGEING AND PURGING WITH MONEY

You can have a relationship with money that looks like a food addiction, with all the highs of big spending and handling a lot of cash, followed by frightening lows, when even paying the rent is a struggle. The drama is intense and never-ending, and what's missing is any sense of moderation. The people who experience the feast/famine cycle most often are entrepreneurs whose income is erratic, with fat times frequently followed by periods in which checks don't come in and money is scarce.

PHYLLIS: As a real estate agent, it's either feast or famine for me. Some months I don't bring home anything and then in one month three escrows close and I'm flush. I know I should put some away so I'll have a steady income. But by the time the money comes in, I'm so starved for things that I buy, buy, buy. Then it's back to a strict financial diet for a while.

NED: I have myself on a rigorous budget. For weeks I live within it. I'm careful to track every penny I spend. Then something will come over me. Last time a friend called me about a real estate venture, asking me to join him in it. Without learning much about the details, I ran to the bank and withdrew $10,000. Didn't even tell my wife until it was a done deal. She was furious. And meanwhile I'm sweating it, hoping I didn't make a stupid move. Then, promising myself I'll never get sucked into something like that again, I go back to the tight budget.

Periods of abstinence with little or no spending, followed by intervals of intense spending, create a kind of emotional rush. You feel as though you are living on the edge. This, to put it mildly, does not promote stability. While the lifestyle can be exciting, it diverts you from pursuing goals that have real meaning and substance.

As you answer the following questions, be truthful with yourself. Which of these obstacles are on your hero's path?

• Do I secretly think that having a predictable relationship with money would be boring?
• When I have closed a deal, do I count on the money as a sure thing, even before I receive a check?
• Do I get a thrill at receiving an enormous amount of money after a particularly lean time?
• Do I create that thrill by waiting until my accounts receivable are large before I try to collect on them?
• Do I believe that money in accounts receivable is money in the bank? (Did you know that the more these accounts age, the less likely you will be to collect on them?)
• How long has it been since I kept my word to myself or someone else about attaining long-term financial goals? How often has it been because of my up-and-down relationship with money?
• What has it cost me to do things this way?

GAMBLING: GETTING HIGH ON RISK

It's exciting to beat the odds. Something for nothing is the way we like to see it, or a lot of thrill for a small investment. Casual gambling can be fun, and for some people it's a pastime with minimal energy costs. But when it becomes driven behavior, and tinged with the qualities of addiction, it can be very costly.

Veteran gamblers report a sort of ecstasy when they win, but they also say that the biggest rush comes after winning when they have been losing for a while. Which brings us to a question: What are they playing for—the big win or the big loss?

> WILL: I live close to Lake Tahoe. On weekends I like to go and play blackjack. I get there on Friday night and I don't move from the tables until Saturday evening. Everything goes okay until I start losing. I get desperate, and I'll do anything to get more money to keep playing. Last time I maxed out my credit card and came home $2,500 in the hole. I keep telling myself this is the last time I'll go up there with credit cards. But I always manage to forget to take them out of my wallet before I leave.

> JULIE: We have a new kind of lottery in our state. It's like keno, where you sit at tables, pick numbers, and wait for them to come up on the screen. I've lost $500 so far. Every time I go into the liquor store and see the screen flashing numbers, I'm hooked for at least an hour.

Gambling is fascinating in the way it strips money of its intrinsic value. When you are at the table, $600 in the hole, you rarely stop and think about what you could do with the same amount of ready cash.

As with everything else in this chapter, the only thing you need to do right now is look. Ask yourself: *Is what I am doing focusing my energy on attaining the life goals that really mean something to me, or is it getting in the way?* Is it possible that you have been shooting yourself in the foot? Write down your answers to the following questions:

• Do I know or suspect that I have wasted time and money trying to beat the odds in life? Look at high-risk investments, lotteries, gaming, consistent wagering at office jackpots, etc.

• Are my friends, family, or co-workers concerned about my gambling? Has a loved one openly complained to me about it?

• If I were to add up all the money I've lost in gambling over the past ten years, what is the estimated figure?

If you're willing, please share these answers with at least one person you trust. Have it be someone whose fortunes are not tied to yours, so they can be an objective listener.

INFORMATION ADDICTION

Never before have we had the kind of access to information we have today. In our wired homes and offices, we can plug in, any time of the day or night, and shop, chat, check our stocks, or research any conceivable topic. We get pulled into the 'Net, caught in the Web, and many of us are vulnerable to a kind of addiction that was almost unheard of only fifteen years ago: addiction to information.

> JEFF: I can easily spend eight hours every day at the computer. I log on to the 'Net, find a chat room, or go in search of great Web pages. I love to shop on the 'Net, too. I've got a good modem, but it still isn't fast enough. I'm thinking about getting one of those ISDN lines, dedicated to my Internet connection. It's expensive, but what the hell? I work hard. I deserve it. My wife gets upset because she doesn't see enough of me.

Is Web surfing, 'Net-shopping, e-mailing, and chat-room time focusing your time and money energy, or have you started to use it compulsively or addictively?

Ask yourself:

• Does my recreation time with computer software, including games, the Internet, and information-managing programs, exceed two hours daily? If yes, do I see where this interferes with my relationships, goals, health, and peace of mind? For example, are my loved ones complaining that I spend more recreational time with my computer than I do with them?

• Can I "lose" myself at the computer, without noticing that I need to eat, sleep, or attend to biological needs?

• Can I imagine what I would do with my time and money if I did not spend so much of either on my PC?

WORKAHOLISM

Take control! Get off your butt! You can have it all! When the going gets tough, the tough get going!

Can you feel the adrenaline pumping yet? Americans spend hundreds of millions of dollars every year to be prodded with messages like these, urging us to work harder. In moderation these sentiments are useful, but they're like psychoactive drugs to those of us who are addicted to work. And there are millions of workaholics in our midst. Putting in long hours is integral to most corporate and institutional cultures—and if you happen to be a small-business owner, salesperson, or tradesperson, this behavior is not only condoned but required. Workaholism, though it appears to be a sure way of focusing ourselves to get more money, sets in motion a cycle that ultimately saps the energy of money, as well as all the other forms of energy in our lives.

Can you go anywhere without your pager, cell phone, day planner, briefcase? Are you always accessible to your office, your clients, your employees? Do you remember what it's like to spend uninterrupted time with your loved ones, or alone—just doing *nothing*? (Gasp! Please breathe here!) Do you repeatedly cancel dates with friends because of work emergencies or deadlines?

The competitive climate we live in puts a high value on the motivated go-getter, and it rewards us with respect, pay, and perks for our 24-7 commitment. But what's lost in the frantic, urgent shuffle is a sense of who we are. We can't stop and rest long enough to remember.

Interestingly, a study of peak performers several years ago found that no matter what their field, they share a single distinguishing characteristic that sets them apart from everyone else: Peak performers take time for complete rest every day.

Rest. The taboo, four-letter word for workaholics. Yet the peak performers who never failed to find time for it included John F. Kennedy, Winston Churchill, Albert Einstein, and Thomas Edison, all of whom typically took naps every day, if only for twenty to thirty minutes.

Rest and play are not the same thing. We tend to get them confused.

PAUL: I work hard and I play hard. That's my rest and relaxation. If I sit still too long, I get antsy.

Rest means letting your body and mind slow down and become replenished. There is no such thing as resting hard.

Are you pouring energy into work, at the expense of the dreams at your core? Take out your notebook and answer the following questions:

• If I were to give myself time to rest, would I feel guilty or edgy because I'd be thinking about all the things I need to do?

• What would I do with myself if I didn't work so much?

• Who am I under the flurry of all the activity in my life?

TELLTALE SIGNS

Workaholism isn't about working diligently. It's really about working without rest and allowing work to interfere with other areas of your life, such as intimate relationships, creativity, leisure time, and physical well-being.

If you're a workaholic, you may pursue more money and more goals the way an addict goes after "speed." You can use goals to prod yourself into action, no matter how tired you are, and pride yourself on your ability to do it all. All the elements of driven behavior come into play here. You repetitively take on work, even if it's wearing you out. You set ever-escalating standards, allowing perfectionism to rob you of satisfaction. The joys of the moment are lost, for years, in the quest for the elusive goal.

Authentic Action connects you with your deepest self and with joy. It doesn't put your "real life" on hold; it feeds you now. Addictive goals, however, are quite different. They pull all your energy into feeding the addiction to movement, adrenaline, busy-ness.

Jim, a very bright office-equipment salesman, came to the You and Money Course with the goal of retiring by the time he was forty-five. He was thirty-eight and working very hard. Our dialogue went something like this:

JIM: I figure if I can save up enough money, I'll be able to retire.

ME: What does retirement look like to you?

JIM: I'll be able to work at something I love. I'll rest. I'll have fun. I'll see more of my friends and family.

ME: What if you could work at something you love, get the rest you need, and enjoy yourself right now? Would you still want to resign or retire?

JIM: No, then I could start doing what I want with my family and friends instead of waiting another seven years. Maybe if I have fun, I won't want to retire. Maybe I'll stay at this job or quit it and go back to school. Come to think of it, I could go back to school right now. Oh, oh! (laughter) This is getting too easy!

Jim's solution may seem obvious. But when you're caught up in working too hard, it's easy to miss the logical flaw in your thinking. Errors like this are often the product of a driven, over-heated mind.

If any of this sounds even slightly familiar to you, take heart. Your opportunity here is to wake up to what you are doing. Ask yourself the following questions. Let your mind get quiet and listen, really listen. Write down your discoveries in your notebook. Share your answers with a friend or loved one as a way of bringing all this into your consciousness.

• What would I find inside if I slowed down my frantic work pace for several hours?
• Who am I when I'm not working?

These questions may lead to important answers. The last one, about your identity apart from your job, can be especially revealing. A workaholic finds it difficult to develop a personal identity away from the work he or she does. I often wonder what it would be like nowadays to go to a party and not talk about what we do for a living. What if we were to introduce ourselves by talking about our dreams, favorite charities, inspiring books we have read, qualities we admire in people, or places we want to visit? It might be awkward at first, but it would move us beyond our all-consuming identification with our jobs.

DO YOU HEAR YOURSELF IN THESE VOICES?

I'd like you to listen to the words of some people who've let work
consume their energy and push them off the path that leads to fulfillment. As you read these anecdotes, substitute your own profession or other details from your life for the details in their stories.
Don't let the differences between their stories and your own stop
you from looking at the underlying themes that have taken over
too much of your life. Only then can you see where your energies
are going.

> LAURA *(public relations officer)*: I've got a beautiful time-share
> at the lake that I haven't been inside in years. I give the time slot
> to friends for their vacations. Last week I finally decided to take
> two weeks off and go there myself. But there's a big publicity
> party for our top clients during one of the weekends I'll be gone.
> Everyone will be there. What if something goes wrong? Why
> does this have to happen, just as I was trying to break free for a
> while!

When you are addicted to your work, work-related issues *always*
threaten to interrupt your plans for rest or recreation. You find compelling, even irrefutable, reasons to keep working. Or you bring the
trappings of work with you wherever you go. At the very least, you
feel pulled by last-minute crises that come up and beg for your attention. And you convince yourself that you are the only one who can
handle them.

Do you consistently leave for vacations absolutely exhausted
because you have been working so hard to tie up loose ends at the
office before you go? Does the thought of leaving your work behind
make you feel uncomfortable or anxious? Those are two telling
symptoms of workaholism.

> STEVE *(building contractor)*: Two years ago my wife left me
> for my best friend. I went into a tailspin. I was mad, all right.
> But then the real truth hit me. I drove her away. I'd been
> working fourteen-hour days, six days a week to build this busi-
> ness. I told myself I was doing it for her, and that we'd iron out
> our difficulties later when I'd made some big bucks. Three years
> ago she asked that we go to a marriage counselor. I said no
> because I didn't have the time. So she left. I haven't been see-

ing other women. But I've sure been working hard. Sometimes, when business is slow, I worry about what to do with my
free time.

Steve's last sentence is a real giveaway. It reveals his workaholism. The following question expresses it best:

• If I had some free time, would I know what to do with it or
myself?

Free time is a challenge for workaholics. And often they keep
themselves so busy they never have to think about anything but one
of the many tasks at hand. But facing the compulsion, and telling the
truth about it, leads to wisdom—and a way out.

Exercise: Am I or Am I Not a Busyholic?

By now you've done a lot of work to identify your driven
behavior, but before we leave this topic behind I'd like you to
take one final look at what I call "busyholism." Busyholism is
the term I use for the need to keep busy, whether at home or at
work. This inventory caps off our look at driven behavior. I suggest that you go a bit more slowly than usual with it. Be careful
not to skip over items you find uncomfortable.

If you can, talk about these items in a group. Each person can
speak about the issues that most concern him or her. A supportive atmosphere gives you breathing room to acknowledge
publicly what you might dismiss privately.

You will need a pen or pencil, and your notebook to record
your responses. This exercise will take about forty minutes—
twenty minutes for this inventory, plus discussion time.

Each item below is presented as a statement. Write it down.
Next, indicate how true the statement is for you. Use a scale
from 1 to 5, with these values: The number 1 means "not true";
2 means "somewhat untrue"; 3 means "don't know"; 4 means
"somewhat true"; and 5 means "true." There is no score to add
up at the end. The scale is there to make it easy to discern
whether or not this item relates to you.

After rating each item, take a few moments to write about

what you thought, especially if an item rated "true" for you. For example, do you recall the last time this happened? Who was there? What did you do? What does it cost you to do things this way, in terms of money, time, love, and health?

BUSYHOLISM INVENTORY

1. I am tired most of the time.

2. I always seem to be in motion.

3. Most of the people in my life (spouse, friends, family) don't appreciate all I have to do.

4. I get very frustrated if I cannot finish a task or if I'm interrupted and I have to put it off until later.

5. On Sunday (or my day off) I have a list of things I must do before I can play or rest. I rarely get to the play and rest part.

6. I often feel isolated from those I love.

7. By the time I do something I like, I am too tired to really enjoy it.

8. I feel guilty when I am resting or just taking it easy.

9. When I am doing something (such as watching a son or daughter play soccer), I often miss out on the fun because I am too preoccupied with what needs to be done next.

10. I use substances such as caffeine or sugar to prod myself into action during the day, and turn to alcohol, marijuana, or other drugs (prescription or over-the-counter) to relax in the evening.

11. I feel resentful because I am not doing the things I really want to do.

12. I feel that I have more responsibilities than most of my family or friends.

13. I usually do things in a hurry, like gulp my food or throw on clothes.

14. I forget to take care of myself (do not eat, drink water, or use the rest room) for long periods of time.

15. My friends and family tell me they are not seeing enough of me. Or, when I am with them, they tell me I seem withdrawn or emotionally removed.

There is no cumulative score for this inventory. It doesn't matter if you rate yourself at 5 on one or all of them. What matters is the self-awareness that comes out of the process.

When we start looking at our own busyholism, most of us will come face-to-face with a very active Monkey Mind. By its very nature, the "inner busyholic" does not want to be exposed, and Monkey Mind wants to protect itself. You'll hear it doing everything in its power to convince you that all this busy-ness and work that fills your life is absolutely justified. But if you are willing, you can see what you're really doing. You'll begin to crave breathing room.

SEEING THE LESSON

Is there even a slim possibility that you are a busyholic? Or that you may be leaning in that direction? If you still do not know for certain, there is one surefire way to find out. It requires courage, but if you do it you'll definitely get more than your money's worth out of this book. Ask your family and friends. Don't turn to the people who work with you, because they may be caught up in the same system that you are. Or they may have a vested interest in your staying busy. For the most trustworthy answers, ask those who know and love you outside of work. And be prepared to look, see, and tell the truth!

If you really want to get a handle on your driven behavior and busyholism, give the people around you permission to call you on it, and to remind you of who you are and what you're up to in life.

It's very important for you to have compassion for yourself as you look at the lessons in this and the next chapters. I've worked with thousands of people as they faced both their own driven behavior and their private versions of scarcity.

Perhaps the greatest reward is this: As you proceed on your hero's journey, you will open yourself to being less driven and more called by joys in the present moment. You'll free up your money, your time, and your heart for your deepest dreams.

PRINCIPLE 5

SCARCITY IS ONE OF YOUR GREATEST TEACHERS

In the last chapter we saw that fear is the engine that powers driven behavior, and sometimes even addiction. In this chapter we will address one of our greatest fears, especially where money is concerned—scarcity.

WHAT IS SCARCITY?

Dorothy Parker is quoted as saying, "I've been rich and I've been poor, and rich is better." Isn't that just the thought we all have at some point in our lives?

Being poor, broke, bankrupt, or destitute is the fear we often have as we enter the next stretch of the hero's journey. Some of us refer to it as "Scare City," and the most discouraged of us know it as "Scar City." For all on this path, it's the ground on which we must stop running and take a stand.

Scarcity is one of our deepest fears. *It is the mind's experience of the limits that are a natural part of physical reality.* No matter how enlightened or conscious—or rich—we may be, we encounter scarcity, naturally and repeatedly, every day.

LIMITS ARE PART OF PHYSICAL REALITY

Let's take apart the definition you just saw: "Limit" is a boundary that defines an object. This is what allows it to exist in physical reality. Pick up a pen or pencil and get the feel of it in your hand. Now imagine it getting bigger, its boundaries stretching ten feet in every direction. Continue to expand the boundaries, pretending that they extend for a thousand miles. Take away all limits and let the object's edges move out toward infinity. What happens as the object grows? If you're like many people, you'll notice that as you try to see it in your mind it disappears. It becomes everything, and no thing, at the same time.

The infinite pencil may be a great idea, but it's hard to wrap your hand around. Taking away its limits takes away its usefulness.

Beyond the three-dimensional limits of the physical plane, we also work within the limits of time, our life spans, and the cycle of birth and death that governs the existence of everything in physical reality. Rocks, people, oceans, and flowers: all are born, exist, and then disappear. Limits give rise to impermanence.

None of this is shocking information, and it's not particularly tinged with emotion. Limits are a fact of our lives. It could be said that one of the purposes of our lives is to learn how to be masterful with what we have—our limited amounts of time and energy—and to learn to appreciate and respond well to the limits in our lives.

That calm, cerebral interpretation, while true, is divorced from the second half of our definition. When we're talking about scarcity we're not talking about limits, precisely. We're talking about how the mind experiences them. And the truth is, the mind goes nuts whenever it comes up against a limit—as it does in nearly every waking moment of our lives.

Try this experiment: Take a deep breath, and hold it in. Keep holding it—and holding it—as long as you can, and pay attention to what's happening in your body and mind. Do you notice the limit of oxygen? How does it feel? (Okay, you can exhale now.) The feelings of stress, distress, and even panic that arise as we encounter a limit are part of scarcity. That fear provokes Monkey Mind, which then tells us: "Oh, God! I don't have enough," or even "I don't have enough, I'll never have enough, and I'm going to suffer or die."

Put the word "limit" next to the word "money" and you can just feel the scarcity triggers begin to trip. Most of us begin to run when

this happens, and many of us feel driven to fend off the impos-
ing dragon of scarcity. We'll look at how to face—and learn from—
that dragon. Remember that if you are willing to learn from your
dragons, you transform them into allies. But you must first ask to see
the lessons they bring.

We keep ourselves moving so we never have to stop and look,
really look, at the question I'm going to ask you now:

What do you hate most about the thought of not having money in
your life? What is the nightmare scenario that keeps you awake
when you think about not having enough of that energy?

These are not intellectual questions. The true answers come from
the gut, and it takes guts to find them. But if you are willing to strip
away any theories you have about how you experience scarcity, and
if you allow yourself to feel it and look at it and tell the truth about it,
you will take its fearsome power away.

Scarcity is a reality in the physical domain. As a minister friend of
mine once told me, "It's as though we got bored living without limits.
We decided to incarnate—which means, literally, to turn into meat.
We further chose to work with the limits of form, time, and finite
energy. This was to see how much of the divine we could bring into
the mundane before it was time for us to leave."

We reach the infinite through living fully in the finite. The infinite
is not reached by trying to ignore limits, as many of us try to do.

IS THE MONKEY SCREAMING YET?

Monkey Mind hates limits because its primary concern is survival. It
wants to live forever, and it wants safety and comfort, so when it
encounters the fear that time's running out, or that the bank account
is dwindling, it will do anything to keep that fear from getting close
enough to look at.

> WARREN: The last thing I want anyone to know is how
> much money I *don't* have. I have this internal monitor that tells
> me just how much to spend to keep myself broke. I can't hold
> on to my money. I know something's wrong with me. Some
> nights I worry a lot about growing old and poor.

Warren's predicament is common. On the one hand, he fears not having enough money. On the other, he hates the idea of facing that fear and doing something about it. He races past Scarcity with his credit cards out and spending everything he has, which results in keeping himself poor. This makes no sense at all. Yet it happens again and again in our lives. We spend bravely and put up a great front. We take other actions that draw to us the very thing we most abhor. On our circuitous route to avoid the dragon, we end up at its door!

Another time Monkey Mind comes up against limits is when people choose to live on a fixed or reduced income. Jeannette had decided that she wasn't willing to keep climbing the corporate ladder and wanted to simplify her life. She was using the You and Money Course to ease her transition into no longer spending lots of money. She reported that she had panic attacks, and dreams about catastrophes that would occur if she didn't keep earning more money every year. She didn't see how she could do without all the luxuries that she had enjoyed.

When she looked, she saw that this whole conversation was Monkey Mind. First of all, when she made a list of all the luxuries, she found that there weren't actually that many of them and that most of them were convenience items like hiring a grocery shopping and housecleaning service—things she now would have the time to do herself. Her internal dialogue was trying to convince her that she was about to go down the tubes because Monkey Mind abhorred the possibility of a limit. Its mantra is "More, give me more!" But in fact, Jeannette founded her own small consulting firm and did very well with limits.

Jeannette's situation answers the question, "If simplicity sounds so great, why don't more of us do it?" The answer is that before we can appreciate simplicity, we first have to deal with the Monkey Mind that stands at the gate and says, "This is going to be terrible. Your survival is at stake."

Monkey Mind has a siege mentality. It tells us something almost all of us believe: *Amassing more will solve the problem and slay the scarcity monster.* Ironically, though, it's just not true. If you try to stave off scarcity by amassing more—more objects, more money, even more spiritual practices—the experience of scarcity grows bigger.

People have all kinds of thoughts when they first hear this:

• Sure, sure. Just let me win the lottery and I'll show you how to handle scarcity!

• I absolutely know that having more money would get me out of this funk.

• Here we go with the metaphysical double-talk. Let's get real! The way to solve money problems is with money!

As much as we try to use the energy of money as a bulwark against our anxiety, however, we can't succeed. The purpose of money energy isn't to add jet fuel to our flight from what deeply frightens us; it's to take us toward our dreams. Try as we may, we can't get money alone to allay the fear that's wrapped up in the question What if I lost everything? Still, we persist, with results like this:

> ESTHER: When I was a student on scholarship, I lived on $500 a month. I remember saying to myself: "All I need is another $100 a month and I'll have it made." Sure enough, I got a part-time job and started pulling in an extra $120 a month. Three months later it was the same thing: If I just had another $75 a month! I could take myself out to the movies and buy some extras. Then I got my first full-time job for $2,500 a month. It was heaven for about six months. The old voice came right back: "Just give me $500 a month more, and I'll be on easy street." That was six years ago. Today, with my MBA, I'm earning $6000 a month, and I *still* wish I had more money. What's weird about this is that I am more in debt now than I was five years ago, and I worry about money as much now as when I was in school.

Esther's story is not just a case of poor money management. It is a reflection of *scarcity unconfronted.* The Monkey Mind that chants "more, more, more" is never satisfied. I remember reading an odd story about a man who owned a cigar store in my town. He lived frugally, and from the way he dressed, people thought he was barely getting by. But when he died, relatives who came to clean up his apartment found $200,000 in cash under his mattress.

How much was "enough" for him? How much would have allowed him to spend some of that money on himself? How much would have quieted the roar of Scarcity?

The experience of scarcity is a condition of life. And one of the properties of a condition of life is that when it goes unconfronted, and we try to put more things in between us and the experience of that condition, it only makes that condition bigger.

By doing the work here, you may genuinely discover contentment with what you have. You could begin to enjoy the abundance you sought for so long. Perhaps you'll see that you could be happier making less money than you presently do. Or you may find that you're willing to have more money and are up to the challenge of using its energy wisely. The point is, these alternatives are possible only when you're willing to face and learn your personal lessons about scarcity. Then you're really free to have what you want in life.

When Esther saw how scarcity influenced her relationship with money, a subtle shift occurred. One year later she bought her first home, began working with a certified financial planner, and was saving money rather than incurring more debt. More important for her is that she felt relief, and life was easier. She wasn't running from her dread of limits.

The span of our lifetime is limited. Our money is limited. Our physical stamina is limited. And no amount of work, or prayer, or frantic activity, or cash under the mattress, can keep that fact of physical reality from pricking us awake every time we take a breath or see a new wrinkle in the mirror.

YOU CAN'T AFFIRM AWAY SCARCITY

We're not used to talking about limits, or about our intense discomfort with them. In fact, one trick Monkey Mind uses to avoid looking at scarcity is to tell us, "If I don't think about it, maybe it won't exist." A lot of us take that a step further and believe that we poison our chances of experiencing prosperity if we spend any time at all with "negative thinking"—such as acknowledging our worries about not having enough of what we want or need. If we affirm the positive, we figure, we can somehow fool reality into going along.

I remember thinking, "Maybe if I wake up every morning and say to myself, 'I have enough money. I have enough money,' it'll be true." But the real truth is, affirmations like that don't work. According to Shakti Gawain, who wrote *Creative Visualization,* affirmations work best when you use them to affirm the truth about yourself. I have found they fail miserably when you use them to suppress negative thoughts or feelings. In the You and Money Course, we call that sugary, "let's pretend everything's fine" variety of positive thinking "candy-coating the cow pie." The scenario goes like this:

Let's say that you come upon a cow pie in the middle of the road—something you don't want to feel. You need to deal with it somehow—it stinks, and it's attracting flies—so you carefully pick it up and surround it with candy coating. You really pour on the candy coating of positive thinking: "Scarcity doesn't exist. I have my greatest good always. I have everything I need." Every time your unwanted feeling of scarcity pops up, you pour on a little more of that coating. The problem is, though, that you haven't gotten rid of the cow pie. You've just covered it up, and it keeps fermenting. You can smell it. So you keep pouring on more and more candy coating. And try as you might, you can't escape the unpleasant, permeating odor of your doubts and other negative thoughts. It's not a pretty picture, but it gets to the heart of the problem with wishful-thinking affirmations.

Yet everywhere we turn, people are assuring us that positive thinking will make everything all better:

HAROLD: I've gone to a number of prosperity workshops. I have been told that if I hold the right thoughts my outward reality will begin to reflect my new thinking. But nothing's changed in my life over the past year. I still don't have the job I want. I'm even further in debt. Maybe there's still something wrong with me or my way of looking at things.

PAUL: I just joined a network marketing system to make more money on the side. I've seen videotapes of people who are successful at it. They're sitting on the beach in Hawaii or in their beautiful homes, telling me to think positively and expect the best. They say it's important to work hard and have a "winning attitude." But how can I have a "winning attitude" when I get so anxious about my finances? I try not to worry, but it doesn't work.

Harold and Paul are trying to use positive thoughts to avoid their honest reactions to scarcity. They're trying to control thoughts and feelings they don't even want to look at. But thoughts and feelings need an outlet, and if they don't get it, they fester and undermine our entire outlook on the world. The effort to make them disappear with positive affirmations is as futile as trying to keep the waves from lapping against the shore of a lake.

You're probably familiar with what happens when you actively try to avoid thinking about something. For the next ten seconds, *do not* think about a sumptuous hot-fudge sundae. *Do not* think about the rich chocolate topping, the cool, sweet taste of the ice cream, the smooth whipped cream, and the chopped nuts.

If you're like most of us, your mind probably responded to that attempt by saying something like this:

Okay, I'll stop thinking about a hot-fudge sundae with whipped cream. This is easy. I don't care about hot fudge sundaes at all. As a matter of fact, I'll just meditate. And of course, the last thing I'll be thinking about then is hot fudge and ice cream and nuts. No big deal. See? I just put that sundae right out of my mind.

Clearly our minds are drawn to the very things we tell them to avoid. So is it possible to cover over your negative thoughts? That's very much like trying to control the waves on a lake. You can do it, but you have to freeze the lake or drain it first. And you *can* control the thoughts you don't want—if you're willing to freeze over huge areas of your life experience. When you freeze out the pain, however, you also numb the joy, and your enthusiasm for life.

LET'S GET REAL

It takes incredible amounts of energy to suppress your thoughts, and that energy would be much better spent in pursuing your dreams. We've all met people who maintain that everything is "fine, just fine"—no matter what. And inevitably we get the sense that their bright-eyed smiles and firm handshakes aren't real. They seem to be outgoing and cheerful and full of energy, but connecting with them is nearly impossible, because we can't get past the happy-happy facade. That smiling plastic exterior becomes a huge barrier. A minister friend of mine tells this story:

> FLOYD: In the past I refused to acknowledge to myself that I had negative thoughts about other people. For years I insisted that I had only *positive* thoughts. About two years ago I found myself getting incredibly irritated by some of the people passing

in front of me after Sunday service. You know, the ones who take a single $1 bill and crumple it into a tiny ball and throw it into the collections plate as though the church could just run on air. I tried not to think bad thoughts. After all, they're God's children. But after a while I just couldn't help it. And I hated myself for it. I'd judge them and condemn myself for doing that, and the cycle went on and on. At the same time, my Sunday contributions began to go way down. I talked to some parishioners I knew well, and the consistent feedback I got was that I didn't seem like a real human being anymore.

When I thought about it, I realized that my judgments about the people who don't donate a lot to the church were my own personal experience with scarcity. I decided to face my own negative thoughts. At first I felt so uncompassionate. But when I faced them, I saw that I'm a real human being just like everyone else. And something happened. I relaxed. People started coming up to me and saying, "You know, Floyd, you're a lot more approachable than you used to be. I sense a softness about you." And the weird thing is, people started giving more money.

There's something about looking at what you think is wrong with you—your own personal experience of scarcity—and being willing to see it and tell the truth about it. You get more room to breathe, to soften up a little. You make space for compassion. And when that happens, the people and situations around you often have room to shift, too.

LILLIAN: I always thought my son was pretty untrustworthy with money. He'd spend his allowance in a flash and come crying for more. I didn't give him more. I would get irritated and lecture him on the importance of being thrifty. When I thought about it, I noticed how much he reminded me of my brother and the way he was lazy and used to beg off my parents. I hated having those negative thoughts and feelings about my son and my brother. Worse was what I thought about the kind of person I must be for having these judgments in the first place. When I saw it was my Monkey Mind at work, I stopped feeling so trapped. Although I didn't give my son more money, I stopped with the lectures. He must have noticed, because he came up to me one day and said, "You know, Mom, I keep asking you for a lot of money. I bet if I were you and you were doing that to me, I'd be pretty frustrated." It made all the difference in the world to me.

What happened? You could say that the son just had a coincidental change of heart. But I've noticed that when you become more comfortable with facing your own negative thoughts and have compassion for yourself, people respond. It provides them with a chance to be more authentic and show who they really are in their hearts.

This is quite different from affirming away your fears and judgments. Just think for a minute of someone you dislike or who irritates you. Picture them in your mind and find ten positive things to say about them. What happens? Your mind becomes confused as it searches for a compliment, and tension may rise as your positive thoughts battle with the negative ones. Most likely you're not feeling too joyful as you do this. Doesn't it feel phony, as though you're trying to put one over on your mind? That's because you *are*. You're trying to use positive thoughts to ward off negative emotions or circumstances. It doesn't work.

Looking at negative thoughts is one thing, but what about that nagging voice inside that urges you to go out and get what you deserve? Is that a form of scarcity as well? Yes!

THE DEPRIVATION CYCLE: "BUT I FEEL SO DEPRIVED; CAN'T I JUST HAVE A LITTLE MORE?"

"I'm tired. I want a toy. After all, I've been good, haven't I? I'm working hard, bringing home the bacon. Don't I deserve a treat?" Monkey Mind purrs in our ear, beguiling and reasonable. And we listen.

Deprivation is one way we experience scarcity. Deprivation is that feeling of need, that feeling deep inside that we don't have enough money (or fun, enjoyment, love, you name it) in our lives. It's coupled with a sense of entitlement to buy something that will fill the void that's been left by days or weeks of relentless driven behavior. So feeling deprived is intimately connected with driven behavior.

You get a sense of deprivation when you've worked long and hard

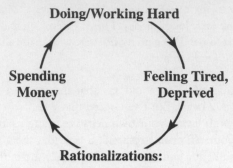

Doing/Working Hard

Spending Money

Feeling Tired, Deprived

Rationalizations:

a) This has been one killer week—
   it's time for a pick-me-up.

b) I need a new outfit, a great
   meal, a new toy.

c) After all, I work hard for
   my money. I deserve it.

without a breather. Depleted, restless, and often lonely, you look for a way to fill up. You need a reward. Spending money offers the best solution.

Look at the rationalizations in the diagram. They usually precede your spending money on something, not necessarily because you genuinely want it, but because it makes up for the deprivation. You have worked so hard, and had so little rest, that a reward is needed.

> BRIAN: I get caught up in "I deserve it" thinking when I'm not careful. Tired and stressed out, I get this idea that I deserve a good meal at an expensive restaurant. One night, staring into a $25 plate of food I really didn't want, I had to ask myself: "Am I working this hard so I can afford to spend money on spaghetti arranged like a southwestern landscape, with basil leaves for cactus? Is this really what I want?" Don't misunderstand me; I love good food. But sometimes I know I've bought the notion that a pricey meal at a trendy place is the best reward for hard work. It's a knee-jerk response to stress. Spending my money that way is one reason I end up working harder in the first place! What a vicious cycle!

The "I deserve it" rationale can provide a reason to buy almost anything. As soon as we start thinking we deserve something, we create a need. Monkey Mind thinks the need will be satisfied only by spending money. That's why some of the most effective ads around begin with the words "You deserve." Yes, you deserve a break, a car, a vacation, a hot new computer, and whatever else your hard-earned dollars will buy.

Instead of having what you deserve, what would it be like for you to simply have what you want? That's a whole different perspective. We often take a defensive, sometimes demanding posture toward getting what we "deserve." In addition, we have to build up a deprivation state in order to justify our demands. And it's often this very state that interferes with our enjoyment. To quote Brian: "When I dine at those pricey restaurants because I deserve it, I'm often too tired to relish what I'm eating. And what's more, I usually overeat because I want more energy."

It's costly to consume out of a sense of deprivation. We get caught up in wanting more-bigger-faster stuff, and have to go back to earn the money to pay for it. In addition, we're often not satisfied, because what we really want is rest, time, meaning, and connection with others. That is really what's most important to us, and that's what we're often too depleted to create.

If you want to get in touch with what is of real value to you, try this experiment: Imagine that there is a fire in your home. Your family and any pets get out safely, and you have two minutes to grab some possessions. What do you take? For me it would be the photographs of my family and the other people I love. I think those would be the most difficult to lose. Next, maybe, I'd want some art objects and computer discs full of my writings. My VCR and espresso coffeemaker? Way down on the list. Even if they were not insured.

I talked with a few of the people whose homes were destroyed in a fire in Santa Barbara, California. The immediate shock of losing everything was devastating. But for everyone, being stripped of possessions yielded a new view of life. I talked to one woman two years after the fire:

LAURIE: I lost everything in the fire, and what I grieved about most was my weaving loom, which was my most precious possession. But my friends heard about it, and they put together enough money to buy me a new one. The interesting thing is that when I didn't have a lot of possessions, it's as though some

energy got freed up. And living in a home that didn't have a lot
in it, I started to do a lot of thinking about what I really wanted
in my life.

Laurie decided that what she wanted most was to write a book
about weaving in Third World countries, and she recently received a
grant to do it. She thinks of it as a blessing from the tragedy and said,
"I never would have gone for it if I didn't have that fire in my home,
tragic as it was at first."

You will be amazed at what happens when you step out of the
"must work/must have/must work" whirlwind. Your choices, and
your life, will begin to look quite different.

"I'LL SHOW YOU MINE IF YOU SHOW ME YOURS"

If you want to come face-to-face with one form of scarcity, just compare your financial situation with that of the people around you. A
feeling of tense competition can rush in when we compare our lives
to others', and that happens repeatedly from the time we're old
enough to compare body parts to the time we are old enough to swap
the details of our retirement plans. Look at these examples and see
where you fit in.

> JAMES: I don't talk about my commissions and how much I
> bring home every month. It's nobody else's business. The truth
> is that I'm afraid I make less than most of the insurance agents
> in my company. I'd never want anyone to know that!

> MARGE: I felt just wonderful about my new 4 × 4 truck
> until I found out a girlfriend got the same one at a better price.
> Now I feel stupid because I didn't go to the other dealership,
> and I'm angry that my dealers took advantage of me.

> ROBERT: Last week, I sneaked a look at the salary structure
> in my firm. There are some attorneys here making a lot more
> money than I am. They don't work half as hard as I do. I got
> my yearly bonus check yesterday for $25,000. Ordinarily I'd be
> overjoyed. But looking at the amount just made me even more

resentful. I bet that others are getting more than I am. It just burns me up!

When you compare yourself to others, do you usually get the short end of the deal? That's just the way your mind works. Even when we compare ourselves to those who are less fortunate, our minds usually discount them quickly and jump to those who are better off than we are. Scarcity tells us that we don't have enough because others have more, and our feeling of being "one down" is especially powerful when we compare ourselves to people we think are barely ahead of us. I did research on this phenomenon in young children, and I've found it to be true of adults as well.

In my study, when young boys played pinball, they became the most competitive when they were just slightly behind their partners. Boys who were way ahead, slightly ahead, or way behind could be more easily induced to stop the game and let others play. In the same way, we adults feel the competitive heat most with people who operate at about the same level of responsibility, especially in fields where salaries are based on individual effort, as in sales or the legal profession.

We have seen that it does no good to candy-coat or wish away negative thoughts. Similarly, it's a waste of energy to try to stop comparing ourselves to others and hope we won't feel the sense of scarcity that the comparisons bring up. Comparisons are reflexes that we really can't stop. The important thing is to recognize and be mindful of them, because the comparisons you make between yourself and other people often reflect your current life's lesson.

Take Robert's story, for example. Robert was angry because others were making more money than he was, but the real source of his suffering wasn't a concern about money. His foremost fear was of being overlooked. He hated that—and just telling the truth gave him some breathing room. Our exchange in the You and Money Course went something like this:

ME: What do you hate about being overlooked?

ROBERT: I work so hard. I deserve respect.

ME: Does everyone else work this hard?

ROBERT: Yes.

ME: Okay, then look again. What do you really hate about being overlooked? What is the fear?

ROBERT: It's more like I don't fit in. They don't even acknowledge all the business I've brought to this firm over the past two years.

ME: Let's look a little deeper. How do you know they don't recognize all the work you've brought in to the firm?

ROBERT: Well, I've never heard any of the partners say anything about my contribution.

ME: When was the last time you really talked to any of them? You know, taken at least one of them out for coffee? You could talk about how you feel.

ROBERT: I don't have time.

ME: Not enough time for relationships? This has all the makings of a good lesson.

ROBERT: Yeah. I haven't been spending enough time with my wife and family lately. I'm working long and hard hours.

ME: You're lonely, aren't you?

ROBERT: Okay, I know where this is leading. Your next question will be "Have you had enough of doing it this way?" You're so predictable. Yes (laughs), I have had enough. To-morrow I'll take one of the partners out for coffee. I'll tell my wife how much I have been missing her lately. Satisfied? (Laughs again).

ME: And, while you're at it, you might ask for a raise if it's appropriate!

When you face your discomfort, you open the door to personal transformation. You create an opportunity to put scarcity in perspective. Do you try to avoid scarcity? Do you manipulate yourself into thinking it does not exist and rationalize away your feelings by saying things like: "I'm being overly sensitive"? Do you misuse positive-thinking strategies or affirmations? Do you try to deal with scarcity by creating a deprivation-spending cycle? Unfortunately, the more you run, and focus attention on avoiding your feelings, the faster the fire-breathing dragon of scarcity catches up with you.

FACING THE SHADOW

Carl Jung, the noted psychotherapist, spoke of the consequences of not facing our dark, or shadow, side. "Everyone carries a shadow," he wrote, "and the less it is embodied in the individual's conscious life, the blacker and denser it is. At all counts, it forms an unconscious snag, thwarting our most well-meant intentions."

The shadow side simply means the side that the light of consciousness hasn't yet shined upon. It's no worse than the nonshadow side, any more than the dark side of the moon is worse or more nefarious than the light side of the moon. To pinpoint your shadow, ask yourself, "What don't I want to look at? What would I pay a million dollars not to have to look at in my own life?" That is the shadow.

Toni didn't want to look at how she was not keeping the promise she'd made to herself to become an artist, but she was willing to look anyway. She saw she had a wellspring of creativity and loved art (watercolor was her specialty), but she wasn't painting. She had covered her dream over for years by saying, "Just let me stop working so hard. Let me get my career in order, and then I'll go back to art." Her worry was that painting would cause her to become lazy or irresponsible.

In the You and Money Course she realized that she'd been saying this to herself for twenty years. She saw that it really was okay to allow her creative energy to express itself, that she didn't have to wait, and that waiting meant putting it off forever.

Another You and Money participant, Steve, didn't want to look at how he used money to "buy" relationships. He gave lots of gifts to people—wristwatches, theater tickets, dinners out—and was very generous with his friends. But it became clear to him that he gave these gifts partly because he wanted people to like him. He loved people, but he saw that he was afraid people wouldn't appreciate him just for who he was. Out of courageously looking at this, he realized that he'd been manipulating people, in a subtle way, into the intimacy he craved. The result was no intimacy, because he didn't give people a chance to value him. Steve also saw that he didn't have much discretionary income for himself, and that he had been putting off buying a boat for years because he didn't have enough money.

When Steve shone the light of awareness on that dynamic, he saw that it wasn't working because he was still feeling lonely and empty. He began to see the possibility that people might like him for who he was, whether or not he gave gifts—that, in fact, in a funny way the gifts took away intimacy. He started giving fewer gifts but more of himself. He saw other ways for him to demonstrate intimacy as well. He joined a hiking club, got involved in many community projects, and found that these pursuits really fulfilled his desire to connect with and contribute to people.

Scarcity, along with all the negative feelings we try to hide, is one of our most profound teachers if we are willing to learn its lessons. When we do, life fills with adventures instead of defenses. When you are afraid, look directly into the face of whatever you fear. It's not necessary to escape the discomfort. You can handle it. Use the support of your friends. Remember that there is a place for both pleasure and pain in becoming conscious. As Pema Chödrön writes:

"There's a common misunderstanding among all the human beings who have ever been born on earth that the best way to live is to try to avoid pain and just try to get comfortable. . . . A much more interesting, kind, adventurous and joyful approach to life is to begin to develop our curiosity, not caring whether the object of our inquisitiveness is bitter or sweet. . . . We must realize that we can endure a lot of pain and pleasure for the sake of finding out who we are and what this world is. . . ."

Trying to escape the discomfort will only prolong your suffering. Get underneath the Monkey Mind chatter and experience the essence of the distress. You do this simply by recognizing Monkey Mind for what it is, which is *not* reality, and by allowing yourself to feel whatever you are experiencing. Lean into the pain rather than away from it. When you do, you'll hear the real question that Scarcity is asking you. It's not "Do you have enough?" Rather, Scarcity is chasing us to ask: "What is *really* important to you? Are you using the limited energy of your life to create your dreams?"

Answering that question returns us to our Standards of Integrity and our Life's Intentions, which lay out the parameters of what we truly want and what will finally satisfy us.

These parameters, too, are limits, and they can focus our energy the way a river's narrow banks speed the water's flow. Affirmations that come from this place, describing what is true about us, have a force and power that Scarcity-driven wishful thinking cannot.

Look at your Life's Intentions. They are grand reflections of your hero's heart. You are here to manifest them, to shape them with your hands, to grasp them, and contribute your talents with them. But before you can do that, you must face the fears that obstruct your power. Seeing them allows you to let them go, and this will set you free.

Exercise: Encounter with a Dragon

You are about to read some questions that will help clarify how scarcity operates in your life. Though you may already have had significant insights in reading this chapter, I'd like you to allow yourself to answer these questions in writing, on paper. Bring your Standards of Integrity and your Life's Intentions with you, and keep them by your side.

This is a multipart exercise, and each section uses a different format to help you arrive at a picture of your relationship with scarcity.

You will need your notebook to record your responses. Take as much time as you need for each part of the exercise. Don't rush your answers, even if you're tempted to do so. Respond to one or two questions at a sitting. The benefits you reap will be in direct proportion to how truthful you are with yourself. You may find some similarities between these questions and those you've answered earlier. However, the work here approaches scarcity and money more explicitly.

Share your answers with at least one friend whom you trust, or a support group. You'll see striking similarities in the way we all look at scarcity. Even coming from different walks of life, and allowing for some differences in perspective, it's important to see that everyone encounters scarcity. It provides a sense of hope as we look at the dragon. Sharing your answers also helps to diffuse the power of what holds you back. Whatever you examine, and especially what you share, loses its power over you.

After doing this exercise with money, you may want to substitute another form of energy, such as time, love, or physical well-being. Is there a similarity in your answers? It might be interesting to find out.

Part One: An Overall Picture of the Dragon

1. *What issues, problems or concerns do I have about money?*

Guidelines for answering: Look at all your worries regarding money, even if they seem petty or silly. Do you have overdue bills? Do you worry about your children's education or your own retirement? Does it seem like you never have enough, no matter how hard you work? Have you been the victim of fraud, theft, or deceit regarding money? Do you envy people who seem to have more than you do? Who are they? Look at all of your negative feelings about money as you respond to this item. Do you hate money? Fear it? Fear not having it? Let yourself write about this until you are emptied out. Have you told yourself that money is "not spiritual"? Write for at least ten minutes without a break. But remember to breathe!

2. *What do I say or think about myself for having these issues, problems, or concerns?*

Guidelines for answering: Do you have judgments about yourself because of your money concerns? Do you think you are silly, incapable, or irresponsible? Do you hope no one finds you out? We all have some of these thoughts and feelings about ourselves. This is especially true when we have been doing the same things, over and over again, expecting different results. Keep listing until you get at least six statements.

3. *What are my major blunders regarding money?*

Guidelines for answering: What have you done in the past regarding money that you would be ashamed to tell anyone about? Have you gambled and lost large sums? Have you signed leases without reading the fine print? Have you made errors in calculation that caused you to become seriously overdrawn at the bank? Have you invested and lost money you could not spare in ventures that were very risky?

4. Whom have I blamed for my difficulties with money?

Guidelines for answering: This is the opportunity to really let loose. Who are they, and what have they done to you? List all the funky things you think about people who have "done it" to you. This is no time to be quasi-enlightened. Do not fall into the trap of saying "But they didn't do anything to me, I allowed them to do it." Just cough it up. What happened? How did it feel? Another hint: Do not list yourself. Look for the culprits outside of you.

Write what you feel as you answer these questions. Do you feel angry, sad, frustrated, bored, irritated, resentful, or tired? Many who go through this inventory find it stirs up many feelings connected with scarcity. It is a very rare person, rich or poor, who has nothing to get off his or her chest. But everyone who takes the time to confront his or her feelings and concerns in this way benefits greatly.

Remember: As you face your experience of scarcity, you prepare the way to have a relationship with money that is fulfilling. This relationship will no longer be merely the extension of past upsets.

PART TWO: DRAGON PRINTS IN THE SAND

In this section you will find a list of words. Each one is followed by a definition. These words represent how we often deal with scarcity when we are trying to get away from it. Write each of the words in your notebook. Then list incidents regarding money that are examples of that word or concept. Draw from real experience in your own life. For instance, look at the word "greed." Here you might write something like "I sold sodas at a softball game for much more than they were worth. I knew people would pay that much because it was a hot day." It doesn't have to be a long description. The shorter the better. Do your best to cut out rationalizations or justifications for the event. Get right to the essence. List everything you can recall under each word. I promise the list will not go on forever, even if Monkey Mind tells you it will. You may find that an incident can be listed under two or more words. Some lists may be short and others long. Write whatever comes to you. Be as complete as possible.

Greed: The desire for more than one needs or deserves, especially without consideration for the needs of others.

Dishonesty: Lying, cheating, stealing.

Guilt: Feelings of self-reproach resulting from a belief that we have done something wrong or immoral.

Regret: A troubled feeling over something that one has done or left undone. Feeling "it should not have happened as it did."

Unconsciousness: The state of not being aware, as with having made a mistake because we were not paying attention. Acting without the knowledge or preparation we should have had.

Manipulation: Managing or controlling by a shrewd use of influence or power. Often done in an unfair or fraudulent way. Done for one's own gain or profit. Getting others to act against their will or best interests for your own selfish gain.

Resentment: Feelings of displeasure and indignation, from a sense of being injured, offended, or used.

Error: The state of believing something that is not true. Doing something incorrectly because of ignorance or carelessness.

Fear: Anxiety, agitation, or a sense of foreboding. Caused by the presence or nearness of a perceived danger or pain that is real or imagined.

Self-deception: To mislead oneself into believing something is true when it is not.

Hooray for you! This can be a difficult process, and you have completed it. Like a person removing heavy armor that is awkward and bulky, you will now feel lighter and more agile—especially if you talk with a friend or support group about what you're finding.

PART THREE: DISCOVERING THE MAGIC IN THE DRAGON

The next three questions ask you to look at how your life would be if you allowed scarcity to be your ally. Take your time to move through these questions. Know that you are accelerating your way on the hero's path. You are joining the thousands of others who have gone on to thrive after fully examining the role of scarcity in their lives. You are providing an opening that will give you some breathing room to make authentic choices.

1. *What choices would I make if I no longer held scarcity at bay?*

Guidelines for answering: What dreams would you follow that you have put on the back burner? What relationships would you pursue or enhance?

2. *Recall a time when you faced and learned from a limitation. What was it?*

Guidelines for answering: Were you pleasantly surprised by the outcome? What were your thoughts about your initial assessment? What new, creative ideas came from that encounter?

3. *If I were to simplify my life, what would I do with my money?*

Guidelines for answering: Look at areas of your life where you could have fun, contribute to others, be more creative.

Congratulations! You have just done more to understand your relationship with the fear of scarcity than most people do in a lifetime. Do you notice that you're more aware of the role your fear of scarcity, or your avoidance of it, has played in your relationship with money?

If you are doing this exercise with other people, take time to share your answers. Once again, you may find a lot of similarity. We are often not as unique as we like to think.

When you have thoroughly shared your answers to these questions, I want you to do something special with Parts One and Two of this exercise. Take them out of your notebook. Tear the pages up. Drop them into a paper bag and throw the bag away in the trash. Notice if you feel uneasy about letting the pages go. Do it anyway. You are giving yourself the message that it is all right to let go of these thoughts and feelings. They may come up again—and they probably will. When they do, simply write them down and throw the pages away once more. Notice if your thoughts and feelings shift in their seeming importance.

•   •   •

Now that you know you have looked squarely at scarcity, instead of running away, you can stretch beyond your customary ways of seeing the world and discover new ways to relate to money and the other forms of energy in your life. Honor your courage. In embracing the darkness, you've made room for the light.

It's almost as if, having faced the dragon and gotten his lesson, the hero sits down by the side of the road with his new ally and says, "I can't believe that all these years you were chasing me to try to help me out. I'm still exhausted from all the things I did to try to get away from you."

The dragon answers back with an enigmatic smile, "You'd be surprised to discover how many things are not what they seem!"

PRINCIPLE 6

TRANSFORMING INNER BLOCKS LIBERATES MONEY ENERGY

Even though the last several chapters have talked a lot about Monkey Mind, in this chapter we're going to probe the Monkey a little more deeply. And we're going to uncover what basic assumption you have made about life, yourself, and others that is most likely to be at the center of your Monkey Mind thinking.

We've seen how Monkey Mind jumps up screaming as we approach Trouble at the Border, when we start to translate thought into action, and when we consider doing anything heroic or risky. What happens within two weeks of your New Year's resolutions? What comes up when you pull out that investing information one more time, or begin a physical fitness program over and over again? I've heard hundreds of examples of this in the You and Money Course.

ROBYN: Sometimes I can just *see* my goal right in front of me. Like the one of being in a triathlon. I joined an expensive fitness club and got a personal trainer. I made a detailed training schedule so I'd be ready in six months. But I lost interest after two months. It was like I put my schedule in my desk drawer, covered it up with guilt, and went on the way I was before.

HOWARD: I promised myself I was going to clear away all my money leaks. I paid off an old debt to my former roommate. It felt great! Then, and here's the crazy thing, I just stopped.

You'd think I'd keep going, but I didn't. I don't know what happened.

THE NATURE OF MONKEY MIND

We've noted that Monkey Mind is the reactive aspect of your mind that the Tibetan Buddhists call "sem," which is like a candle flickering in an open doorway, moving this way and that with every passing puff of air. Monkey Mind is in perpetual motion, plotting, scheming, and gathering evidence for its decisions.

Once you realize that your Monkey Mind is with you for the duration, you no longer have to fight it, try to run from it, or stay mesmerized in its company. You can relax and stop wasting energy trying to change it. Trying to alter what your mind says forces you to dance with it, keep its rhythm, focus your attention on it. But as soon as you step out of the dance, your attention and energy are free to focus on the possibilities that surround you.

You can devote your energy to changing Monkey Mind, or you can use that energy to infuse your dreams. Your choice is to dance with your Monkey Mind or dance with your goals and dreams. Pick one.

Shifting your attention from Monkey Mind to your goals and dreams is both a gentle and subtle act. It implies that no change to your ceaseless inner dialogue is necessary. In fact, you take it with you on your hero's journey. There is no need to wait for it to leave before you go for your dreams. Just place it in a basket under one arm and proceed. You can focus your attention outward instead of inward.

DANCING WITH THE MONKEY

As you start to pay attention to the way the chattering of Monkey Mind affects you and throws obstacles into your path, you may feel like grabbing a stick and chasing the monkey out of your way. But I've seen repeatedly that successful people don't spend energy trying to change the course of the waters in the rivers of their minds. Instead they observe them and learn how best to navigate them. They're the ones who observe Monkey Mind—then let it fade to white noise that they can acknowledge and ignore. They know the chatter won't stop, so they don't waste effort trying to control it.

In the You and Money Course, Paul talked about how Monkey Mind kicked into action five months before, when he agreed to climb Mount Shasta with some friends.

> PAUL: I planned to start training right away, since it's such a difficult climb. But I never got around to it. I remember thinking "I don't have the time. It's only a one-day hike. How difficult could it be?" To my credit, I did walk a few miles each week. But it obviously wasn't enough. Comes the day of the hike, last week, I set out with everyone else, but an hour into it my heart is pounding in my ears. I tell myself: "Keep going. Everyone else is." I'm having a terrible time. My buddy Mike is hiking next to me. He looks great. Sure, he's sweating. But he's enjoying himself! He trained for this.
>
> I hung in one more hour, but that was it. I had to stop. I felt lousy. Talk about struggle! I was out of commission. Had to hike back down and wait for the others. They got in that evening, tired but happy. Me? I'm sore and exhausted. And hitting myself over the head with thoughts like: "You jerk. Can't you do anything right?" I've had enough of doing things that way.

On the trail, Monkey Mind prodded Paul on past his endurance. Back at camp, he made himself wrong. And the stage was set for this battle when he first listened to the words "I don't have time for this."

As you might guess, this wasn't the only place in his life where Paul found himself going along with the "reasonable" voice in his mind. He remembered putting off his taxes because he was "too busy with work to focus on them right now," then slapping his returns together bleary-eyed at the last minute, fearful that he'd missed something important.

It's easier to separate from Monkey Mind if you can look objectively at the guises it likes to wear. Like Paul, you might recognize forms, shapes, and voices that seduce you. The following checklist shows the symptoms that erupt when Monkey Mind is speaking to you and you're buying its view of the world. We all have these sorts of thoughts and conversations—but we don't have to make them into major productions.

Remember: Once you know that the sexy voice of reason belongs to the Monkey, you can stop paying attention to it.

SYMPTOMS OF MONKEY MIND

Here is a list of some symptoms of Monkey Mind, so that you can begin to identify the Monkey's voice, and how it shows up for you.

MONKEY MIND CHECKLIST

1. Being vague: "I'll balance my checkbook sometime soon. Right now I don't have the time or energy."

2. Dealing with the past and future as if they're the present: "Income-tax time has always been, and will continue to be, an ordeal for me."

3. Being defensive: "I am not being defensive about my credit-card debts! Just back off!"

4. Taking things personally: "Look, are you questioning my professional judgment here?"

5. Feeling resigned: "It doesn't make a bit of difference whether I plan for this vacation or not. I'll never go. I'm too busy. Don't have the money. Why should I bother?"

6. Making qualifying statements: "Well, I'll try to do it." "If everything works out—if I get the time/the money—I can probably hire an accountant." (Have you ever noticed that if you invite someone to the movies and they say "I'll try to make it" they're really saying *no*?)

7. Making excuses: "I was late for the job interview because I overslept and ran out of gas."

8. Using either/or thinking: "Either I get to keep my credit cards or I'm not going to feel secure. I couldn't possibly stop using my cards for a month."

9. Being paranoid: "Nobody listens to me. They think I don't have anything valuable to say."

10. Fragmenting our personalities: "Part of me wants to stop overspending. But you know, part of me really doesn't think it's a problem. And there's a third part that's too tired to even consider this."

11. Making comparisons: "Why does it seem like no one struggles with taxes as much as I do?"

12. Rationalizing: "I'll accept this money under the table just this once. After all, doesn't *everybody* do it?"

13. Justifying our actions: "I deserve that expensive meal. I've been working hard all week."

14. Deflecting concerns with jokes: "I know I spent a lot of money. But, hey, I didn't spend it all. I still have checks left!"

15. Being a martyr: "No one really knows how hard I work."

16. Becoming petulant (cantankerous, cross, or grouchy): "If I want your advice, I'll ask for it. Until then, just leave me alone!"

17. Being impulsive: "I want what I want right now!"

If you spend a just few days paying attention, and letting a small alarm sound inside when you hear Monkey Mind in any of these guises, you'll begin to notice the way it grabs your attention, and you'll recognize the arguments you respond to most readily. You'll know you're in the grip of Monkey Mind if you find that any of the above symptoms are coupled with physical dis-ease—that is, a lack of ease. Monkey Mind makes you feel locked in place, adamant, tense, as though it's a matter of survival to maintain your position.

A WORD OF CAUTION

Some people have discovered that one way of dealing with Monkey Mind is to infuse it with an intense perception of danger. After an initial burst of chatter, it gets quiet and focuses intently on the task of keeping them alive. It has no time for anything else. This experience is reported by many who mountain-climb and hang glide.

> ARMAND: When I climb, it's just me and the rock. Very simple. No thoughts. I put my hand where it fits and lift myself up one more foot. Then it's on to the next crack or foothold.

Armand recognized that this method for warding off the internal dialogue could be habit-forming. He had known others who tried to recapture the mind-bending experience of quiet exhilaration again and again by increasing the fear quotient. Many had met with accidents.

He was always vigilant about taking unnecessary chances while climbing. But he was aware of the temptation:

> ARMAND: It's part of my discipline to keep within safe limits. I remember reading an article on hang gliding, which said that most master gliders are no longer alive. They kept pushing the edge until it was just too much. I saw that could happen to me in climbing.

Take a moment and look at your own life. Are there times when you create emergencies, real or imaginary, to give your mind something on which to focus?

> JANETTE: I admit it. Crises do calm me down. It sounds crazy, but when there's an emergency I feel focused. I get into a problem-solving mode. During those moments everything else in my mind goes away. It's like when the copier broke at work yesterday. We had a report to get out by 5 P.M. My administrative assistant and receptionist were panicked. Me? I'm calmly taking the thing apart to see what's wrong. So now I'm looking to see where I actually *create* crises in my life. One place is tax time. I wait until the last possible moment to do them. I'm always there at the post office at 11:59 P.M. on April 15. Tired. Exhausted. But calm.

> PETE: This is real embarrassing. I like to gamble. I like to bet big. Big. When I play blackjack, the world goes away. It's just me and the dealer and maybe a few other suckers at the table. But I just noticed that my mind *does* cool down when I concentrate on my cards. Especially when I place big bets and have to keep myself very focused. Hours go by like minutes.

As you can see, dancing to this melody with Monkey Mind is costly. Dealing with constant "ups" and "downs" can sap your money energy.

MONKEY MIND IS TENACIOUS

Monkey Mind is behind our dogged refusal to change our money behavior, even when it's just not working for us. This kind of behavior sets us apart from the rest of the animal kingdom. You can train a pigeon to peck at a bar for food pellets by rewarding him with a pellet every time he pecks. But if you stop giving him the reward, he'll keep trying for a while—and then he'll stop pecking and do something else.

If only learning were as easy for people. We'll persist with behavior that hasn't rewarded us in years, and we'll even put a lot of additional energy into justifying why we are "right" about doing it that way. Monkey Mind can provide endless reasons for these behaviors:

- It was supposed to work this way.
- It will work if I just try harder.
- It works this way with other people.
- It worked this way once, and I know it will again.
- I don't have the time to do it another way.
- This is just the way I am, and there's nothing I can do about it.
- If I just keep pushing though it, the pain of doing it this way will stop.
- This is how my mother/father did it.
- I don't want to do it like my mother/father did it.
- I have to analyze why I'm doing it this way before I can stop.

Think of the energy we use to explain why things are not so bad, or why we have to do what we do. Sometimes we forget that life can be any other way.

As we proceed on this journey, know that you will rediscover what life is like when it's clear of money insanity. You may still get caught up every once in a while in the diverting dramas you create around money, but you'll have the clarity to wake up and refocus your energy.

YOU ARE NOT YOUR MONKEY MIND

Your Monkey Mind thoughts about money have nothing to do with your true nature. It is only one aspect of your mind, and who you are is greater than anything it can throw at you.

When you recognize how Monkey Mind works, you minimize the chances of getting off track as you go toward your goals. This is important when you deal with money, since that form of energy seems to spark our most compelling and disempowering internal dialogues. As a psychologist, I've watched countless people talk themselves out of dreams that could easily have been within their reach. Any attempts to motivate them were fruitless: they'd keep going a few paces and then stop.

When you understand Monkey Mind, and know that you are *not* that chatter, then you have choices. You can then master Trouble at the Border. You free up energy to channel into your goals and dreams.

How much of your life is lived out of Monkey Mind? The next exercise will give you the beginning of an answer. This is an opportunity to consciously catch yourself "dancing with the Monkey." The key here is to discern the times you are not acting or thinking in accordance with who you really are. It is valuable to bring your Standards of Integrity and Life's Intentions with you as you do this exercise. Looking at them will bring you back to yourself.

Exercise: Dancing with Monkey Mind

You will need your small spiral notebook to carry around with you and jot down the observations you will be making over the next few days. Have the Monkey Mind Checklist (see pages 156–57) handy so that you can identify the symptom.

Over the course of two or three days—no more, no less—jot down at least three times you engage in Monkey Mind thinking each day. Do it at the moment you notice the symptom. What was the symptom? Did you say it aloud? Did it appear instead as an internal dialogue? If you find you have forgotten to keep records, have compassion for yourself. You are removing the mask from a style of thinking you have used for years. After you notice you've forgotten to record your symptoms, go back to paying attention. If you remember any conversations, note them. If not, record the next instance. Make your notations brief. They may look like this:

Monday, 10:15 A.M.: Comparison. Bob doesn't look worried about our presentation. I sure am. What's wrong with me? (Spoken to self)

Monday, 12:45 P.M.: Being vague. I'll get this budget done sometime next week. (Spoken to supervisor)
Monday, 4:30 P.M.: Defensive. I am *not* always too busy to talk with you! I've just had a hectic day, that's all! (Spoken to wife)

Examine what you wrote during the past two or three days. If you have even a few notations, commend yourself! This is rigorous work. Now look at the notes. Let the following questions guide your observations. It is best if you can share what you see with someone with whom you feel comfortable.

1. Were most of these thoughts internal, or did I voice them?
2. What are the themes here? Is there a "Medley of my Favorite Monkey Mind Conversations"?
3. How does my body feel when I am gripped by each of these symptoms? Am I tense? Do I have a sinking feeling? Do I go on the attack? Do I tighten my stomach? Clench my jaw?
4. Was I able to catch any of the symptoms before they became full-blown? In other words, was I able to intervene early on? What was it like to do this?
5. Are there any special Monkey Mind conversations I have about money? If so, what are they? When did they arise?

Almost universally, people are amazed at how much unbidden, unrelated, even contradictory conversation goes on in their minds. What did you see? Are you beginning to grasp the nature of Monkey Mind? Share your discoveries with someone. If you are reporting back to a group, have each person contribute at least one observation. The goal of this exercise is not to eradicate the inner dialogue but to observe it. This seems counterintuitive. We are all so accustomed to analyzing and making sense out of everything we think.

What if we were to discover that 90 percent or more of the thoughts that leap through our heads are, in fact, irrelevant to anything that's of real value to us? When I ask this question, most people say they'd be really relieved.

After doing this for one week, you may notice a heightened sense of awareness of times when Monkey Mind is present. When you see and tell the truth about the symptoms you

exhibit, they no longer have a hold on you. You have dismantled them—until the next time. And each time will get easier.

Exercise: "Peace with Honor"

Just as a pool of water becomes clear when the mud is not
stirred up, so the mind settles when you just let it be without
trying to mess with it. You can experience this by trying a meditation technique I have found particularly suited to observing
and calming Monkey Mind. Use it whenever you notice your
mind becoming overheated, like when you consider the possibility of doing something that you would normally put off—like
creating a will or a budget—or any other task involving money
that has stressed you out in the past.

For this exercise, you will need nothing except a quiet place
to sit. You may settle on the floor or in a chair. Start by setting
aside ten minutes. Increase to twenty when you are comfortable with this technique. Do this once a day for one week. If
possible, pick the same time each day so you establish a routine.

This exercise is a meditation that asks you to focus on your
breath. Sit in a comfortable upright position with your spine
straight. Rest your hands, palms down, on your thighs. Close
your eyes. Breathe in, allowing the air to fill your lungs gently.
Keep your tummy soft. A soft tummy gives Monkey Mind less to
hold on to. Remember to fill even your upper lungs with air.
Breathe out, feeling the breath as it leaves your nostrils. Pause
at the end of the breath for a moment before you breathe in
again.

In your mind's eye, be like a wave. As you breathe out, you
are gently breaking upon the shore of your favorite beach.
Wait a moment before returning to the sea. As you breathe in,
draw back into the ocean. Wait a moment and then breathe
out again. Do this throughout the exercise. Feel and observe
your breath as it moves in and out.

I've found a phrase from the Bible that works well here: "Be
still." As you breathe in, you can say quietly in your mind's eye,
"Be," and as you breathe out, "Still." Your inner chatter will
become less noticeable. Periodically, the babble will get louder.
You'll see how it comes and goes in waves. Thoughts that have

nothing to do with the present will float through your mind. Each time this happens, let them pass.

Most people report that they find themselves following thoughts unconsciously. When this happens, just release the thought and be the wave again. When the time is up, you have a sense of the constant noise that underlies daily life. Sometimes we think this noise really means something. You have had a chance to see how it changes from moment to moment, not based on anything in particular. You may notice how hard it is to be attentive to life when you think that the chatter means something.

Observing your mental process, and letting it pass, increases your power to peacefully coexist with Monkey Mind. I suggest you practice this as we encounter the next principles. This power will serve you well on the hero's journey toward your goals and dreams.

If you have any final doubts about whether Monkey Mind is *you*, ask yourself the following question: If the Monkey Mind conversations are you, *who is listening to or hearing them*? Who you really are is much greater than Monkey Mind, and therein lies your power.

Sometimes all it takes to wrest yourself from the grip of Monkey Mind is to tell the truth when you are acting or thinking foolishly. This takes courage and a big heart. As a hero, you have those qualities. It is time to demonstrate them.

YOUR BASIC ASSUMPTION

How does Monkey Mind show up for you? One way is in how it reflects your Basic Assumption. Your Basic Assumption is a fundamental decision you made about life when you were very young, a core conversation about yourself, others, and how life is. Since it is an example of Monkey Mind thinking, your Basic Assumption is a self-limiting decision. You have been gathering evidence for it, or against it, most of your life. We act out our Basic Assumption by either "being it" or by "being its opposite." Basic Assumptions are extensions of the fight, flight, or freeze instincts.

Your Basic Assumption colors how you see life, and how you live it. As you come closer to seeing yours, you'll realize how it can snare your energy, making your relationship with money more difficult than it needs to be. Your Basic Assumption is so much a part of the filter through which you see life that you don't even know the filter is there.

I love this quote from the *I Ching*: "Before the beginning of great brilliance, there must be chaos. Before a brilliant person begins something great, they must look foolish to the crowd." I experienced this on a cool morning in Sacramento fifteen years ago. I found myself squarely on the border of a new beginning, poised to stride into my destiny. After months of planning, dreaming, and hard work, I stood in front of my first You and Money class. It was the third session of a ten-session course. Each of the twenty women present had been assigned to balance her checkbook to the penny. I knew it might not be an easy task for a lot of the people there, but I was astonished when only a handful of the participants had done the work.

As I looked around the room, my chest got tight. My arms got heavy, and something came over me. Angry, disappointed, maybe possessed, I flew into a rant, an unplanned lecture about this lazy group's lack of commitment and guts. The room was absolutely still.

My friend Rita stood at the threshold of the room, and when I stopped to take a breath, she motioned me to come outside. I excused myself and stepped into the hall.

"What's going on?" Rita asked. "You sound so angry. You're being very rough on them."

"This is it!" I replied. "I'm not going on with this course. I can't lead it. It's just too much for me. If someone better led it, everyone would have done their homework. But not with me."

Rita looked concerned. "Sounds like you're having a fit," she said. "What's going on?"

"I'm *not* having a fit. It's the truth! I can't lead this course."

"What do you mean you can't?"

"What do you *mean*, what do I mean? I just can't do it. I don't have what it takes to do a course on money. Or any course. I should have listened to myself when I began this. I knew I couldn't do it."

I stopped my fit long enough to look up at the course room window. There were twenty noses comically pressed against the glass. Twenty pairs of eyes peered out at me. It looked so funny I started to laugh. I felt like a fool!

But that laugh dismantled something, and I pulled myself together, apologized, and went on with the class. Everyone was relieved, including me. It was the kind of thing that would've been easy to chalk up to nerves, but later that day I remember telling Rita how familiar the whole thing felt.

That sinking feeling and the "I can't" pattern that went along with it had been with me as long as I could remember, and it always popped up whenever I started something new. That day I connected with an idea that has changed my life—and may change yours. I saw the Basic Assumption I'd made about my life, and how deeply it affected my relationship with success and money. My Basic Assumption was "I can't."

Like a black hole in space that invisibly, but powerfully, changes the orbit of anything that comes near it, our Basic Assumptions exert a force that can tint, warp, and alter our best intentions. Basic Assumptions can make attaining a goal seem impossible and dissipate our resolve. At times they even spark behavior like my tantrum in front of my class.

In the You and Money Course I came to see that, even as adults, we look through a scared child's eyes every time we enter unfamiliar territory—as we do whenever we cross the Border between metaphysical and physical reality. And when the unfamiliar territory involves money, our Basic Assumptions become especially potent.

Even with my previous work on Basic Assumptions, I had not felt the fundamental effects as deeply in my cells as I had that morning in the first You and Money class. I felt the "I can't" response in my body, as my shoulders slumped forward. My tone of voice was definitely whiny, and I could feel my face tighten. Those two words had been in the background most of my life. They struck me to the core. They made me feel like a fool. But when I saw this Basic Assumption, there was a shift. After the initial chagrin of recognition, it has lost a lot of its power to provoke my behavior.

I knew that if we could all see our Basic Assumptions we could, perhaps for the first time, stop automatically reactivating the scared child's view of our options and power when we feel challenged. We could see how we created a limited, false sense of who we are, and learn how to leave that inauthentic perception behind. That would free us to act as the heroes we are. Fifteen years and thousands of people later, this has proven to be the case. For myself, "I can't" no longer frightens me when it emerges. In fact, it has become a sign that I'm stretching outside my comfort zone.

Later in this chapter I will give you the chance to begin work to discern your own Basic Assumption. While it is unlikely that you will get to that core decision here, you will at least see what is around the outer edge of it. Everything you uncover here will bring you breathing room in your relationship with money.

THE STARTLE RESPONSE

The idea of the Basic Assumption has its roots in 1950s psychological research that studied how people respond to emergencies. That research developed the now well-known idea of the "flight-or-fight response," in which the body produces adrenaline and other chemicals in response to stress, enabling it to defend itself or outrun danger. Initially, humans' well-developed flight/fight response was a key survival tool, but in the late twentieth century we've seen that it takes a toll on the body. The literature on stress is full of research on the harmful effects of being in situations that frequently evoke this response. Researchers have also noted a third response to emergencies: freezing, as animals often do, hoping to protect themselves by literally blending into the scenery.

In my work I have found that when people are under stress, sensing some sort of danger, their psychological responses fall into the fight/flight/freeze model as well. And one of these responses dominates in each person. Some people want to run away, avoiding what they fear. Some become combative. Others seem paralyzed. Do I know how a particular choice is made? No. We will probably find that each of us has a genetic predisposition to one of the three responses. Your personal bias toward fighting, fleeing, or freezing shapes your Basic Assumption.

For example, my Basic Assumption of "I can't" is a flight response, and I hate it. I'd prefer to be a fighter, but I have discovered that *the Basic Assumption you like least is the one that fits you best.* You have a natural aversion for your own Basic Assumption. You hate it because it's the idea you've used again and again to limit your possibilities. It is your private showstopper. It also reflects the person you're afraid you are. It is the awful truth about you, your "fatal flaw"—or so you fear.

Everyone has a Basic Assumption. It never goes away, and it usually doesn't change. However, when you see what it is, it often loses its power over you. You still feel your mind producing versions of "Don't move!" or "Run!" or "Let's fight!" in response to danger, but as the brilliant teacher Ram Dass says, "The internal dialogue just doesn't stay around as long." It stops impeding your progress.

THE RISE OF YOUR BASIC ASSUMPTION

Your Basic Assumption forms when you're a toddler and you're suddenly faced with a shock or a loss. It could be something that seems trivial to you now, but then it felt like a matter of life or death. Perhaps you woke up in the middle of the night and your night-light was off because the bulb had burned out. Alone, confused, and afraid, you tried to make sense of the circumstances and save yourself. Your body, depending on your inclinations, wanted to fight, flee, or freeze. You may not have had the language skills to explain what happened, but the memory remained vivid.

As time went on, Monkey Mind wrapped words and images around the experience. And then it formed a conclusion such as:

• I don't know (what to do, how to save myself)—a freeze response
• Life is hard (and I can never be safe, or count on anything)—a flight response
• People are jerks (Where is my mom when I need her? Whose fault is this?)—a fight response

Over time that conclusion took on a life of its own, and it became the filter through which you viewed the events in your life. Long after making that decision about how the world works, you still gather evidence to prove it is correct—even though you have no idea what your Basic Assumption is, or even that you have one. Or else you gather evidence to prove that it's *not* true—because it's so noxious to you that you don't want to believe it.

For example, the opposite of my "I can't" Basic Assumption is "I can, too!" I say it with a defensive tone in my voice and a shrug of my left shoulder, daring anyone to stand in my way. At those times I'll do anything to prove to people that I am capable, even super-capable. That was the attitude I exhibited as I invested that $35,000 on an unsecured promissory note. Friends cautioned me, but I was out to show them they were wrong and that "I could" make a good financial deal.

Because the Basic Assumption is the package in which you come wrapped, it's almost impossible to see. That creates one of the hero's most challenging and important tasks: to identify the limited, inauthentic picture of him- or herself that so often soaks up the energy that could be spent moving toward our dreams.

SEEING THE INVISIBLE

Our Basic Assumption is invisible to us. We don't think it, we *be* it.

You see your Basic Assumption as *the truth* in your life, and it seems to transcend any possibility of choice. It looks like a given, not an option. For example, when I am gripped by "I can't," there is no way to convince me that this is simply a decision I made long ago as a child. No matter that it is not logical or coherent. It is absolutely real to me at that moment, and I can always find a way to prove my feelings are justified.

Parents have told me that they can tell when their children are making limiting decisions about life. But it's impossible to stop the process, which has a life of its own. I watched it happening recently on a visit to Disney World. I was walking in front of a man and his five-year-old daughter, who wore a Mickey Mouse hat and a Disney World T-shirt and held a balloon in her free hand. As she walked along, she turned to her father and asked:

"Daddy, will you get me an ice cream?"

"Not right now, honey. It's almost lunchtime."

"Oh," she said. "You *never* get me anything I want!" A budding "People Are Jerks" Basic Assumption? That's hard to say with certainty. After all, every child has moments like this. But we do know that the child was making a decision about life right then, no matter what her father said or did. And it would be fruitless for the man to point out that he'd just gotten her the hat, shirt, and balloon she'd asked for. She'd made up her mind based on her most recent request, and that was that!

Let's observe how the Basic Assumption can affect us in a more "grown-up" situation.

After discovering her Basic Assumption, Marlene reported the following to her course mates:

> MARLENE: My Basic Assumption is "Life is hard," a definite flight pattern. Now that I'm looking at it, I remember

signing up for a quilting class a year ago. Our first assignment was to get some cloth that was beautiful or meaningful in some way. We were each going to create our personal "work of art." I had two weeks to gather the material. Five days before the class, I got it in my head to go to a swap meet thirty miles away. I'd heard there was some old, beautifully patterned cloth for sale there. Sunday morning I woke up at 6:00 A.M. to get there on time. It was foggy and cold, but I toughed it out and made the drive. The punch line is, they weren't open! It was the wrong weekend. Actually, that was no surprise. That's how I seem to handle new situations: by making it harder on myself, and others, than necessary.

Prior to discovering her Basic Assumption, if you had asked Marlene if "Life is hard" as she was driving to the swap meet, she might have answered, "No." As a matter of fact, she'd probably have replied, "It's not that hard at all. Why do you ask?"

YOUR BASIC ASSUMPTION'S TRIBUTARIES

Over the years your Basic Assumption becomes so ubiquitous that it disappears into the fabric of your life. But you can see the effect of

Example of a Basic Assumption Tree

tributary decisions, ones that are more conscious to you. For example, you may have a fight Basic Assumption at your core but have surrounded it with flight and/or freeze decisions. The diagram on page 169 shows a Basic Assumption tree. It's different for everyone.

As you do the Basic Assumption Exercises below, you're not likely to arrive at your core Basic Assumption. But as you encounter your tributaries, you can begin to get closer to it. This is like entering a labyrinth, exploring all of its paths. If you're willing to investigate the tributaries fully, looking at how each has affected your life and your relationship with money, you will, at some point, make your way toward the center.

You can hear the tributaries in your head. They're the voices that comment, criticize, and prod you as you set out toward your goals. You may recognize it as Monkey Mind's chattering. Your Basic Assumption and its offshoots shape the sorts of things you hear Monkey Mind telling you.

Here are some examples of the decisions that form your Basic Assumption or its offshoots. Numerous people have gotten relief from actually saying the words aloud instead of "being" them.

FLIGHT BASIC ASSUMPTIONS
- I'm dumb!
- I can't!
- Something's wrong with me!
- Life is hard!

FREEZE BASIC ASSUMPTIONS
- I don't know!
- I'm not sure!
- This isn't it!

FIGHT BASIC ASSUMPTIONS
- I'll do it my way!
- People are jerks!
- You can't make me!
- Back off!

The Basic Assumption expresses itself directly through your body. When you're speaking through it, your tone of voice shifts. Your posture undergoes some changes. Your facial expression may alter. You may sense tenseness. Your heart could start pounding. Groups of symptoms reappear like old, familiar, if unwanted, company. Many people try to muscle their way through the Basic Assumption reaction. Others stop and wait for it to go away. Of course, they wait forever.

Your Basic Assumption can limit how you see life—but you have an antidote to these limitations in your Standards of Integrity and Life's Intentions. When you compare them with the dictates of Monkey Mind, you'll have a clear picture of "who you are *not*" vs. "who you are."

The following exercises are designed to bring "who you are not" into sharp focus so that you can see it for what it is. This creates a spaciousness in your heart to see who you really are, even when you have a lot of chatter in your head.

Exercise: Trials and Tributaries

You will need your notebook and pen, and you can do this exercise in ten- to fifteen-minute segments. You may want to do it a number of times over the course of the next few weeks, taking one or two questions each time. This will not interfere with any other work you do in the book. Doing this exercise many times helps you map your responses and to see the patterns that develop.

Write your responses to the following questions. Keep them short and to the point. Be absolutely candid. Note your body sensations and posture. This is no time for quasiliberal or "enlightened" answers. As Joan Rivers would say: "Can we talk?"

1. You have just inherited one million dollars. A relative asks for a $50,000 unsecured loan.
    a. What is your first thought? Be honest.
    b. What are your body sensations right now. Are you tense, tight, hot, cold?
2. Think of a time when you failed to complete something you promised you would do. Be specific. Think of names, dates, and places.

    a. What are your reasons for not keeping your promise? What happened?

    b. As you think of it now, whose fault was it that you failed to do it? (Do not answer "me" unless that is what really occurred to you to say.) Why?

    c. Do you have any body sensations? Where are they?

3. The past ten years have shown an upsurge in the number of personal bankruptcies filed.

    a. In your opinion, what causes someone to go bankrupt?

    b. What do you feel as you say this?

    c. Note your body sensations. What are they?

4. Think of a place, at work or in a personal relationship, where you know you are not operating within your Standards of Integrity.

    a. What has kept you from clearing this up?

    b. What are your body sensations as you write this answer?

5. You are about to stand up in front of a group of people you hardly know. You are going to tell them precisely how much money you bring home to the penny each month.

    a. What thoughts come to your mind as you contemplate doing this?

    b. Do any emotions emerge?

    c. Note your body sensations.

6. You have been asked to give the year-end summary presentation to the president of your company. You have two hours to prepare.

    a. What did you just think as you read this? Note anything down, even if it seems unrelated.

    b. Why would you fail at this task?

    c. Note your body sensations.

7. You are being asked to compute your net worth.

    a. How hard would this be for you? Why?

    b. What feelings come up for you?

    c. Note your body sensations.

8. You have just received a letter that your income taxes for the last two years will be audited.

    a. What do you think happened to cause this to occur?

    b. How will you handle the situation?

    c. Note your body sensations.

9. You are leaving a record store with some purchases. As you

go through the security gate, the alarm sounds. A salesperson rushes toward you to stop you from leaving.

 a. What is your first thought? What would you do?

 b. What are your feelings as you think about this situation?

 c. Note your body sensations.

 10. Name one dream you have had for some time that you have given up on.

 a. What is it? Be specific.

 b. When did you give up on this dream? What were the circumstances? Note your body sensations.

 11. You bought a book on financial prosperity three months ago. You were excited at the time but haven't read past the first three pages.

 a. What are your reasons? What's keeping you from reading, and even putting into practice, what the book suggests?

 b. Have you done this before? When? Tell the truth. Note your body sensations right now.

 12. You've been meaning to talk to your children (spouse, partner) about an issue involving money, but you haven't done so yet.

 a. What keeps you from doing this?

 b. What worries emerge as you think about this?

 c. What are you feeling in your body right now?

These questions are by no means easy to answer. They are designed to bring your tributaries to the surface. Were you able to arrive at some distinct phrases? List them. Make sure they are declarative. For example, "I think that few people are really trustworthy," or, "It seems to me that there are very few people in the world who are truly trustworthy" are not declarative. A decision is precisely that: "You can't trust *anybody*!"

Did you find your answers to be fight, flight, freeze—or a combination of all three? While your Basic Assumption is one of those responses, your tributaries can be any of the three. Discuss what you have found with a friend. Are you willing to give them permission to tell you when they think you are doing a flight, fight, or freeze response? That will give you great feedback. You may ask them to tell you what your facial expression looks like during those times.

Do these phrases seem familiar? Are there other times in your life when you heard them in your head? What were you doing? What did you do next? Really take the time to explore any ways these statements have worked in your life.

You may not find your Basic Assumption using this exercise alone. Unearthing it often requires the support of a group in a structured situation. But you will come closer and closer to it, and get a very clear view of the tributaries that flow from it, as you repeat this exercise over time.

You have just done some challenging but very valuable work to identify your mental blocks to progress. Congratulations! In the next section we will look at clearing your hero's path by releasing old beliefs, practicing forgiveness, and making and keeping promises.

PART III

Clearing the
Path

RELEASING OLD BELIEFS
BRINGS MIRACLES

In the last few chapters we've seen how deeply and pervasively Monkey Mind has colored our thinking about and our relationship with money.

Monkey Mind wants to be "right" at any cost—even if it needs to manufacture *incorrect* "facts" about the way life works. To Monkey Mind, fear-based decisions we've made about our world, and even our Basic Assumptions, are real and correct. The Monkey sees scarcity as its greatest enemy, and it constructs an entire belief system around its fears and defenses against all "enemies." The "facts" we've been absolutely positive about, the thoughts that have driven us and shaped our whole relationship with the energy of money, are often just smoke screens that Monkey Mind throws up to protect itself.

Even when the Monkey is relatively quiet, our minds set to work creating what I call "structures of knowing" to define and clarify—accurately or inaccurately—the world around us.

WHAT ARE "STRUCTURES OF KNOWING"?

A structure of knowing is a mental model of how things work. It contains all of the thoughts, feelings, opinions, beliefs, attitudes, memories, body sensations, and points of view that surround our present view of something. It organizes everything we know about the world.

Structures of knowing filter information for us. Imagine a grid that sits between you and the world, like a fencing mask, admitting certain information into your conscious awareness while keeping other bits out. In our evolutionary prehistory, this filtering system was a matter of life and death. We had to be on the lookout constantly for danger. We had to interpret and segregate observations that would preserve our lives from information that was unimportant to our survival.

We create structures of knowing about everything—what it is to be "successful," what it means to be a good parent, how the holidays should look, how much money we should have, how to bake a turkey, how to drive a car, what kind of work we should be doing, everything. We especially have structures of knowing about money.

Sometimes we know what our structures of knowing are, and sometimes they are unconscious. Jeff, an attorney who took the You and Money Course, was aware that he had a structure of knowing that he had to work on weekends in order to succeed at his firm. But he was unaware of another structure of knowing—that until he was forty he couldn't expect to make more than $100,000 a year. Seeing both of these, questioning their validity, and moving beyond them affected how he worked. Almost without effort, he became more efficient, spent weekends at home with his family, and put himself in line for a raise.

Our structures of knowing can be so deeply entrenched that it seems impossible to think about things in any other way. Alice runs a housecleaning service, and had decided that she didn't want to deal with any more than five employees. She didn't think she was a very good manager and had seen friends run into all sorts of trouble with people who worked for them. Her service was so successful, however, that soon she was turning away clients. A management consultant convinced her to go outside her structure of knowing, her comfort zone, and try hiring a few more people. She hired three more workers, and the team thrived. "I can't believe I didn't do it sooner," she told me. "I was just stuck in that old thinking, and it was holding me back. I'm actually a pretty good manager, and I even enjoy it!"

HOW STRUCTURES OF KNOWING WORK

Structures of knowing aren't always limiting. They can help us process and handle information—especially when we are young. But we need to dismantle them in order to mature and progress along the hero's path of dealing with energy and increasing our power.

For instance, when you were two or three years old, you had a particular view of where money came from and what it was good for. Probably you believed that it came from your parents and was good for toys and candy. When you were five or six, you may have thought it came from ATM machines and was good for bikes, cool shoes, and candy. As you got older, your views continued to evolve.

The interesting thing is that at some level we carry bits and pieces of our old structures of knowing with us into adulthood. To have a powerful relationship with money, we need to discover what our structures of knowing are and be willing to let them go if they don't serve us. We can then use the energy we've been using to hold together those structures of knowing to focus on our goals and dreams.

Monkey Mind always wants us to cling to our old, outmoded ideas—but this kind of dependency is as counterproductive as insisting on using an old hand-cranked adding machine when you could switch to a computer.

YOUR STRUCTURES OF KNOWING MONEY

As you wrote about your experience of scarcity, driven behavior, and Monkey Mind in the previous chapters, you may have noticed recurring themes in your answers. You may have discovered thoughts and feelings that repeated themselves and formed patterns. For example, as you looked at your blunders regarding money, you may have seen that they revolved around repeated patterns of behavior.

> MYRA: My blunders are mostly about not reading the fine print, whether it has to do with leasing agreements, consulting contracts, or insurance policies. It's odd to see this, because at the same time I wrote in the exercise that I feel victimized by other people. I "know" when I'm about to enter contractual agreements that they won't turn out the way I'd planned. But I now see that *I'm* the one who puts myself in jeopardy by not attending to important details!

The patterns of behavior that you see in your answers reflect your structures of knowing—the paradigms that your mind creates in response to information from the outside world. The hero's task is to become aware of what our structures of knowing are so that we can decide whether or not they are currently useful in our relationship with money.

Here are a couple of examples of how we restrict ourselves when we drag with us our outmoded structures of knowing about how money and life work:

> BLAIR: I've already gone to a financial planner. He didn't seem to know what he was doing. Look, I've tried it that way once. I just need to make my own financial decisions from now on. I know now that nobody really knows that much about investments. It's all a crapshoot.

> KAREN: There are lots of jokes about it, but I really know that you can't trust lawyers. My sister had trouble with her attorney when she was getting a divorce. So why should I give mine all the reasons my landlord is suing me for damages? He doesn't need to know.

These people have made financial decisions based on a single negative experience. Their decision has become a prop in their structure of knowing and is restricting their ability to take Authentic Action. If Blair and Karen were to rethink and challenge their own assumptions, they might come up with new and creative solutions to their problems. By adamantly standing by their mental construct, however, they'll get only reasons, facts, and figures to justify their stand—and those facts will sound irrefutably correct.

Ironically, being *absolutely certain* about the correctness of your feelings or opinions is the best signal that you're being limited by a structure of knowing. It's a sign that Monkey Mind is using them for some specific purpose. The tone of Monkey Mind's voice brooks no doubts. "This is the reality of the situation," it tells us. "Don't even question it." Of course, that's the very time you need to ask some questions.

WHEN TO LET GO

Even the most profound structures of knowing can outlive their usefulness and circumscribe our world in predictable, comfortable ways that keep us from seeing and responding to new possibilities. When do we know when to let go? In *The Enlightened Mind: Anthology of Sacred Prose,* Stephen Mitchell relates this story, told by the Buddha:

"A man walking along a road sees a great river, its near bank dangerous and frightening, its far bank safe. He collects sticks and foliage, makes a raft, paddles across the river, and reaches the other shore. Now, suppose that, after he reaches the other shore, he takes the raft and puts it on his head and walks with it on his head wherever he goes. Would he be using the raft in an appropriate way? No. A reasonable man will realize that the raft has been very useful to him in crossing the river and arriving safely on the other shore, but that once he has arrived, it is proper to leave the raft behind and walk on without it. This is using the raft appropriately. In the same way, all truths should be used to cross over; they should not be held on to once you have arrived. You should let go of even the most profound insight on the most wholesome teaching; the more so, unwholesome teachings."

We need to form some lasting paradigms or structures of knowing to make the world make sense. People with neurological disorders don't have a mental framework for understanding what they see and experience and are continually disoriented. But to most of us, outmoded structures of knowing can also disorient us and weigh us down, like a raft on our shoulders.

In Monkey Mind's view, a truth should last a lifetime. But all structures of knowing have a developmental life span, a specific period of usefulness. Keep them past their time and you experience stagnation. Dare to release them and you create the future.

It's not always easy to see when we've put together a structure that isn't working:

> GREG: I know it's silly, but I can't bring myself to throw things away. My garage is full of old books, papers, and exercise equipment. I've even rented storage space to hold even more things. I mean, what if I need them someday? Even my rusted Volkswagen from my college days is in my garage. My friends

joke with me about it. They ask if I'm going to use it for a planter someday. I just remember what it was like when I was a starving student. I didn't own much then. I'd save everything. I'm still doing it.

ALICIA: I've been going to Alanon for three years to help me deal with my husband's drinking. I went to a therapist who's had the nerve to suggest to me . . . me! . . . that I look at my own gambling! Look, I know the problem really is Harry's drinking. If he'd stop our lives would be easier and maybe I wouldn't feel so much stress and need to relieve it by playing the slots.

Greg's and Alicia's structures are leading them to believe that this is the way life is—they're right about what they're doing and there's no need to change. But there are definite telltale symptoms that tell us when it's time to let go. You need to expand beyond your present structures of knowing when:

1. *Your reluctance and fear block the desire to follow your hero's path.*

PHOEBE: I don't know how to balance my checkbook to the penny. I've never done it, and I can't do it now. I don't care what effect it has on my future wealth. There must be some way around this.

2. *You use the structure of knowing as an excuse for not keeping your promises.*

TERRY: I'm a busy man. I don't have time to train for that 10K run. I know I promised to raise money and do the run, but I'm just swamped. Maybe next year. Besides, I have a hard time asking people for money.

MARK: Yes, I've promised myself to do something creative. But art classes will probably be too expensive. Besides, I know I don't have any talent for it.

3. *You use the structure to keep old grievances alive.*

ED: Talk to my brother about a loan? He is one of the stingiest people I know. He never gave anything away. I know he'd turn me down flat. So why even give him the satisfaction?

4. When circumstances have become predictable in a stifling way.

BOB: This financial seminar is going to be like all the rest: I'll get excited, but I won't end up doing anything with the information.

DORIS: I'm always broke after Christmas. But, hey, I don't want to be stingy with my family and friends. This is just one of life's trials and tribulations. If I made more money it wouldn't be so bad.

5. When there is no joy or satisfaction in everyday events:

ELLEN: Okay, I just got a personal trainer. I know I should be glad, but I don't know if she's as good as they say. I'm probably just wasting my money, as always.

6. When the future just looks like more of the past:

JOHN: I can't even think of taking a trip to Hawaii for at least five years, given the way business is going now. Yes, I know I've been saying that for at least three years already. But it's true!

REGINA: I've got too much to worry about right now. When my life calms down, then I'll consider if I really want to go back to school. And I can't see things clearing up for at least a year.

Look carefully at what these people are saying. The part of the structure of knowing that really trips them up is often the parenthetical statement at the end. For Terry it is "I have a hard time asking people for money." For Mark "I don't have any talent for it" seems to be the main showstopper. What are the tripping points for the rest of them? Go back and see if you can spot what's stopping each person.

Seeing is the first step. But even when you realize that you're bumping into a structure of knowing that is no longer useful to you, it's not always easy to take apart. The older you get, the more complex, fine-tuned, and rigid your structures of knowing can become, and the more sophisticated the evidence you muster to support your restrictive view of the world!

GENTLY BUT FIRMLY PRYING THE MASK AWAY

What does it take to dismantle a structure of knowing? The definition of dismantle is: to take the cover off. One person described it as "removing the mask I've been hiding behind." You don't blow it apart. If you did, you'd give your Monkey Mind the chance to gather irrefutable evidence about the danger of this process.

Think of a structure of knowing as a fine old wristwatch. When it doesn't work, you take the cover off and look carefully to discover what's no longer functioning and needs to be exchanged for a working part. Dismantling occurs when you look carefully for patterns in your behavior, then see and tell the truth about how well they're working for you.

Conscious observation is the key to going beyond your self-developed limits. I'm not talking about analyzing the reasons you've developed the structures that you've built around money. You just need to observe the "just so" quality of them, and they will begin to loosen and shift. You'll get some breathing room to go forward.

As you begin to observe these structures you'll notice Monkey Mind demanding, insisting that your fearful thoughts, feelings, and evidence are correct. It may even screech in your ear: "Turn back! Turn back! You're headed for trouble." You may become convinced that it's a matter of survival to keep things the way they've always been. This is most especially true when it comes to your relationship with money.

It takes flexibility and courage to dismantle what you have created in life, yet many heroes among us have seen the necessity of taking apart what they've built so that progress can be made. Yitzhak Rabin, for example, gained territory for Israel in 1967 and was hailed as a great warrior. In 1995, however, he realized that the land would have to be returned so his country might have a chance for peace—and he dismantled the warrior's structure to build a life view that would allow him to be a peacemaker.

Ted is a successful entrepreneur and You and Money graduate who dismantled his structure of knowing that he had to do everything himself. He owned a plant-export business that became extraordinarily successful after he got a Website and did some fantastic mailers. His business went through the roof. Up until this point Ted had done everything himself. He kept the books, answered the phone, and filled all the orders. When huge amounts of business started coming in, he hired three people—but he wouldn't delegate work to them. He had to be in charge of everything. At some point he saw that his insistence on running the whole show was keeping his business small. He dismantled his structure of knowing by working with a consultant to develop systems for other people to take over.

Ted said that it was hard for him to let go because he just *knew* that no one could do things as well as he could. After all, he had started this business from the beginning and knew it intimately. Until he let go of that structure of knowing about what it took to run a business, he could not expand. Today he has a multimillion-dollar business.

Another man, Paul, was looking for a car and found that he could get the same model for $8,000 less if he went to another city five hundred miles away to buy it. The problem was, he was convinced that he had to buy the car in his own town because the dealership where he lived wouldn't be responsive to him if he got the car elsewhere. He was about to give up the out-of-town car when he finally saw in the Course that this was a structure of knowing. He called the local dealership and found that they'd be more than happy to work with him even if he'd bought the car at another place. He almost lost $8,000 because he just *knew* that it wouldn't work.

His experience is reminiscent of something said by English philosopher Herbert Spencer and quoted in the Alcoholics Anonymous big book: "There is a principle which is a bar against all information, which is proof against all arguments and which cannot fail to keep a man in everlasting ignorance—that principle is *contempt prior to investigation*."

THE TWIN DOGS: PARADOX AND CONFUSION

To move beyond our structures of knowing about money, we must confront the twin sentinels on the hero's path: paradox and confusion. Often represented as two stone dogs at the doors of many Buddhist temples, a reminder that we must embrace these states to gain enlightenment, paradox and confusion have a lot to do with the clear-eyed, bottom-line topic of money.

As we dismantle old, perhaps dearly held beliefs, it's easy to become confused. Confusion is a state in which, for the moment, nothing is clear. It's uncomfortable to live with because Monkey Mind so loves clarity. When circumstances are cloudy or unclear, Monkey Mind panics. We feel driven to have our questions answered and our way swept clear of doubt or ambiguity.

That's exactly how Ted felt when he let go of having to do everything himself. He didn't know whether or not the business would continue to be successful, or how he would handle the natural stress of letting go of his old structure of knowing.

What I'm asking you to do as you proceed with our work here may cause momentary discomfort. You may feel confused later on as you lay open and then dismantle your money structure of knowing. Your Monkey Mind might tell you that you're not going to learn anything new from this. Allow yourself to stay with your confusion. Your confusion will actually give you breathing room to get beyond the thoughts, judgments, memories, feelings, and other evidence that you need to leave behind. These constructs have gotten you this far, but they cannot take you any further on your hero's journey.

Also, watch to see if paradoxes arise when you look at everything you think you know about money. A paradox is a self-canceling statement or thought that forces the mind into a sort of logical gridlock. It seems to turn the world upside down, and when that happens a new point of view has a chance to appear. A typical paradox would begin with a statement like this:

My name is Maria. I live in Sacramento, California. Everyone who lives in Sacramento is a liar.

Now, here's the paradox: Am I lying about this, or am I telling the truth? How would you know? Wrap your mind around the puzzle for a few moments. Gridlock? You bet! Zen koans produce a similar effect. Koans are teaching phrases designed to produce a state conducive to enlightenment. You probably remember the famous question "What is the sound of one hand clapping?" There is an answer, but it lies outside the logical structure that created the question.

When we're trapped in a structure of knowing, with Monkey Mind cranking out logical justifications for keeping ourselves chained in place, we're wasting energy. Sometimes we have to step outside logic entirely to find a new way of looking at what we're doing.

Hanging out with open questions like "What is my lesson here?" is not always easy. We feel unfinished or incomplete until they're answered. Nothing is distinct and tidy, wrapped up with a bow, the way Monkey Mind likes it. Yet allowing ourselves to sit with our questions, confused and uncertain, moves us away from the handy answers Monkey Mind would pull out of our structures of knowing. And it makes room for what we need to know now. Here is a beautiful description of this process from the poet Rainer Maria Rilke's *Letters to a Young Poet*:

"Have patience with everything unresolved in your heart and try to love the questions themselves as if they were locked rooms or books written in a foreign language. Do not search for the answers, which could not be given to you now, because you would not be able to live with them. And the point is, to live everything. Live the questions now. Perhaps then, someday far in the future, you will gradually, without even noticing it, live your way into the answer."

Interesting things happen to your relationship with your mental productions when you dismantle your structures of knowing. You see that it's not *what* you know but *how you hold* what you know that makes the biggest difference between success and ease on the one hand, and frustration on the other. For example, if what you know is "written in stone forever," all of your energy in life will be aimed to prove you're right.

A much more powerful position comes when you are willing to question everything you "know" about money. Are you willing to hold all your theories in a sort of living suspension while you observe them and see how they interact? It takes less energy than that required in the first scenario, and will bring you closer to your life's goals.

In the You and Money Course I continually see heroes who are willing to hang out with paradox and confusion. One woman, Lana, wasn't enjoying her job and had an offer in another city. She was thinking how great it would be just to get out of her present job and get out of town, but instead of quitting immediately she was willing to sit with the dissatisfaction and discomfort. Instead of jumping to the next job, as she had done in the past, she spent some time allowing herself to look at what the discomfort was really about. She was confused, but she realized that her Monkey Mind was still the loudest voice in her head. She observed her thoughts jumping from one decision, back to the other, and back to the other. "This is the best. No, *this* is the best. No, *this* is the best."

Instead of answering the question "Should I or shouldn't I move?" she began to ask what she was so uncomfortable about. Some very interesting answers came to her. One was that she wanted to become a minister. Just going to another job in a different city would have put off some discomfort, but it wouldn't have brought her that answer. The second thing she saw was that a relationship she was currently engaged in really wasn't working. She had thought of inviting this person to move along with her, but she saw that it wouldn't have worked. Third, in the area of money, she saw that with the way she was spending money there was no way she could go to ministerial school because she had no savings. So out of all this she saw that she wanted to stay at her present job, work out a compatible resolution to the relationship, simplify her life and save some money, and go to ministerial school. Today she is a minister.

Hanging out in paradox and confusion also worked for a couple I know who wanted to buy a house. It seemed to be a great house and a perfect location, but when they opened escrow they started running into one problem after another. There was a lien on the mortgage that hadn't been reported, and a number of other issues. They began questioning whether or not this was the house they wanted to buy. Ordinarily they would have gotten very angry and frustrated at the process, made demands on the owner, and created a very adversarial situation.

Instead they sat with it for a while. They observed their confusion, anger, and frustration without taking immediate action. Finally they saw that they didn't want the house. It was a compromise for them, and they were trying to make it fit what they wanted—but it really didn't work. When they saw that, they could step back and avoid a contentious process that might actually have resulted in litigation. They rented for a year, then found the perfect house at the right price. Had they pushed through, trying to force a resolution, they might have had a house they didn't want and a legal bill to boot.

Heroes develop the capacity to sit with paradox and confusion as they occur. They do not jump to premature conclusions. Allow the amorphous space, the gap, to be there, and do not try to put something in its place. In this space you can journey beyond what you currently know.

A POWERFUL SHIFT

The process of creating and later dismantling structures of knowing occurs throughout our lives. And the mind chatter that fiercely defends every structure we create will also attempt to prevent our leaving each one. So as I suggested earlier, it's interesting to consider the possibility that 90 percent of the mind's running commentary on our lives is not in the least relevant to our circumstances, and is the equivalent of a mental burp!

That's enough to make you want to shut Monkey Mind off once and for all. But one paradox in life seems to be that the harder you try to make your doubts and worries go away, the longer they stick around. If you simply allow your fears and worries to remain—observing them, telling the truth about them, yet letting them be—your relationship with these products of your mind will shift. They will no longer compel you to do anything to make them go away. Instead you can use them to wake you up as you proceed on your hero's journey. You see that your experiences are your personal interpretation of the situations in your life. You become curious about your experiences, whether they are joyful, painful, hard, or happy.

WHERE MIRACLES LIVE

A miracle is an ordinary event that lies outside your current structure of knowing. Rainer Maria Rilke once wrote: "Whoever you are, some night step outside the house you know so well . . . enormous space is near." Let's proceed into this enormous breathing room!

"Miracle" is a word that seems loaded with portent and magic. But when I talk about miracles, I'm not necessarily referring to a religious or even a spiritual experience. Willa Cather put it best when she said, "Miracles rest not so much upon healing power coming suddenly near us from afar, but upon our perceptions being made finer, so that for the moment our eyes can see and our ears can hear what has been there around us always."

The potential for miracles is always around us. They are hidden from view only by the way we think about the world.

Much of what you now consider to be commonplace once seemed like a miracle to you, including your first breath. Do you remember the first time you were able to ride a bicycle? I do. I had been tooling around on my tricycle, watching the older kids zoom here and there on their two-wheelers. I could not understand how they *stayed up*. Did they have invisible wires? Were they all gifted with unimaginable athletic prowess? How did they do it? Then came the day when I got my first two-wheeler. I was nervous. How could I possibly accomplish that miraculous feat? I remember clearly the moment my father pushed me off and, amazingly, I stayed up! I felt in my body the miracle of balance. Of course, after a few weeks I didn't even think about staying up, let alone consider it a miracle. By then riding a two-wheeler was well within my structure of knowing.

What was it like to receive your first paycheck? What about doing something like visiting the mountains for the first time, making your first financial investment, or staying upright on water skis for the first time? Before you experienced these events, you probably thought you knew what to expect. But in retrospect, it's likely you didn't have a clue. These events were awesome and wonderful. They were miracles. Take a moment to note other miraculous events in your life that now seem ordinary or predictable.

When you discern a miracle and interact with it, the scope of your structure of knowing expands to incorporate the event. A miracle eventually loses its aura of wonder and mystery and takes on a quality of ordinariness. It can even become a habit. But if you can keep stretching your structures of knowing, there will always be another miracle within reach.

JAKE: I remember first learning to drive. Finally I got to take the car out alone. Was I excited! I turned on the ignition and saw my whole life as a traveler before me. For the first two weeks I'd jump at any chance to drive. If Mom needed groceries or any errand done, I'd be there, eager to do it. But, in a few weeks the novelty started wearing off. One afternoon Mom asked me to run to the cleaners for her, and for the first time driving across town seemed like a hassle. The thrill was wearing off. Now? I take driving for granted. It's just a means to an end.

There's certainly no thrill as I start the car each morning for my commute to work.

Now, if Jake went to work for the Peace Corps in some undeveloped Third World country, driving a car there might once again take on miraculous proportions. Similarly, if he were to take up flying lessons, he'd probably be thrown back to his predriving level of wonderment. The point here is that you have already had plenty of miracles in your life. You undoubtedly will have more. We're just giving you a more systematic way of reaching them.

Can you remember how impossible some of your accomplishments once seemed? Having a peaceful and satisfying relationship with money is just as possible as any of those others. Consider that it will affect your relationship with all forms of energy. It's simply a matter of being able to move beyond your current structures of knowing.

MIRACLES AND THE HERO'S JOURNEY

Living your life knowing it is a hero's journey molds you to prepare to succeed in attaining the miraculous, and that preparation is crucial. In the story of the Holy Grail, for example, Percival didn't just meander up to the Holy Grail and nab it. He first made sure his own house, his mind, and his affairs were in order. He sorted out his intentions and opened himself to recognizing the signs that guided his quest. His training and focus allowed him to withstand temptations that might have distracted him from his path. He thus succeeded where other Knights of the Round Table had failed: he found the Grail and brought it to King Arthur.

Your journey to discover miracles in your relationship with money is much like Percival's search for the Grail. You are preparing your mind to distinguish your true Life's Intentions from your Monkey Mind's distracting chatter as you trade the comfortable and familiar for the miraculous.

How do you stay your course as you approach miracles? You'll run into some hair-raising moments. Many of the world's greatest film directors will tell you there are often shooting days when nothing goes right. The weather turns wicked. The cast gets sick.

The equipment breaks down. Permission to shoot at a specific location is suddenly denied. At these points Monkey Mind jumps into action, yelling, "If you had any sense, you'd cut your losses and quit right now. Let's get out of here!" This is the decisive moment, and everything hinges on whether the director listens to the chatter.

The best directors move outside their structures of knowing, ignoring what Monkey Mind says things should look like. They reach for their vision despite the setbacks—and they put themselves in the position to produce a miraculous result. Claiming your miracles, despite the insistence of Monkey Mind, requires being willing to operate outside customary reason and wander into the confusion. It also requires being willing to take things one step at a time, with the support of your friends.

If you look under all the activity, that's what the movie directors did. There were really no huge heroic moves—just putting one foot in front of the other. They kept going steadily along. My friend Josie did this with her book of short stories. She called me six months after her You and Money Course to say, "I just finished my book, and I'm submitting it to three literary agents! I never thought I would get this far, but I've been writing three pages a day, every day, even when I didn't feel like it. At first I thought three pages a day wouldn't be enough, but three and a half months later I have a complete manuscript. It's a miracle."

IS IT THE MONKEY, OR IS IT YOU?

Monkey Mind chatters at us incessantly as we approach the edges of our structures of knowing. But sometimes what we hear in our minds sounds a lot like the "still, small voice" of inner wisdom. How do you know if it's Monkey Mind or your inner wisdom cautioning you? Let's look at what happened with Matt.

> MATT: We've just been asked to submit a bid for all the finished woodwork in a big new housing development. What a break! It looks like a sure thing, and means a lot of money for our shop. We'll have more work than we can handle for at least a year, maybe longer. I'll have to hire at least ten new experienced carpenters. We may need a new bookkeeping system and another clerical person. Hmm, I don't know. It makes me kind

of nervous. It'll be a lot of work. Don't get me wrong. I want to go for the contract. I'm excited, but thinking about it makes my head spin.

Matt needs to adjust his way of life to dance with this miracle because it's outside of what he currently knows and does. The prospect is a little scary. Doing what you know feels safer. Monkey Mind gets so raucous when you push outside the familiar! The alternative, though, is no expansion, which could lead to stagnation. Your dreams are much bigger than that. How do you know what to do?

There are two ways to tell whether it's Monkey Mind or your inner wisdom whispering in your ear:

1. When it's Monkey Mind, your body gets tight. Your mind feels overheated. You have a sense of worry and doubt. It feels as if your survival is at stake, and you must do something *immediately*.

2. Learn to discern the difference between what is *valid* and what is *relevant*. Matt's anxiety, doubt, and worry are *valid*. By valid we mean that they are real and genuine. It's possible that, with his current structure of knowing, he cannot deliver on such a big project. Since he's never done such a big job before, he has no proof that he can pull it off. His concerns are legitimate. They are reasonable given his current structure of knowing. Now comes a different question. Is Matt's internal dialogue *relevant?* That is, does it have a direct bearing on whether or not he should proceed toward grasping this miracle? Maybe not. Look at the following questions:

a. Should Matt wait until his thoughts and feelings subside before he submits his bid? Probably not. No matter what's going on inside of him, something needs to be done now if he is to go ahead.

b. Is this chatter a sure sign that something is wrong with his intelligence or ability? No. It is a normal response to considering a big step. Everyone has active internal voices during such times. Still, it's interesting that we often think that there is something wrong with us because we have anxiety or fear at a new opportunity.

c. Will the intensity of this chatter ever diminish? Maybe it will, but it is always ready to come back. Chatter may resume when Matt is again poised at the edge of his comfort zone.

Sometimes seeing that it's all Monkey Mind chatter doesn't help. You still don't know what to do. What do you do then? First you look and see if what you are about to do corresponds with your Life's Intentions. One of Matt's Intentions was "to be financially successful." Obviously this new job, which would expand his business, was relevant to that. Next he looked at whether or not expanding his business with this contract was in keeping with his Standards of Integrity. Among his Standards were "creative" and "adventurous." Going for this contract certainly reflected these two qualities for him. At that point he could see the chatter more clearly. He decided not to wait for it to go away. He saw it as valid but irrelevant. He took the big step and applied for the contract. Matt also hired a business consultant to help him with the expansion. They awarded him the business.

Dancing with your Life's Intentions and Standards of Integrity, instead of Monkey Mind, provides opportunities for miracles. Look at the difference between a miracle and an opportunity. An opportunity is an auspicious opening. It combines circumstance, timing, and place to produce conditions that are favorable for a particular event or action. Opportunity can include events that are predictable, not requiring a stretch, as in: "Have you had the opportunity to read this morning's paper?" Some of these events can be boring or even commonplace. Miracles, though, are events that show up in the opening that opportunity creates. They are not an extension of the past. And they fill you with wonder and awe.

You begin to see miracles everywhere as you dismantle your structures of knowing about money. Even reading this far has undoubtedly started that process for you.

Exercise: Your Structure of Knowing Money

This exercise is designed to make your structure of knowing about money clear to you. Remember, conscious observation is the key to going beyond your paradigm. To continue your journey, you must know where you stand right now.

As you do this exercise, you are beginning to dismantle your structures of knowing. Remember, this is an ontological, not a psychological, process. It has not so much to do with analysis as with observation. As you write your answers, you will notice a shift in the way you see money.

You will need several poster-size pieces of paper, some colorful felt-tipped markers or pens, and a smooth surface on which to work. Make sure you are in a place that's quiet enough for you to concentrate. Give yourself an hour for this process. If you like, break your sessions into no less than twenty minutes each.

Take one of the pieces of paper and lay it on a flat surface. Imagine that this paper forms the edges of a large box or structure. You are about to reveal everything that goes into your structure of knowing about money, and you'll do it by using a simple mind-mapping technique developed by a writer named Gabrielle Lusser Rico.

Write the word "money" in the middle of the box. Now, using one consistent color throughout, start writing down your associations with this word. Do this by drawing lines moving outward from the word "money." An association is any word or phrase that pops into your mind when you think of money.

You may find that these new words have associations or connections with other words, as well. Write those down, too, allowing one idea to flow freely into the next. When you run out of associations, return to your base word, "money." See if anything else comes up. Do this quickly. This is no time for analyzing or editing. If you run dry, see if the following phrases stimulate any more material:

1. What it will take for me to have all the money I want
2. What I know I am right about regarding money
3. Why I want money
4. What I must give up to have money
5. What I think and feel about others who have lots of money
6. How having more money will change my life or the lives of loved ones
7. What I will be able to do with more money that I cannot do now

You may recall poems or sayings that remind you of money. Book or movie titles may come to mind, or quotes from the Bible or other religious texts. Put them on this structure of knowing map. Attach them to any item that seems appropriate.

When you have finished, you will have something that looks like a big web or net. Some associations will be clustered with lots of descriptive language. Others will stand alone.

Get out the other felt-tipped colored pens. Using one new color, circle words that get repeated or are similar in tone or mood. For instance, are there some that point to how hard it is to make a good living? Are there themes of bitterness, resentment, confusion, excitement, or pleasure? Use a different color for each theme. Do other kinds of energy, such as love, health, creativity, self-expression, and spiritual well-being, get mentioned? If not, could they easily be substituted for the word "money" in the middle of the page?

This picture, with all of its associations and colors, is a graphic representation of your current structure of knowing about money. It is your personal model of how money operates in your life and the way you see it in the world. You could list many more associations. However, the work you have done here is enough to give you a handle on what money means to you. This structure affects you every time you read an article on money, go to an investment course, or listen to a lecture on prosperity. It serves as a filter as you try to make authentic choices about your goals and dreams.

Place this map, with all your work on it, where you can see it for at least three days. This is part of the observation process. If a few more associations occur to you during this time, add them. If you see more themes, circle them with a colored pen. Show this structure of knowing to a friend or someone else who knows you well. Talk with them about it as you point out the patterns. This will also aid in your ability to observe, or bear witness to, the way your mind has designed your relationship with money.

Keep notes on what you discover about you and money. Ask yourself: "Is there a pattern to my thoughts about money that limits my options? As I look at what I wrote, are there items about which I feel righteous or defensive? Am I willing to consider what it would be like if I did not hold tightly to this belief [or thought, memory, or body sensation]?" Notice your answers. Are there aspects of this structure of knowing that you prefer to keep? Is there some hope, joy, or enthusiasm peeking out at you? Write about this as well.

Try standing back at least ten feet from this sheet of paper. Does this shift your experience of the structure of knowing? Does there seem to be a lot of energy in your creation? Does it seem to dissipate as you look at the structure over time? Write what you notice. You might place a red dot next to any items that continue to make you feel uncomfortable or anxious. Place a blue dot next to those items that make you feel joyful or peaceful. They will be useful later as we continue the dismantling process.

As you observe your money structure of knowing, I'm going to ask you to do something very different with any tension or feelings you might have. Just let them be there, just as they are. Imagine that you have a basket on your lap. Put them in the basket. Breathe. Don't do anything with them. What do you notice about this? You may think this is a very simple thing to do, and that it's insignificant or irrelevant. But I promise you that if you do this over a period of several days you'll be desensitizing yourself to those elements in your structure of knowing that are uncomfortable. As a matter of fact, you'll be making them so familiar that they will begin to lose their charged energy. It will be increasingly easier to step beyond them, toward the miraculous.

Finally, notice within two weeks of doing this exercise if you see some miracles in your relationship with money. Is breathing room or clarity showing up in a situation that's been worrying or baffling you? What is it? Be specific.

Exercise: Dismantling Through Authentic Action

There is another way to shift your relationship with your money structure of knowing. It consists of deliberately doing something that runs counter to how you know you usually operate. This may not be easy, and your mind chatter may get loud even contemplating the actions below. But if you are willing, proceed. Do not wait for your Monkey Mind to stop.

You will need your notebook to jot down what you discover. The time you take for this exercise varies, depending on what you choose to do.

Choose one or more of the following actions. Take them within the next seventy-two hours.

1. For three days, resolve to pay for everything you buy with cash. Do not select those days when you pay your monthly bills. Is there a shift in your experience of money? What is it? Do any new thoughts or feelings arise?

2. Put all your credit cards (including gasoline cards) in a place where you cannot easily get to them for one week. What do you experience even as you think about doing this? Is your Monkey Mind chattering? (Are your teeth chattering?) Do it anyway and write about what you find.

3. The next three times you go grocery shopping, put 10 percent of what you just spent in the charity box that is usually at the checkout counter. Write about your reactions to having done this.

4. Tell someone you know and trust how much money you make each month. Make sure it is someone who does not already know. This need not be someone you work with. The norms in your organization may prohibit this sort of disclosure. Whomever you talk to, tell them you are doing this as an experiment. What do you experience?

These are not trivial acts. They are designed to help you pass the boundaries of what you know about money in your life. Write your reactions in your notebook. You are increasing your ability to observe how your relationship with money is wired up.

BECOMING EN-LIGHTENED

A paradox occurs when you consciously observe what you are experiencing. Whatever you look, see, and tell the truth about begins to lose its emotional charge. This is what clearing away your thoughts, beliefs, and ideas means.

"Most people think of enlightenment as a kind of magical attainment," writer David Cooper tells us, "a state of being close to perfection . . . but for most of us, enlightenment is much more in line with what Suzuki Roshi describes. It means having a quality of being, a fresh, simple unsophisticated view of things."

The key to finding miracles in your life is to develop your ability to recognize and benefit from them. The Buddhists call it "beginner's mind." You can enjoy its gifts at any age. To approach our lives with beginner's mind is a major breakthrough in how we experience the world around us, and this certainly includes our relationship with money. In this respect, we are working toward a certain level of enlightenment. We are clearing away the thoughts, beliefs, and ideas that cloud our ability to see things as they really are.

FORGIVENESS UNLEASHES
MONEY ENERGY

It may seem odd to you that forgiveness has anything at all to do with the energy of money. Forgiveness releases the energy that's bound to judgments and assessments of people for what they did in the past, whether distant or recent. It's a bit like splitting the bonds of an atom, and the net effect is movement and power on your path toward your dream. You will move more quickly on your path if you forgive.

When you forgive someone, you dismantle your structures of knowing about him or her. You lay down your weapons and armor and proceed onward. You lighten up. If ever there were an act of courage, this is it. As Laurence Sterne said: "Only the brave know how to forgive."

I use as a foundation for this exercise three questions on forgiveness that I learned from Father Gerry O'Rourke. At the time, he was the Ecumenical Officer for the Archdiocese of San Francisco and a priest at St. Philip the Apostle Catholic Church. Father O'Rourke has made it his business to teach people how to forgive others. I learned from him that forgiving from your heart is possible even when your mind insists that there are reasons not to forgive. With immense gratitude, I have taken his view of forgiveness and adapted a process that includes those questions. They appear later in this chapter.

THE POWER OF LETTING GO

Forgiveness occurs when you systematically lay aside conclusions you have reached about other people and the motivations for their actions. It begins and ends with your own structures of knowing. Most of us are confident that what we know about others is accurate. This is especially true when we're angry or displeased with them. Social psychologists will tell you that it's instinctual for us to attribute negative intentions to the behavior of others, especially when we don't like what they've done.

When you forgive someone you don't necessarily forget what he or she has done. As we've seen earlier, we can't easily direct our minds to stop or avoid thinking about an incident in the past. Forgetting isn't necessary, or even advisable. People can do hurtful things. Therapists' offices are filled with those who have tried to blank out painful portions of their lives. It's often important to remember distressing incidents and times for our continued growth and healing.

What I'm really talking about when I refer to forgiving someone is dismantling the negative assessment we have about him or her. Forgiveness occurs when you are willing to let go of what you have said about another person because of what they did.

To forgive, you must take two big steps:

First, you must look directly at your evaluations, judgments, and catalogued scenarios about the person. You take stock of the thoughts and feelings going on inside you when they come to mind, and you examine what you have said to yourself and others about them.

Second, you must become willing to relinquish the permission you give yourself to entertain those thoughts, feelings, and judgments ever again. Every time you hear Monkey Mind whisper, "But he really is a jerk!" you say: "Thanks for sharing, but I have already forgiven this person."

Three components of forgiveness make this courageous act accessible to everyone, no matter how they feel they have failed at previous efforts:

1. Forgiveness is letting go of negative structures of knowing that you have created about another human being.
2. Forgiveness comes from your essence—who you are in your heart. It is a product of being willing.
3. Monkey Mind takes longer than your heart to catch on. Just

because it still chatters at you about how awful the other person is does not mean you have not forgiven them.

WHAT WE SAY ABOUT OTHERS

Begin your act of forgiveness by answering the following questions: Whom would you need to forgive in order to have a powerful relationship with money? Whom do you secretly blame for your misfortunes in life? Whom do you hold responsible for your money problems? The answer is not "me"! Resist the temptation to blame yourself or to fall into the trap of thinking that you have consciously chosen everything that has happened to you. This is no time to be noble, self-effacing, or co-dependent. Tell the truth. Who do you feel did you harm? What has he or she done?

> MARIANNE: My mother was never very independent. She stayed home and took care of us kids. She wasn't enthusiastic about my going to law school. I think she was jealous. If she had encouraged me, law school might have been a lot easier to get through.

> MITCH: My business partner hasn't kept his part of the bargain over the past three years. Now I'm ruined. If it wasn't for him, this construction company would be solvent today. Now I might have to let go of the whole operation. And it's all because of him. He has ruined my hopes of being a successful businessman.

These people have plenty of evidence for their assumptions. As you listen to their stories, you might be tempted to agree with them about the character of the transgressor. You could add insights of your own about the nature and motivations of those who hurt them. We all do this, whether it is at the dinner table or the coffee room at work. But let's look a little closer to see what's really going on here.

Ruined my hopes . . . shattered my dreams . . . cramped my style . . . jealous and dependent . . . these are all structures of knowing. They are metaphors permeated with thoughts, feelings, attitudes, states of mind, points of view, and memories. You can almost sense their weight and feel how much energy is invested in developing them and keeping them alive.

These structures are also being used as reasons, justifications, or excuses for the speakers' failures or broken promises. From what you've already learned about structures of knowing, you can see that it's time to dismantle them. As long as they're in place, their owners will be sitting by the wayside—something none of us wants to do—instead of advancing down their paths with greater ease.

The structures of knowing we just saw were negative, pointing to the other person's shortcomings. They carry the speaker's sense of finality, even resignation, about the situation. We call these structures of knowing *characterizations*.

WHAT IS A CHARACTERIZATION?

When you form a characterization of another person, you see them through the grid of your assessments and judgments. This produces a two-dimensional experience of them and keeps you from seeing them as fellow humans. They appear to you as the cartoon outlines of what you perceive to be their shortcomings.

Characterizations don't change the other person. In fact, the only person they deeply affect is you, because they contribute to the driven behavior in your life. When you ascribe your behavior to what others have said or done, as in "I would be more successful if my parents had only . . . ," you keep in place the same behavior you fear, despise, or otherwise want to deny. This applies whether the behavior that keeps you down involves making bad business decisions, choosing poor investments, letting a great opportunity slip by, or getting into partnerships that do not work:

> DON: Of course I don't know how to manage money. After all, my dad was a gambler. He spent everything he had. Never taught us anything about money, except how to lose it. That was his gift!

Your characterizations limit both the way you can interact with others and your memory of them. They keep the two of you tied together in a way that stunts your growth and theirs, and they'll even affect your growth when the person is no longer in your life.

How do we develop these limiting and rigid characterizations about others? Let's say you're in a relationship with your friend Elise. Elise rushes into the house one day and knocks over your favorite vase, which breaks into a dozen pieces. She apologizes and offers to replace it, but Monkey Mind, noting what she did, won't let it go. It chimes in with comments like "You know, Elise is nice, but she's really careless. Not only that, but she's unconscious. Look at the way she just swooped into the room and destroyed that great piece of art. No question about it, she's an accident waiting to happen."

Once it's offered this assessment, your mind acts like a magnet, attracting examples from the past of when Elise did anything similar. Labels like "careless" and "unconscious" and "accident waiting to happen" are powerful mental constructs. They're actually decisions to see the other person in a particular way. Once we've made decisions like this, we gather other decisions to prop them up. This is what I mean when I say structures of knowing begin to take on a life of their own, unbeknownst to their creators.

When Elise comes over two weeks later, she opens your refrigerator and a glass bottle that was balanced precariously at the edge of a shelf tips and falls, making a mess. Monkey Mind springs into action. "See? I was really right about her," it says. "She's a total klutz, and she's careless and unconscious."

The mind continues to collect data to flesh out the structure and prove itself correct. It gathers incidents, names, dates, and places to hang on the frame. You start to see a host of other behaviors or incidents that irritate, hurt, or frustrate you. As in: "Yeah, and come to think of it, she did this before. She's always in such a rush, she just doesn't look where she's going. You know, she's a lousy driver, too. And she's so forgetful! I don't know how many times I've seen her leave her purse in a restaurant and then knock over people when she rushes back in to get it. Remember the time she . . ."

The characterization is a Monkey Mind–initiated/created pattern of unrelated incidents. Over time the characterization of the person becomes more and more detailed, and anything that doesn't fit–like Elise's kindness or high energy and enthusiasm–falls out of the grid. The characterization becomes increasingly two-dimensional, and like the villain in your favorite novel, it comes to life, haunting your waking hours and popping up unexpectedly in your dreams.

Characterizations are contagious. When you describe the one you have about Elise to others who know her, they may start to agree with you. They might even add their own stories. They call out to everyone to join in. During the You and Money Course, when a participant talks about someone with whom he or she has a grievance, everyone gets angry for them. If the object of the characterization were to enter the room at that moment, almost everyone there would react coldly—even though they'd never met the person before!

Finally, and this happens to all of us, we get to the point of relating only to our characterization, rather than to the person. It is a lonely prospect. We don't want to be around him or her because we cannot tolerate being present with our own negative thoughts and feelings. It is too uncomfortable, mostly because it is not within our Standards of Integrity to keep such characterizations alive. It's not that we don't like who *they* are; we don't like who *we* are in the presence of that person. Our negativity becomes our burden.

How does all of this affect Elise? She knows you're not happy with her. She may not know why. Becoming wary or weary around you,

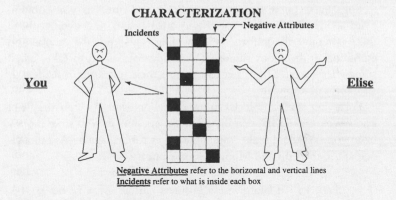

CHARACTERIZATION

Negative Attributes

Incidents

You

Elise

Negative Attributes refer to the horizontal and vertical lines
Incidents refer to what is inside each box

Elise may avoid you, sensing that all is not well. This is *not* a blueprint for empowering relationships!

The process of forming characterizations is quick, almost reflexive. You can't stop yourself from doing it. Everyone has structures of knowing about other people. But while you can't keep the thoughts from arising, you can observe and tell the truth about them. You can be willing, if only for a moment, to see your characterizations as irrelevant.

But when you give up permission to dance with your characterizations, they no longer shape you. As you forgive, you stop the process of being trapped in what you fear and dislike. You liberate yourself from the hold the old structures had on you. You become your own person. And you release the people you've forgiven to continue on with their own lives.

FORGIVENESS: AUTHENTIC ACTION FOR THE COURAGEOUS HEART

Through forgiveness you get in touch with who you are in your heart. Your movement toward forgiveness is first expressed as being *willing* to forgive. Remember, being willing is the most powerful Authentic Action you can take.

The moment you are willing, you are able to draw a distinction between your Monkey Mind and your heart. You may not *want* to forgive. You may be afraid to forgive. Many thoughts and feelings may course through your body and mind as you contemplate laying aside your most closely held beliefs. But even with all these potential discomforts, being willing transcends the mental and emotional stuff of our minds. It is a powerful stand to take, albeit somewhat scary. That's because we're then operating outside our structures of knowing.

Forgiving someone feels vulnerable. For example, you may not know what would happen if you forgave a person who stole money from you. Would it make you liable to get robbed again? As one participant in the You and Money Course put it:

> SYDNEY: If I forgive my business partner for what he did, does that mean I give him license to do it all over again?

Of course you don't. We are talking about forgiving, not forgetting. If someone steps on your foot, forgiveness does not mean feigning amnesia and sticking your foot out again to wait for a replay. As you forgive the other person, you are simply relinquishing the permission you give yourself to use their behavior to prove that he or she is an unthinking, unconscious jerk. You may still tell them: "That hurt me! I didn't like what you just did one bit!" But you give up the right to use the action to dehumanize or demonize them, or to prove what a rotten person they are and how they've ruined your life.

Forgiveness happens at the moment you are willing to forgive. It starts in the metaphysical domain and moves into the physical one very quickly. The metaphysical domain is timeless. The moment you declare you are willing to forgive someone, they are forgiven. That's it! No lag time. It is done. No magical formulas to recite over and over again in hopes that you will finally forgive the person or situation. Nothing to work on. The answer to the question "Are you willing to forgive this person?" is either "Yes" or "No." Answers such as "I'll try," "Maybe," "I think so," and "Yeah, I guess" are really "No"s in convincing disguises.

MONKEY MIND NEEDS TIME TO CATCH ON

Forgiveness requires patience, no doubt about it. Monkey Mind will want you to continue talking about "that awful person who offended you." It takes a while for your mind to catch up with your heart when you engage in forgiveness. Your heart forgives—and then your Monkey Mind sets in once again with a litany of all the terrible things it's collected to prove the other person's failings.

What do you do when your mind will not stop? Answer it in the following way: "Thanks for sharing, but I have already forgiven this person."

Whatever you do, don't fight with Monkey Mind. Act with compassion. This aspect of your brain has been programmed over the years. Remind it that these old, habitual thoughts are no longer relevant, and after a while you will notice your mind beginning to loosen its grasp on them. It will become quieter.

It was a relief to me when Father O'Rourke taught me the role the mind plays in forgiveness. I had forgiven people in the past but then heard my mind jumping in to list their faults once again. I worried that I had failed at forgiving them—but it was simply not true.

You have the ability to forgive. You know how to look at, see, and tell the truth about your structure of knowing and then let it all go. The only question is Are you willing?

Most of us notice loud Monkey Mind conversations about ourselves. People have asked me whether they need to forgive themselves before they can forgive anyone else, and the answer is no. If

you look at your characterizations of yourself, you will find that ultimately you hold others responsible for your "faults." This is true for
most of us, even when we think we have already taken responsibility
for our own shortcomings.

And even if that were not true for you, forgiving another person is
much more powerful and far-reaching than forgiving yourself. Forgiveness allows you to let go of the ties that have bound the other
person to you in a negative way. In doing so, you set them free and
take a stand that your judgments about others will no longer weigh
you down. One of the oldest spiritual teachings in the world is that as
you forgive, you will be forgiven.

Since forgiveness is an act of generosity, the result is often far-
reaching and occasionally surprising. One woman in the You and
Money Course had a well-developed characterization of her sister:

> MARILYN: I just knew my sister was childish and irrespon-
> sible. She'd owed me $800 for at least five years. She didn't give
> any signs that she was going to pay it back. I didn't want to, but
> I saw that I was willing to forgive her—to let go of all the things
> I've said about her in the past, to myself and others. One week
> after forgiving her, the strangest thing happened. She called me
> to talk. About ten minutes into the conversation she said, "You
> know that $800 I owe you? I'd like to begin paying you back
> now. I can see I've been irresponsible in letting it go for so
> long." Even stranger was my own reaction. I was thankful to get
> the money. But it wouldn't really have mattered if she'd paid
> me back or not. I felt like we were getting close again, like in the
> old days.

Did something magical occur the moment Marilyn forgave her
sister? Or did her sister just call Marilyn and sense that something
had shifted in their relationship? Did that shift make it obvious to her
sister that it was time to take care of the incompletion? To Marilyn it
was a miracle, outside her former structure of knowing. Whether or
not it affected the debt, forgiving her sister had a healing effect on
both of them.

FORGIVENESS IS *YOUR* BUSINESS

People often ask, "Should I tell someone that I've forgiven them?" Think about it for a moment. If I walked up to you and announced, "I have forgiven you," what would your probable response be? Right. Something like "What for?" You might feel defensive, because to explain what I've forgiven I have to pull up all the elements of my old characterization of you—the one I'd sworn to let go!

Announcing how I'd forgiven you could convey my hidden agenda. The unspoken message might be "You're a terrible person who did horrible things. You need to be forgiven because you were such a jerk to me, and I'm just proving what a good person I am by forgiving you in spite of it all." That's why we get a hollow feeling in the pit of our stomachs when someone tells us they have forgiven us. We may feel a moment of guilt for some unknown transgression that we are about to be reminded of. Resentment follows. It's pure Monkey Mind.

The bottom line is that it is irrelevant, and a mistake, to tell someone you have forgiven them. After all, forgiveness is being willing to let go of what you have said about someone. It does not require even a single word from them to complete this process and bring you a sense of closure.

> MEG: I remember after forgiving my brother, I had an occasion to have dinner with him. After a few moments of embarrassed silence, I found myself asking for his forgiveness for all the times I had been mean to him! He was so surprised. He started to cry!

Occasionally someone will ask about forgiving a person who has been physically or emotionally violent with them or a loved one. It can feel threatening or dangerous to let such a person off the hook. Remember that forgiveness does not mean forgetting or rationalizing away what they have done. It involves letting go of a characterization of them that you have created and are holding on to. That lets you off your treadmill of grievances—but it doesn't put you in danger. It doesn't ask that you put yourself in harm's way. Indeed, the process of forgiveness may help you understand how certain people can be hurtful to you. And it can make you compassionately aware of how you can be hurtful to others. This increased awareness allows you to be clearer in your interactions with the person you have forgiven. You need not stay in close relationship with them, and you need not run.

If you want to get more than your money's worth from this book, practice forgiveness regularly. Notice how this affects your personal and business relationships. Are you more energized as you go for your goals?

THE POWER TO FORGIVE

It is empowering to know that you can forgive others. In our heart of hearts we want to be complete with everyone. It is a much easier road to travel. Being complete simply means knowing that all is well. They did and said what they did, and so did you. To forgive is to release the regrets of what is in the past. It is to know what it is to be who you really are, no longer using past hurts or misfortunes as an excuse.

Forgiveness involves two elements. First, you must forgive someone primarily for his or her sake and only secondarily for yours. You must be willing to see that you have held them in your mind, roasting on a spiritual spit for what they did. You must be tired of the dynamic created by your grievance.

Second, you must be in touch with your characterization of the other person instead of brushing it off or trying to forget it. You will need to see your judgments, evaluations, anger, disgust, resentment, fear, and all other components of this structure of knowing. Why? You cannot let go of anything unless you are aware of it.

When you are ready, experience the way forgiveness releases you. It will create the breathing room that allows you to look and see the supportive energy of other people all around you. This will ease your way toward your goals.

Forgiveness Exercises

The following exercises will help you practice forgiveness:

Exercise 1: Stepping Toward Forgiveness

You will need your notebook and ten to fifteen minutes of quiet time.

Choose a dream or a goal that you haven't yet attained, one you've held on to for a long time that's been dear to you. It could be a dream that you've discarded lately because you thought it would never come true.

1. Write down a word or two that describes your dream in the middle of a piece of paper. Then, using the mind-mapping technique you learned earlier, start looking at all your reasons, rationalizations, or excuses for not completing that dream. List all the reasons you can.

2. Look at your reasons. Can you think of one or more people who've contributed to your difficulties? Write down who they are and what happened. You might say, "My dad was a put-down artist who undermined my self-confidence," or "My uncle Joe wouldn't give me a loan for my education, so I don't have the credentials I need." Look for the person or people you blame. Was it a teacher who was cruel? Or your brother, the family star, who got what he needed at your expense? *This is no time to look good.* List the person or people you feel stood in your way or caused you to get derailed. Say what they did, or failed to do, for you. Don't worry about being uncharitable. Just be honest.

3. What do you feel as you write? Is there heaviness in your chest or gut? A lack of breathing room? Anger or frustration? No matter how you manage to disguise your true feelings, when you are in the same room with that person, or even hear their name, the feelings you have now are always present. They're right out front, or buried just beneath the surface. This is definitely not traveling light.

4. Ask yourself: "If this person were never in my life, would I have gotten what it is I say I want? Would I be free of all these reasons and excuses? Would I be successful? What would I be doing with my life that I'm not doing now?"

If you've made your mind map and don't locate any people you deem responsible for the condition of your thwarted dream, look deeper. For example, if you say, "One of the reasons that I haven't gone to Tahiti is that I don't have enough money," look under that statement for the reason why. What's causing you not to have enough money? You may have to go back three or four steps, but I guarantee that you will eventually trace your reason to the personality of another person.

Maybe it was that your mom never showed you how to manage money. Maybe it was that your father was stingy with the money that he had. But allow yourself to go back until you locate the person or people whom you really deem responsible for things being the way they are.

It takes courage to do this. How did you feel as you did this exercise? Share what you found with a friend.

Remember, when you forgive another person you cease to use what they did as the reason that your dreams and goals failed to materialize. Through forgiveness, you are waiving the right to use what they did against them or yourself.

As forgiveness replaces negative judgments and assessments, your stories or scenarios about how difficult it is for you to deal with that person fade away. You no longer spend time talking with others about that person's character flaws and how much they hurt you. This may not be easy. I remember one woman who said, "If I can't talk about how rigid and selfish my mother is, I'm afraid I won't have anything to say to my brothers and sisters when we're together at Thanksgiving!"

Once again, when you give up your characterizations you're no longer shaped by them. One consequence of holding on to your limiting decisions about another person is that you may turn out exactly like them. You know this is true. You have seen it in yourself and others. You wake up one morning to find you've become like the person you blame for your misfortune. You can hear it in your voice or in the words you use.

Conversely, releasing others releases *you* to be successful. No more reasons or excuses!

If you wish to go on, try the exercise in forgiveness that follows. It is powerful, and freeing.

EXERCISE 2: THE FORGIVENESS PROCESS

You will need your notebook and a quiet room. Part of this exercise involves an eyes-closed process. Ask a friend to read the passage to you, or tape-record it and play it back. This exercise will take about forty minutes the first time you do it. You will find that you're experiencing a practice effect and that future experiences with this exercise may take as little as ten minutes. Father O'Rourke says he can go through this process himself in one minute. He can see a characterization in its early stages and nip it in the bud.

1. Identify someone you are ready to forgive. By readiness I mean that you're in touch with all your feelings about them, the negative as well as the positive. Sometimes this is hard for us because we want to suppress our negative feelings. But choose, as the first person you forgive, someone about whom you have well-developed judgments, evaluations, and assessments. Begin with someone who is not a parent. You might start out with someone you hold responsible for a specific thwarted goal or dream, or a person who has irritated you lately at the office, at home, during a sports activity, or during a financial transaction. You're just learning to do this, and starting with someone who is simpler to forgive will give you a feeling of success. Please allow yourself to have that. Take that positive experience and let it help you with the more difficult cases in your life.

2. Take a clean piece of paper and draw an oval that fills the entire sheet. Next, put that person's name on top of the oval. This figure now represents your characterization of that person.

3. With a pen or pencil, fill the oval with all of the thoughts, feelings, judgments, and attitudes you have about them. Write small if you must, but put everything on that oval. For example, were they thoughtless, dishonest, hypocritical? Where did they drive you or others crazy with their behavior? What are their character flaws, as you see them? Take your time and leave nothing out. Be as picky, unmerciful, and derisive as you like.

Someone once asked me, "Why drag up all this old stuff? It's painful and I'd rather forget it." The answer is simple: If you are remembering it right now, it is still there inside you, festering away, and maybe it's been there a long time. It needs to be put on that paper where the light of your awareness can shine on it. If you see it and acknowledge it you can consciously let it go. Trying not to look at it will only keep it around longer. When you deny your grievances, they affect you profoundly, and the more you try to push them down, the more powerful they become.

Please take a moment and realize that you have taken a big step in healing your relationship with him or her. Remember that the act of observing is the first step toward enlightenment.

As you look over what you have written—and I hope you have

filled up your whole page—see if you have left anything out. Add whatever is necessary before continuing. When you have finished, write: "And everything else." It signifies that you are including anything your Monkey Mind may create in the future.

4. Now I'd like you to ask yourself the three questions. Again, you can do this by prerecording your voice or by having a friend read the questions to you. Allow yourself to pause, grasp the questions, take a moment to get in touch with your true feelings, and then answer. You may feel a whole variety of emotions as you go through this exercise. These feelings are natural and have probably been there for quite a while. Just let them be there. You do not have to do anything with them except give yourself room to experience them.

The answer to these questions is either "Yes" or "No." Remember, a "Maybe," " I think so," "I'll try," or any other vague or qualifying answer counts as a "No." Qualifications do not come from your heart. If they occur, it is a sign that you are not yet ready to forgive that person. But be aware that you may need to have room to say "No, I'm not willing to forgive this person" before you can have the space to give an authentic "Yes."

Here are the words to the guided meditation, to be recorded or read to you by another person. The dots in the text indicate pauses of about three seconds. The text is also available in my "Energy of Money" tape series, available through the Sounds True catalogue:

Sit in an upright, yet comfortable position. Place on your lap that piece of paper on which you have written all your notes about the person you are going to forgive. Now close your eyes . . . Let your hands rest on the paper . . . As you do, you might be able to feel the energy from that characterization sheet.

In your mind's eye, place an empty chair about three feet in front of you, facing you . . . In your mind's eye, look at the horizon on your right. Allow yourself to see the person who is there for you to forgive coming toward you . . . Let them sit in that chair in front of you . . . How do they look as they see you? Do they appear worried or wary? Do they seem sad or concerned? As you sit in front of them, feeling the heat from the characterization sheet coming through your hands, you'll hear me ask you three questions, the answer to which is either "Yes" or "No." Take a deep breath . . . If you notice any emotions coming up right now, just allow them to be there . . . Now answer the following questions to yourself as you hear me ask them.

1. *Are you willing to forgive this person totally?* . . . By this I mean are you willing to let go of everything you have written on that sheet of paper, and even things you have not written, not keeping any part of it for later? Are you willing to let them off that spit you've had them roasting on? Are you willing to let go of the chains that have bound them to you in this way? . . . You may not want to, may not even think you know how, but are you nevertheless willing, from your heart, to let this person off the hook? . . . Once again, are you willing to forgive this person totally? Answer silently, "Yes" or "No" . . .

2. *Are you willing to forgive this person absolutely?* . . . By this I mean are you willing to give up your favorite stories and scenarios about them—the things you say again and again about how they are and how that affected you? . . . This takes a lot of heart and courage, because these stories and scenarios have had a lot of juice for you in the past. Are you willing to give up permission to use them, either with yourself or with others, as the reason you have not achieved your goals and dreams in life? . . . When you hear yourself about to use one of these stories, are you willing to say to Monkey Mind, "Thank you for sharing, but I have already forgiven this person"? As you do that, you're drawing a distinction between who you really are in your heart and Monkey Mind . . . So, once again: Are you willing to forgive this person sitting in front of you absolutely? "Yes" or "No" . . .

3. *Are you willing to forgive this person unconditionally?* . . . Now and forever? . . . Are you willing to give up permission to entertain characterizations of them, not just now, but forevermore? . . . This person may do what they usually do, which has upset you in the past . . . But you are hereby giving up permission to use what they do or say to form characterizations of them . . . In answering this question "Yes," you are willing to see that forgiveness has nothing to do with this person himself or herself . . . It has everything

to do with what you say about him or her . . . So, once again, are you willing to forgive this person unconditionally? Answer "Yes" or "No" . . .

Whether you have answered "Yes" or "No" to any of the questions, the fact you have brought this person to sit in front of you says that you are willing for some healing to take place between the two of you . . . We sometimes need room to say no before we can say yes . . . As a matter of fact, whether you said "Yes" or "No," your heart is open to them. There may be something you want to tell them from your heart right now . . . This person is here for you right now. So what I'd like you to do is open your heart and just tell them everything that's there for you to say. Say it all as though you may never see them again. (Pause for fifteen seconds.) And now, because this person is sitting in front of you, there may be some things they want to tell you from their heart. Just be willing to hear what they have to say. Give them room to say it. Just listen. (Pause for fifteen seconds.)

If there are any questions to which you answered "No" that you are now willing to answer "Yes," allow yourself to do it now. If not, just let it be . . .

In your mind's eye, you can hug that person or shake their hand. Is there something else that you need to whisper to them? Say it now . . . The truth is, they did what they did, and so did you. That's just the way it is with human beings. Allow yourself to know that all is well. They had their thoughts and you've had yours . . . Now watch that person stand up and walk away from you. As they walk away, do you notice that they turn and maybe even wave to you? Does their face look lighter? How do you feel? . . . Just let them disappear over the horizon again. And as they do, just allow yourself to sit here with your eyes closed . . . Take another deep breath . . .

Would it be all right with you to discover how courageous you are, and that all is well?

Now gently open your eyes. Take the piece of paper in your lap and tear it up, then throw it away. To complete this exercise, wash your hands. This symbolizes that you have finished with this process, no matter how you answered the questions. Literally and figuratively, you're washing your hands of it.

If you have been working on this exercise with a friend, or if you are with a group of people, take some time to talk about what you have gotten from this exercise. If you have done this alone, write down what you have seen.

You may still have "No" answers for one or more of the above questions. If this is so, ask yourself when you would be willing to do this exercise again. A persistent "No" might indicate that some specific counseling on the matter is needed. Above all, this is a time for compassion for yourself.

If you have answered "Yes," what do you see? Is there an opening for a conversation with that person that was not present before? Do you notice a shift in your energy level? If so, what is it?

Learning to forgive is an ability that, with practice, will become easier for you. At the same time, you'll become more and more aware of people whom you have not yet forgiven. This awareness will stick with you until you act upon it and heal the relationship.

Finally, you may discover after doing this exercise that it's time for you to make contact with this person. Is there a letter you want to write to him or her? A phone call you want to make? Laura, in meeting with her mother after doing this forgiveness process, made a point of telling her mom everything she appreciated about their relationship. She said the going was rough at first but she was determined to let this person know what a good mother she had been, even with all their disagreements. At the end of about five minutes, her mother interrupted her. Laying her hand on Laura's arm, she said, "Will you please forgive me for all the things I did that made you unhappy? I just love you so much."

Pay attention to what you discover about your relationship with money as you move through the forgiveness process. You may have a sense that as you forgive the people in your life you have more energy to actually pursue your goals. And in freeing up that energy, you travel with more ease down your hero's path.

MAKING AND KEEPING PROMISES
MOVES YOU ALONG YOUR PATH

In this chapter you'll learn more about how to dance with the energy of money. As the result of doing the work thus far, you may see that dreams that have seemed beyond you are beginning to take shape. You are starting to see them more vividly. Just seeing your life in new ways allows energy to flow toward what you long for. You begin to dance with the energies around you.

When you dance you move to a rhythm, and there's a rhythm to the energy. Your life has its own rhythm. Energy flows through you, sometimes briskly and sometimes in a slow and somewhat sluggish way. You are a moving, living, breathing conduit, but you're really more than that. A conduit merely transports energy from one place to another. You have the ability to direct this energy intentionally so that you create what you truly want. In doing this, you co-create the dance of energy.

THE JOY OF KEEPING PROMISES

In the Bible, King David danced toward the temple of the Ark of the Covenant. The hero's journey is not a trudge or a forced march. It is animated and joyful. As George Bernard Shaw said, "I rejoice in life for its own sake. Life is no brief candle to me. It is a sort of splendid torch, which I've got to hold up for the moment, and I want to make it burn as brightly as possible before handing it on to future generations."

The promises you *make* in life start you dancing with the joy of that "splendid torch." The promises you *keep* will ensure that you keep dancing. A promise is your word, whether spoken or implied, cast forth into physical reality. It's a covenant you make with the world. It says: This shall be done.

When you make a promise you set up an energy imbalance. Think about this for a moment. Let's say you tell your best friend you'll take him or her to dinner next Wednesday night as a birthday present. Notice that you create a tension, the expectation of something yet to be done. When you put your word out before you, you create a gap that can only be closed when you do what you said you'd do. Now imagine that it's Wednesday and you're at dinner with your friend. See how the tension resolves? The energy field is now balanced.

The energy dance that keeps us moving on our path involves creating and resolving imbalances. When we produce a gap we're pulled forward to close it. This is one of the reasons I asked you to make a Treasure Map for each of your goals. The map's graphic and colorful representation of your promise keeps you mindful of the gap. The more it is in your consciousness, the more likely you will engage in Authentic Action to achieve your goal. At that point, the rift is closed and you move on to create the next one.

BROKEN PROMISES

We often neglect to consider the effect of *not* keeping our promises. When we don't do what we said we'd do, we're left with the tension of incompletion. Unfulfilled promises are energy drains because, Monkey Mind's warnings to the contrary, we expend more energy keeping open a gap than we do when we resolve it.

Each unfulfilled promise draws energy to it and becomes a block to the flow. It saps your power. You become too physically, emotionally, and even spiritually tired, and have no energy for the dance! Interestingly enough, it doesn't matter with whom you made your promise:

ALEX: Well, when I say I'll do something for someone *else,* I usually do it. I just don't keep promises I make to myself. Like about saving for a vacation next year. I haven't begun yet. I always think of myself last, I guess.

Let this be a wake-up call. The universe doesn't care with whom you made the contract. Not keeping your word to yourself is still not keeping your word. It produces the same gap. It's no more laudable than failing to keep a promise with anyone else.

Broken promises often sound like the following:

• You've sworn to get your income taxes done by February every year, but there you were at 11 P.M. on April 15, sweating out whether you'd make it to the post office on time.

• You vowed, with all the resolve in the world, to put aside money every month for a vacation. And how did it go? Looks like you'll be using the credit cards again this year.

• You promised your family you'd cut back on your work hours, but your kids have stopped believing you, or asking you to come to their ball games.

We're now going to do some work to help you fulfill the promises you've already made. It's great to do this phase of the work with a group. If you are not working with a You and Money support group, try to find at least one close friend with whom you can share your observations.

In doing this will you become a clear conduit for the energy of money? At this point in the journey, it's important to know that *the bridge between you and financial miracles is built from the promises you keep.* Unfinished business—that pile of unpaid bills, forgotten loans, missed appointments—weighs you down. Your step becomes heavy. But keep your word regarding money and you gain the energy to bring your dreams from the metaphysical into the physical.

When you are traveling light, miracles just seem to occur all around you. That's what will happen as you do the work of this chapter. Each promise you make good on by taking care of incomplete business will clear your conduit and allow money energy to power your dreams. I know this works. I've seen the results with thousands of people.

BEING A CONSCIOUS CONDUIT OF ENERGY

Imagine a pipe that's plugged into a huge lake of fresh, clear water. The pipe is designed to take this water from the lake to a garden, where it nourishes beautiful flowers—but it has to be operated carefully. If it's opened wide, and lets a flood of energy through, everything in the garden will drown. Similarly, if it doesn't allow enough energy to pass, whatever is growing will wither.

We are like the pipe, and the lake is the unlimited amount of energy in metaphysical reality. Whereas the amount of energy around us is infinite, *we aren't!* We are designed to channel a limited amount of energy during our lives. We have a limited amount of time, physical energy, creativity, and even money to work with.

Countless people have been frustrated because they don't understand this idea. In our culture we have become confused, looking to the infinite energy supply to get us out of the messes we create in life. The supply *is* infinite. We, on the other hand, have been designed to create in physical reality, with all its constraints. So our access to the supply is *not* infinite. The hero's purpose is to discover just how much he or she can create by infusing energy into this limited, dense physical realm. The myth of Prometheus, who brought fire to earth, is the clearest example of bringing energy from the metaphysical into the physical realm. That's the real adventure!

When we depend on an infinite supply of energy to "rescue" us

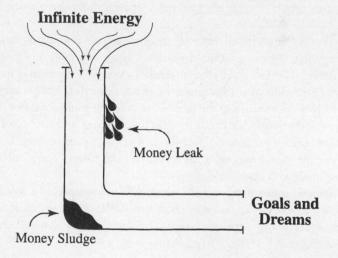

during difficult times, we're actually fostering our own unconsciousness. We waste what we've got, rather than use our resources on
what's important to us. We get caught up in seeking to earn more
and more money. We may think, "There's lots more where that
came from! Why should I be concerned with where it's going? All I
need to do is make (or pray for) more."

On the other hand, too much of the energy of money can drown
ambitious goals, or make them waterlogged, as people who have
inherited great financial wealth often report. We'll cover this later in
this chapter when we look at what I call the Icarus Syndrome.

Our task in life is to become the very best conduit possible. To
learn how we can do this, let's look first at what hinders us from
being clear conduits of energy. Look at the diagram on page 221.

Here's what happens to most conduits in physical reality: After a
while they develop "sludge" in the form of debris. Sooner or later,
impediments block or lessen the flow of energy. These blockages of
money energy can take two forms:

1. Old, worn-out modes of thinking about money that used to
work when we were younger but no longer apply to ourselves or to
our lives

2. Incomplete money business: promises from the past that we
haven't kept, in areas such as paying back loans, delivering on con-
tracts, or making good on agreements. This includes not doing that
which will bring ease into our lives, such as having a will, appropriate
insurance, little or no credit-card debt, a savings account, and the like

As this "financial cholesterol" builds up, the amount of money
energy that we can conduct dwindles. The pressure on our conduit
increases. We feel frustrated, pressured. We need breathing space.
The frustration you experience in being powerful with money is
directly proportionate to the amount of "money sludge" you've built
up over the years that needs to clear away. Later in this chapter we
will confront your financial buildup in a gentle, yet direct way. If you
follow the steps I suggest, your frustration will lower. You'll energize
your goals with clarity and ease.

Something else happens with conduits. They spring leaks. We leak
energy whenever we use it unconsciously. We may receive energy,
but before it can begin to nourish our dreams, it's diverted. How
does that look with the energy of money?

1. Unconscious spending, as in going to the mall with $40 in your wallet and finding that you have $15 left at the end of one hour, without remembering where it went

2. Buying items out of "habit" whether or not you really need or even want them, such as magazine subscriptions, video clubs, and groceries you buy "just in case"

3. Wasting money, such as being overinsured, or insisting upon the deluxe version of a product when you really don't need all the features it offers

We instinctively think that more money energy will solve the problems of our leaks and blockages. That's when we start praying to win the lottery, or to inherit a surprise $10 million. But if those blocks and leaks aren't fixed, the sudden infusion of money energy only turns up the pressure, and the conduit fails altogether.

LEAKS AND BLOCKS

Leaks or blocks in our conduit of money energy siphon off its power. These stories from You and Money participants show how this can happen:

> STUART: I sell airtime for commercials on a local radio station. My monthly take-home pay? Five months ago, I was supposed to get a 10 percent raise. Not looking at my pay stubs, I just assumed it had been added to my paycheck. Preparing for my taxes, I found that due to a computer error I had not received the raise. In addition, there was an unauthorized deduction being taken from my check. This had gone on for seven months!

> MIRIAM: I'm the day manager of a supermarket. I take home $2,314 a month. For years, I've been avoiding balancing my checkbook by rounding up to the nearest dollar. That way I know I'm not overdrawn. As part of this course, I balanced my checkbook to the penny. I was amazed to find $785 that I didn't know I had! That is the good news. The bad news is that two months ago I passed up going on a cruise with my best friend because I thought I didn't have the money.

CAROL: I'm a school principal. I make $3,800 a month and I don't ever see it. It's gone after a few days and again I'm waiting for the first of next month. My credit cards are charged to the hilt. But I can't bear the thought of taking them and cutting them up. I know I'm using at least one-sixth of my income in interest payments alone, yet the thought of being without those cards panics me. I mean, what if I need them in an emergency?

In each of these stories the person is experiencing the consequences of money leaks and blocks. Every one of them has, knowingly or unknowingly, tied up a great deal of energy in the worry, anxiety, and general uneasiness that goes with not being fully conscious about money. Knowing the solutions to their problems isn't difficult. You could probably make two or three suggestions to each person that would get them out of their personal money swamp. If you are like me, you've been in that swamp a few times yourself, or you are there right now. And you know how easy it is to remain stuck, even with help in plain sight.

These people's courage in talking about where they were leaking or blocking money energy was the first step in taking Authentic Action.

THE ICARUS SYNDROME

We've talked about unblocking the conduit and closing leaks, but what about the possibility of inundating the garden and drowning our goals and dreams? It takes skill and wisdom to handle any form of energy in a powerful way. The early Greek myth of Icarus reflects this. Icarus learns to fly like a bird with wings constructed by his father. In the flush of his newfound power, he ignores his father's warning and flies too close to the sun. The wax on his homemade wings melts, and he plunges to earth.

We have a present-day equivalent of this in the lives of people who win the lottery, or inherit huge fortunes, only to find that the heat of this new energy is more than they can handle. Maybe they go on a buying frenzy that lasts for years. Or they give money away left and right, discovering after a year or two that they have no money left to pay their own taxes.

Can you be absolutely certain that, given the opportunity, you wouldn't fall victim to the Icarus Syndrome? We all read newspaper articles about families that are split apart when big sums of money are suddenly introduced into their midst. Without clarity and focus to handle this energy, greed, anger, and resentment can strain even the most valued relationships. One man who inherited $750,000 from an uncle told his story in the You and Money Course:

> ALLEN: "I just went crazy. I bought all kinds of toys: a car, a boat, a Jet Ski. You name it. I had huge, expensive parties. I even gave money away in obviously bad business deals. I thought the money would never run out. I also felt guilty, like I didn't deserve to have it, so why not try to get rid of it? I finally came to my senses when I had about $200,000 left. I went to a financial planner and made some sound investments. It was like coming out of a nosedive."

Clearing your conduit can help you handle whatever amount of money energy is available to you without drowning your goals and dreams on the one hand, or depriving your garden of energy on the other.

CLEARING THE CONDUIT

The work we're about to do is mundane. I love that word because it carries the sense of "of the earth—of the world." Clearing away unfinished money business is your chance to get your hands dirty like a gardener in his or her favorite patch of earth. It will move you out of your mind and into physical reality. Your energy might drop a little as you look at the incomplete details of your life, but take heart. You're removing the blocks that have diverted your energy so you can focus on what you really want in life.

Incomplete business in your life draws energy because you have to exert force to keep it suspended in an unfinished state. As you do that, you become tired, concerned, and preoccupied. There's no way you can go full speed ahead when the past is claiming so much of your attention. But when you shift your energy and finish what's been left undone, amazing things happen.

An architect once told me that she has a sure way of getting a new contract: She does a thorough job on the ones she already has.

ELLEN: You know that old saying about Nature abhorring a vacuum? Works for me! If I want a new project, all I have to do is make sure I'm thoroughly finished with what I'm already working on. Then other projects seem to show up. Is it magic, or does this happen because I'm freer to look at new possibilities? I don't know. I really don't care. I'm just glad it does!

Paying attention to the details, and keeping promises—even the smallest ones—is something successful people do intuitively. Writers Gay Hendricks and Kate Ludeman found that when they interviewed business leaders for a book, every person, no matter how far they had to travel, showed up on time. These successful people showed immediately that they took themselves, and others, seriously. And they made it a point to keep promises in all areas of their lives. As you might imagine, their energy was fully present.

Trying to focus on your dreams when you've got a dozen untended commitments floating in the background is like trying to play an inspired game of soccer on a field that's full of trash. You spend so much energy trying to keep your footing that there's no way to do your best. If you've ever had an unpaid loan, for example, you know how wary and worried you feel as you try to avoid your creditor, even if it's a relative or dear friend. And anytime you think about them, you feel yourself being pulled down:

TONY: Uncle Alex loaned me $5,000 around eight years ago so I could finish college. I haven't talked to him about repaying it. I just don't have the money yet. Besides, every Thanksgiving when I see him, it's hard to talk with everyone around. Last summer he invited me to his beach house for a family reunion. I've wanted to go there for years! Two days before I was supposed to go I got sick, and I hardly ever get sick! I missed the party!

Would Tony have gotten sick if he hadn't been harboring so much worry and tension about talking to his uncle? His illness may have had nothing at all to do with his unpaid loan, but you can sense the dis-ease he feels where his uncle is concerned. He may never know if there was any connection between his getting sick and his unfinished business with his uncle. But we do know that if he had cleared up his past obligations, he could have gone to the family gathering and had a wonderful time.

Many of us expect that our relationship with money will always be burdensome, and we see that weight around our necks as a natural state of affairs. Our load of unfinished money business goes with us when we go to the bank to apply for a mortgage. It's there when we plan to go on vacation, or look at retirement plans, or save for our children's education. And that heavy burden is usually held in place by resignation. Monkey Mind says, "There's nothing you can do about it. Everyone has some trouble with money."

Monkey Mind is wrong. You *can* experience the true power of money! This happens when you complete unfinished money business, both personal and professional. That unblocked energy will then flow toward your goals. I promise!

INCOMPLETE MONEY BUSINESS

Completing your incomplete money business clears the field for you to have a much simpler, more constructive relationship with money.

Allow yourself to be willing to do the following exercises. This is a choice that requires heart and courage. Your mind may find reasons for you to stay where you are. Remember that such advice isn't malicious—it just expresses Monkey Mind's fear of change. And Monkey Mind is perfectly content to see you doing the same thing over and over again, expecting different results. Now, though, you know you are bigger than Monkey Mind—big enough to open your life to miracles and the flow of money's energy.

Monkey Mind might also object that I'm asking you to be nitpicky in clearing up your small, as well as large, incomplete money business. This can come up, for instance, when you look at balancing your checkbook to the penny. However, consider this: *If you want to learn how to deal effectively with large units of energy, you must practice being conscious of the small units.* In fact, the more conscious you become, the more you will be drawn to make completions in life.

Ursula LeGuin wrote of this in *A Wizard of Earthsea*: "As a man's real power grows, and his knowledge widens, ever the way he can follow grows narrower, until at last he chooses nothing, but does only and wholly what he must do."

Some of the items I ask you to deal with may not seem to have simple solutions. Don't worry. Just begin. Take one step at a time and the answers will come. They always do. At the end of this chapter I'll help you with some of the thorniest problems that lead us to leave our money business unfinished and our promises unkept.

Exercise: Taking Care of Business—An Inventory

You will need your notebook, your Standards of Integrity, your Life's Intentions, and your list of the Symptoms of Monkey Mind. Give yourself about an hour and a half to go through this inventory completely.

PART ONE: THE INVENTORY

You are about to see where unfinished money business is siphoning off your life's energy. As you look at the following list, read each item carefully. What is your immediate reaction? Write down your discoveries before you do anything else.

If you see that an item applies to you, look at your Standards of Integrity and Life's Intentions. Ask yourself this question: "What am I more interested in, my Monkey Mind conversations or my goals and dreams in life?" Use this question to meditate on any internal dialogue about why you shouldn't bother to handle this item.

When you find an item that applies to you, write down whatever is true about it. Just the facts. Be specific. For example, if item 5 relates to you, list the credit card(s), their interest rates, and how much is owed on each.

Go through the list now, noting any areas where you might find some unfinished business:

1. Is your checkbook(s) balanced to the penny? For some of us that's no problem, but it drives some of us to tears. It may seem picky and insignificant, but it's not. When you balance your checkbook to the penny, you are balancing the energy of money—as well as energy in other areas of your life. Remember the hologram!

2. Do you have adequate car, health, fire, theft, and disaster insurance? Ask yourself this question: "If I don't have insurance, am I doing life the hard way? Am I putting myself at risk so that if something happens to me or my belongings, I'll have to

put all of my moneymaking energy into an area that I've neglected?"

3. Do you have a will or revocable living trust? You may not feel you need these, and that's fine. But having them in place can prevent half your estate from going to probate taxes, instead of to your loved ones, after you die. If you're incomplete with this item you might get a little wrenching in your heart, or feel uncomfortable when you think about it.

4. Do you have a durable power of attorney if you need one?

5. What's your credit-card situation? Do you have high balances? That form of debt is one quick and easy way to drain off money's energy. Pay them off. You may want to do what many have done in the You and Money Course: take your credit cards and freeze them in a block of ice in your freezer. Having to wait for the ice to melt cuts down on the impulse to use the card.

6. Have you put off having medical, dental, or eye exams? You may feel that you don't have the time or money to invest in taking care of yourself. If that's so, please reread the chapter on driven behavior! You must take care of your conduit. It's the only one you've got!

7. In what condition is your car? Picture it in your mind's eye. Do you need new tires, bearings, or brakes? Is it leaking a lot of oil? Have you put off repairs? Do you have any unpaid parking or speeding tickets?

8. Have you returned all your rented videos and your library books? Have you paid up all your dues and fees?

9. If you have real estate property, are you paying your taxes on time?

10. If you're a professional in a field such as counseling, do you have malpractice insurance? You may think it's unnecessary, but many who were surprised to be sued will tell you that it's very important.

11. Do you owe people money that you haven't arranged to pay back in a systematic way? Look at all the areas of your life. Do you owe your family? Friends? Co-workers? Boss?

12. Do any friends, family, or co-workers owe you money they have not arranged to pay back in a systematic way?

13. Do you need to return any borrowed items? This could be anything: jewelry, garden equipment, books, clothes, etc.

14. Are your financial records in order? Are they accessible to you, and not in a mess somewhere, like a shoe box?

15. If you bill for your services, is your billing done and on time? Do you have a lot of accounts receivable?

16. Are you charging enough for your services?

17. Are you giving your children the allowance you promised? Are you teaching them to handle money?

18. Is your desk in order? Your closet? Your garage? One woman I know cleaned out her desk. She'd been shoving unopened stock reports there from some stock gifted to her many years previously by a deceased uncle. Opening the notices, she found that this stock had doubled, and then doubled again. She had $45,000 more than she'd known!

19. Have you repaid your student loans? Many people find that once they bring their student loans up to date, it becomes easier for them to collect the money that's owed to them.

20. Have you begun an account to pay for your children's education if you're planning to help finance it?

21. Are all of your home repairs up to date? Do you have leaky faucets? A leaky faucet wastes precious resources—which are a form of energy. Does your home have untended electrical problems? How's the roof? Are you disaster-proofed?

22. Do you know that you need professional advice in some area—legal, accounting, financial planning? Have you arranged to get it?

23. Have you set up retirement accounts and plans? The moment you begin a retirement account, you begin to lower your anxiety about the future—and free up energy in the present.

24. Have you set up accounts to save for holidays?

25. Have you arranged to pay overdue bills?

26. Do you have a budget? For many people, the idea of setting one up feels like going on a diet, but it's possible to set up a spending plan that doesn't make you feel deprived. And it can bring a sense of sanity into your money life while providing for the things you truly want.

27. Are there any items I haven't listed that you know are unfinished business for you? Write them down right now, before you forget. List even items that seem impossible to clear up or that have been around for years. One reliable rule of thumb: If something comes to mind during the exercise, even if

it seems illogical or not related to money, include it on your list. You will see how it relates to money as you continue.

PART TWO: TAKING AUTHENTIC ACTION

You've probably uncovered items that you know you need to complete. Some of them may even have surprised you. But remember: insight alone won't get you to miracles. Your next step is to decide how you're going to complete each item on your list.

Before you do anything else about money, balance your checkbook to the penny. Do it, even if you need to have a friend or spouse help you, or if you have to go to the bank or a bookkeeper for assistance. No matter what your head is telling you right now, just do it! To the penny. Go back as far as you have to in order to get your checkbook to reconcile with your bank statement.

Balancing your checkbook to the penny will do more to clear your conduit than almost anything else you could do. When I say this in the You and Money Course, eyes roll and the atmosphere in the room gets heavy. Many think that it would be a waste of time, that it's easier to close the unbalanced account and open a new one. Not so! The unconsciousness follows you wherever you go. Within two months the new account will be unbalanced, just like the old one.

As you balance your checkbook to the penny, take some time to look at where you've been putting your money energy. This, in itself, can be instructive:

> MARCIA: As I looked at my checkbook ledger, the strangest thought crossed my mind. What if, years after I'm gone, my daughter or granddaughter were to find and read this checkbook? What would it tell them about my basic values and spending priorities in life? Lots of impulsive spending. Not much planning. What an eye-opener!

If someone were to read your checkbook ledger and attempt to write a biography about you based upon it, what would they say? Take a moment and write about this in your notebook.

Balancing your checkbook may never have been a problem for you. Do the biography exercise anyway, and I know you'll find a new perspective on your spending habits and priorities. If it has been difficult, congratulations on doing it anyway. You are demonstrating that you're willing to be a conscious custodian of energy.

For the rest of the unfinished items, take at least one step toward the completion of each item on your list. Do this within the next two weeks. For example, if you owe someone money and have not begun to pay it back, call or write this person and set up a mutually agreeable timetable for payment. If you do not have a will, living trust, or durable power of attorney, make an appointment with an attorney to draw up these documents. Notice what Monkey Mind is saying to you about doing this. And then do it anyway!

Let me repeat: Please take at least one Authentic Action toward completing each item on your list within the next two weeks. It is one of the most powerfully direct things you can do to prepare yourself for miracles in your relationship with money.

You may be tempted to put your list away and forget it, but keep to the hero's path. Look at your calendar now. What is two weeks from today? Promise yourself that when you arrive at that day, you will have taken Authentic Action. Complete all the items as soon as possible. Map out exactly what you're going to do. Get specific and concrete, even though Monkey Mind wants you to delay and be vague.

There are many resources available to help you. If you have unpaid student loans, you may be able to get twenty-four months' forbearance, or negotiate lower monthly fees and payments. Talk to your credit-card companies about your repayment options and lowering your interest rate. If you are stumped about handling debts and unpaid loans, consult with your local Consumer Credit Counseling Service agency. Their staff will work with you and your creditors to consolidate and come up with a manageable monthly payment plan.

Wherever possible, use people who will help you get outside of your usual structures of knowing about what it takes to clear things up. They may suggest easier ways to complete items than you currently imagine. Be open. Why suffer needlessly?

Share your results with friends. Ask for their support as you take action. To center yourself and cheer you on, keep your Life's Intentions and Standards of Integrity in front of you. Every step you take prepares you for miracles.

Exercise: Fixing the Leaks in Your Conduit

Do you want to be an investor? Do you want to use the money you have to create more? Doing the next exercise will help you save and channel money to those ends. Whether your dream involves helping yourself or others, you can reach important goals when you gain conscious control of your money and your time.

You will need a small spiral pad, like the one you got to note daily symptoms of Monkey Mind. Let it be small enough to carry in your pocket or handbag. You'll also need your notebook.

This exercise will take about two weeks. This is a tracking exercise, so exact amounts of time each day will vary. One thing is certain: it will definitely take a lot less time than your Monkey Mind is telling you right now.

For two weeks, carry the notepad with you and keep track of every penny that runs through your hands. Divide your daily sheets into three columns: cash, check, and credit cards. Note each expense, no matter how small, under each category. Make sure you do it at the time you spend it, not later. For example, if you buy a newspaper while commuting to work, write that expense down immediately.

You are not keeping track of this money in order to create a budget. You are doing it to increase your consciousness about the ways money energy flows through you. If you have your own business and write business checks, keep track of these as well. Money leaks occur both at home and at the office. If you work for someone else and write the checks for him or her, do not list those.

Even if you forget to do it periodically, start up again. Don't worry about duplication, like charging something on your credit card and later paying the credit-card bill with a check. All of this should be written down. Notice what Monkey Mind says about this right now. Which symptom is it exhibiting?

JOEL: I remember Monkey Mind telling me, "You don't want to do this. It will take too much of your time. It's stupid. Just skip this part. You've done this before. It doesn't accomplish anything." I said, "Thank you for sharing," and did it anyway. It wasn't so bad. I woke up about my money leaks.

During these two weeks I want you to pay attention to whether you *are* leaking or spending money. To leak is to permit a substance to escape or pass through a breach or flaw. It's usually not conscious. It may be impulsive, or habitual—and it happens much less when you wake up about how you're using money.

As you track your expenses, ask yourself the following questions. Write your answers in your notebook so you can look at them more closely later.

1. Regarding the way I use money, what is the difference for me between leaking and spending?
   a. When do I go unconscious about spending money? Is it during a particular time of day? A particular mood?
   b. On which items do I spend most unconsciously? Are they items I really want at the time I buy them?
   c. If the items are other than food, do I put them to good use? Do I get my money's worth out of them? Do they lie around unused? What do I see about this?
   d. Where do I spend money consciously? How does this experience differ from leaking money?
   e. Do I really value everything I buy? Does what I buy bring me pleasure?
2. Is there a parallel here with how I leak or spend my time?
   a. Do I leak time with unimportant activity? If so, what is it? For example, do I waste time looking at television?
   b. Do I leak time by compulsive activity? Do I spend hours and hours exercising, organizing, or fixing?
   c. When am I most likely to leak time? How does this contrast with time that I spend consciously?
   d. Do I make promises to myself or others, only to become distracted with meaningless activity?
   e. Do I spend as much time as I want with friends and family?

3. If I fix the way I leak money, what will happen to the time I use to earn it?

4. Is it possible for me to work less and have more of what I truly want?

As you study your two-week spending record, do you notice any patterns? Are there any black holes that suck away at your money? For example, how much do you spend on convenience food?

> RICK: I spend three dollars a day for cappuccino and pastry at work. It came to $60 a month. I added $2 more each day for incidentals like soft drinks or fruit in the afternoon. I found I was spending enough money each year to fund a down payment on a decent used car, not counting the occasional unplanned lunches or dinners at restaurants. I found that I go for quick convenience food on my way home when I'm tired and feel too bushed to go home and prepare a meal.

> MARGO: How I waste time really surprised me. I buy all these good books, take them home, and never spend time reading them. I'm in front of the television set, staring at a program that barely interests me!

You're becoming aware of your patterns of spending money not to deprive yourself but to give yourself the power to make conscious choices. You don't want to leak the energy that could bring your dreams from the metaphysical into the physical. And by becoming aware of where you're leaking, as opposed to where you're spending, you will gain real choice, and satisfying spending habits. Many You and Money participants have found creative solutions to the problem of leaking time and money:

> RICK: I saw how much money I waste on stuff, so I developed a system. Every time I spend money on convenience food or entertainment, I put twice that amount away in a savings account. I use the savings to make investments, like buying mutual funds. It's amazing how much I've invested in the past two years! Knowing I'm going to spend three times as much on a movie also gives me the chance to see if I really want to see it. If I do, no problem. I've just made an investment at the same time!

MARGO: I go through the TV listings every week and circle
the programs I want to watch. Then I watch them, and only
them. I cut down on my television watching by fifteen hours a
week! I have also budgeted time for reading. I've joined a
reading club. We have a blast together! Something else: I think
better of myself. I had criticized myself for not doing anything
worthwhile with my time. That's over now.

TAKING CARE OF THE TOUGH ISSUES

Congratulations on all that you've done so far. I know the next
couple of weeks will be interesting—and life-changing—as you open
your eyes to see how you handle money's energy, taking Authentic
Action to finish up all the incomplete money business that's been
holding you back. Some items on your list of unfinished business
may seem fairly simple to solve—even if it's not easy to take the steps
to put that solution in place. Other items may leave you puzzled. You
know the problem exists, and you'd solve it if you could—but you're
not sure how. I'd like to help you work through the most common of
those situations now.

1. Charging What You're Worth

It's not unusual for people to tell me that they're good at what they
do, but they just don't seem to be able to charge what they're worth.
The issue comes up a lot for those of us who charge by the hour or
the project, rather than collecting salaries. Why is it so hard to set a
fair price and collect it from our clients?

After working through this problem with many people, I've come
to realize that the crux of the matter is this: If we charge what we're
worth, then we'll have to deliver on our promises. We'll have to go
100 percent for it. Setting a lower fee leaves a trapdoor open, an
escape hatch. We're not getting paid enough, so we don't have to be
diligent. In effect, we don't have to guarantee that we'll go all out to
do what we said we'd do.

When you charge exactly what you're worth, you're putting
yourself on the line. You're telling your client, "I'll do what I said
I'd do, and give you my full effort and attention. If I don't

end up doing what I promised, I'll rectify my work so it will satisfy you."

If you're fretting about why you just can't bite the bullet and raise your fees, I'd like you to ask yourself this: "When I agonize about how much to charge, am I giving myself permission to sit on the sidelines of my path and not participate? Is it possible that all it would take for me to change my situation would be to take a stand for myself and my work and promise to perform to the best of my ability?"

These questions can lead you to a lot of growth. But when you allow yourself to make the leap and charge what you know is appropriate, you'll probably find that you feel pretty shaky at first. All of a sudden you'll be operating outside of your structure of knowing, focusing on how to do a good job.

Allow yourself to be paid what you're worth. You'll grow. You'll be honor-bound to do your best. Yes, I know that you may want to do your best no matter how much you're paid. But there is something to be said for being paid exactly what you know your work is worth. It causes a special kind of maturity to develop.

If you wish, you can donate work to worthy causes, or take on some work for charity at a steep discount. But you will be at a more powerful choice point. You will be taking yourself and your contribution more seriously. For example, my own company does management and communications training for corporations. My success in that arena allows me to call the local food bank and offer such training as a donation.

2. Negotiating for Money

One of the fundamental aspects of negotiation is being willing to tell the truth about what you need. When you do that, and don't manipulate, you usually get what you want.

You may believe that you have to play games. For instance, maybe you think you have to ask for $5 or $8 an hour more than you really want—just so there's room to compromise. Lots of books and experts tell us to do this. But when you do, something in your behavior signals to the other person that you're fooling them. There's not a consistency between who you are and what you're saying—and that inconsistency is impossible to hide.

Despite what you might believe, negotiations aren't a game, and they don't take place in a game spirit. Real negotiation occurs when you ask for what you want, you hear the other person say what they want, and you arrive at an agreement. That agreement is not always a compromise. As a matter of fact, I've found that when you're willing to be truthful about what you want, you often get it.

My guidelines for negotiation: Tell the truth. Say what you want, bottom line. Don't bring in a lot of stories. Operate within your Standards of Integrity.

3. Loans to and from Friends and Family

It's easy to get tangled in problems with loans to and from loved ones. Often we don't spell out the terms clearly, and we treat them casually, as though a loan might be a gift. I've found that being unclear about the exact context in which money is borrowed leads to heartache. So if you're planning to borrow money from someone close to you, write down the details, just as you would if you were borrowing from an institution.

What are the terms of the loan? When are you going to pay it back? Exactly how much are you going to pay? Look at dates. Be as clear with your friend or family member as you would in any other business transaction—even if your mind and theirs say, "There's no need to be so formal."

If one of the items on your unfinished business list involves this sort of loan, go back and spell out the terms now. Put them in writing. You'll all feel better.

If you've made loans and not been able to collect them, go back and be specific about a repayment plan. Putting your agreements in writing shifts the whole money conversation into the domain of consciousness, and it greatly increases the probability that you will be repaid.

We often get vague when we first loan money to people, as though Monkey Mind is running riot and telling us, "This is my friend/my kid/my brother—I don't need to be specific about how I'll get my money back." Allow yourself to be concrete about the terms. Or make the money a gift, with no expectation that it *will* ever be repaid. Either way, you'll free a lot of energy that's tied up now in anger or resignation or resentment.

If you frequently loan money to people in your circle, stop for a moment and think about why you do it. You may honestly want to see them accomplish something that means a lot to them—like go to school or establish a business. But sometimes we make loans because we want to rescue people, and those loans often don't turn out well. Even though the other person may seem desperate, there are often other solutions that won't strain your relationship with them. They may need financial counseling, not someone to bail them out of the current situation.

FRAN: I was always loaning my girlfriend money at the end of the month. For some reason she was always $300 or $400 short. My heart would go out to her, and I'd think, "Well, I have the money—why should I withhold it?" But one month I decided to try an experiment. When my friend called I talked with her about why this kept happening. As a result, she decided to go to the Consumer Credit Counseling people for some help. It turned out that she was trying to pay down her loans too quickly, leaving herself in the hole at the end of the month. Once she realized that, she changed her repayment schedule and stopped having to ask for money. I'm so proud of her!

The result in Fran's case was happy. But I've seen other cases that were more difficult to resolve, yet just as important.

JACK: My friend Bob kept bugging me for loans at the end of the month, and I was a soft touch—I'd loan him a hundred or two if I had it. But when that started to get old, I had a talk with him. And I found out that Bob was drinking his money away. Every Friday he'd go get drunk, and he'd stay drunk till Sunday. I had a serious talk with him about getting help, and I stopped funding his behavior. He's a buddy. I don't want to add to the problem.

If these scenarios sound familiar, have compassion, both for your friends and for yourself. We don't set out to complicate our relationships with people. We want to empower them. Becoming clear about our motivations and expectations will do the job.

4. Battling with Significant Others About Money

A financial adviser named Howard Ruff once said something to the effect of "There are two kinds of people in the world. One wants to have a boat before they save for it, and the other wants to save for the boat before they get it. Inevitably, those two marry each other." Our intimate relationships give us a great chance to confront the way we handle money, and to see how our ways differ from others'.

What do we do when, for example, we want to save and our partner wants to spend? It's a wonderful issue to confront as a couple, and one way to start looking and seeing and telling the truth about your mutual relationship with money is to have your significant other join in reading this book. When you stop and reflect on the questions, or do the exercises, do it together, and use the process as a way of becoming clear with each other.

If you find you have difficulty making good money decisions together, or seem unable to take Authentic Action to get beyond your impasses, get help. Many people have found that if they take stubborn conflicts and dilemmas to a consultant—possibly a counselor, maybe a financial planner—miracles can happen.

Remember that we choose our partners in part because we see ourselves as members of a success team, in which each of us is getting what we want. We want our dreams to come true, and we really don't want to frustrate our partners. When we remember that—and who the other person is—the blocks to our happiness can begin to dissolve. We can reach resolutions about the savings plan, or the vacation, or the credit cards—and put more energy into our dreams.

5. Getting Through Family Crises

It's devastating when a family member dies, and terrible conflicts sometimes arise at moments of overwhelming grief. One typical scenario comes up when the mother or father of a big family leaves an estate and it's up to the children to divide a home and the assets. It's not uncommon for lasting rifts to develop over who got the silver, or the photos, or a cherished heirloom.

If you find yourself facing the need to handle a parent's estate, I'd like you to hold on to a bit of guidance that has helped many people: Don't negotiate money matters when your family is grieving. It's not always easy to do this. Try to come to an agreement not to work out estate or money matters until nine months to a year has passed. As you divvy up belongings and money, old hurts and wishes and unfulfilled needs come to the fore and become attached to those material possessions. There's no avoiding the emotions that come up in the process.

If you can, try to handle estate matters in advance. When they're old enough to hear you, talk to your children, and be very clear about how you want your possessions divided. Even if you're young, make your wishes known in a will. You can't assuage the grief your survivors will feel, but you can take many burdens—emotional, psychological, and even financial—off their shoulders.

6. Dealing with Kids and Money

Having kids can make us crazy about money. We want them to have every opportunity, and we want to ensure that we can look back on our lives and know that we've done a good job with them. To us, that may mean doing better than our parents did in introducing us to money's energy. And it can lead us to some interesting situations:

> HEIDI: My mom was so crabby around the holidays with us kids, and I really wanted it to be different with my own family. I've tried to make things perfect and happy, but I just see myself going overboard. Last Christmas I got Sara probably twenty presents—we filled up the whole bottom of the tree. I thought she'd be thrilled, but I could see on her face when she started opening them that it was way too much. After about the sixth or seventh box she started getting cranky. She tore through the rest of the packages and hardly looked at what was inside. Then she went to get her old favorite doll. I was livid, and the day was a disaster. I thought I would do so much better than my parents, but I've got a ways to go.

The way we handle money with our children sometimes reflects our own unresolved past and present upsets. It's easy to perpetuate exactly the frame of mind and the situations that we most try to avoid. Changing them takes work. It might also require trial and error—and being willing to be honest and compassionate about what we see ourselves doing. In addition, there are three things that can absolutely shift what you show and teach your children about money: being consistent, telling the truth, and acting in accordance with your Standards of Integrity.

Consistency simply involves doing what you say you're going to, especially in the case of allowances. If you set an allowance of $5, $10, or $20 dollars a week, let your child know that you're doing it, and then keep your word. If you want, you can negotiate with your child about what you expect in return for the money. You'll teach them that it's important to honor agreements about money.

Telling the truth is slightly more complicated. In my practice I've often seen parents arguing about money in front of their children, and I've noticed that in such arguments what we're hearing is one Monkey Mind against another. The first may be arguing about why it's important to have whatever we want in life. The second might be passionately disagreeing, and saying, "We don't have any money! If we keep going like this, we'll never have any money!"

And the kids are caught in the middle, confused. When I say tell the truth in front of your children, I mean make a distinction between the truth of the situation and what Monkey Mind is telling you.

> ALICIA: Until I was twelve I thought we were dirt poor. My mom and dad kept arguing. She wanted to buy things, and he would say if she did we'd be bankrupt. It was the weirdest thing to discover that we had hundreds of thousands of dollars in the bank. What was even weirder for me was seeing the difference between what we had and how scared my parents were about it. Some of my earliest memories about money are of being afraid we'd run out of it and be poor. And yet we always had more than plenty.

If there's something you don't want your child to have, don't say, "We're going to be in the poorhouse," or "We'll never survive if I get you whatever you want." Simply say, "Yes, I'll buy it for you," or "No, I won't."

Finally, if you want your kids to handle money well, be sure that your behavior matches your own Standards of Integrity. If you're concerned about your children's integrity around money, look first at your own. I remember one six-year-old telling me that "the reason I took this comic book is, it's not really stealing. My dad takes newspapers all the time without paying for them."

We have a unique opportunity to let our behavior reflect who we really are—and to pass that coherence on to our children. It will make our lives better, and theirs, too, if we do it.

BUILDING THE STRENGTH TO DANCE WITH YOUR GOALS

As you do this work, you may feel as though you're lifting weights, and stretching yourself into places that make you squirm. Your Standards of Integrity are definitely getting a workout, and I know you're using a lot of energy to clear the way in front of you.

Please remember that with every Authentic Action you take, and every bit of unfinished business you clear up once and for all, you are unleashing tremendous energy. Keep going. You are bringing lasting changes to your life and gaining the strength to dance with your dreams.

PART IV

Staying the Course

OBSTACLES CAN LEAD TO BREAKTHROUGHS

What happens when you step onto the road to your goals and dreams and the first thing you encounter is a huge obstacle—say, an emergency expense that requires all the money you've saved for your dream, or a position that you wanted being eliminated in your company? These obstacles and surprises can be disorienting, and even seem to slow down your progress. While you may initially see these surprises as pitfalls and obstacles, they are integrally linked to the way your life is changing.

For instance, you may strive to achieve a career goal that doesn't manifest in the way you intend, but a different reward or path may result.

> MILT: I wanted that job as senior account executive. Worked hard for it. When I wasn't chosen for the position, it broke my heart. I wanted to leave the company. But two weeks later I get this call from the management team at headquarters. They want me to interview for western regional vice president of sales. I got the job. It's even better than I'd have wished. Glad I hung in there.

When you run into trouble on the path, don't lose heart or assume that you're not worthy of or not meant to achieve your goals. Obstacles and surprises are inevitable on the hero's journey. They're the sign that you are on the path. The energy of money can flow around

these surprises. Just allow yourself breathing room to see the ways
that you can be flexible enough to permit the flow.

In this chapter you'll learn how to become flexible and consciously
gather your energy to anticipate and handle the unexpected. You will
learn a step-by-step program for turning obstacles that *do* appear into
opportunities. You need never be stopped again from going for your
dreams.

CHANNELING ENERGY: FLYING TOWARD YOUR GOALS, NOT FLAILING AT THEM

You've already chosen a SMART goal that is firmly grounded in one
of your Life's Intentions. You've made a Treasure Map and cleared
away incomplete money business. You've prepared yourself in many
ways to make this goal real in the physical realm. The power of these
first steps is captured beautifully by the author W. H. Murray, who
wrote:

> Until one is committed, there is hesitancy, the chance to draw back,
> always ineffectiveness. Concerning all acts of initiative and creation,
> there is one elementary truth, the ignorance of which kills countless
> ideas and splendid plans: that the moment one commits oneself,
> then Providence moves, too. All sorts of things occur to help one
> that would never otherwise have occurred. A whole stream of
> events issues from the decision, raising in one's favor all manner of
> unforeseen incidents and meetings and material assistance, which no
> man could have dreamed would have come his way.

In the process of attaining your goals, you will grow in ways
you hadn't imagined—because any goal worth having lies outside your
current structure of knowing. Going for it will expand the framework
that holds your current image of yourself. You can't do things the way
you've always done them. You have to be open to the "unforeseen
incidents and material assistance" that may come your way.

MARGARET: I've looked forward to this promotion for
years. I'm finally project manager at the plant. I head up a team
of twelve people. I remember the days when I'd get irritated on

the job. I'd say it was the manager's responsibility to keep things going right. Now I am one! My whole perspective has changed. Am I up to this? Yes. Now I'm taking courses in management.

Margaret's whole concept of herself had changed, and she saw that she needed to be prepared for all sorts of opportunities. She took the management courses to be ready when the next opportunity presented itself.

You help the energy of money flow around obstacles when you arm yourself with the tools and practices that can help you anticipate them. Here are examples of what happens when you're *not* prepared for achieving your goals:

• You start a new business. You have not researched what it will take to run it. You find yourself working so hard and investing so much money that you are too broke or exhausted to enjoy what you have created.

• You have finally gotten your pilot's license. In the process of paying for it and for a time-share interest in an airplane, you're driven to work long hours. You never find the time to fly.

• You are practicing to run a marathon. You do not get the support or coaching you need. You get injured early in your training and must stop.

Any onlooker could see trouble brewing in each of these cases. Have you experienced similar situations yourself? The enthusiasm of the goal spurs you onward, but you forget or fail to do your homework. You try to find shortcuts or cut corners. As an Olympic coach once lamented, "Everyone wants to be a star, but no one wants to show up for practice."

The hero's journey toward a goal starts with the questions Am I willing to go beyond who I currently recognize myself to be? Am I willing to prepare to have what I want? Am I willing to ask for help? Am I willing to live with confusion and paradox as I learn?

It's easy to bump along before finally taking the steps required to grow into a goal:

MITCH: My goal is to have a successful private practice. When I first began as a therapist, the hardest thing for me to do was to collect money from my clients. Sometimes I'd let client bills pile high because I felt awkward charging for my services. On a few occasions bills would get so high that the client would quit therapy, discouraged about how much he or she owed me, so I wouldn't get paid. It was a mess. Same thing with insurance billing. I put it off forever. By the time I hired a business consultant my accounts receivable was $27,000. That's a lot of money for a solo practice in counseling.

I'm glad I got help when I did! Now I collect payment at the end of each session. My clients are more relaxed and realistic about what they can afford. In cases of need I have a sliding scale. I bill the insurance companies every week. The $27,000? I collected $21,000 of it. I learned one thing for sure. Accounts receivable are not the same as money in the bank!

Remember that you haven't done all this preparation for your goals only to shoot yourself in the foot. You want two good feet to walk up and claim your heart's desire. When you are willing to prepare, and to be shaped by your goals, as Mitch eventually was, you are in for an adventure. You are responding to a dream, created by you and projected forward in time. As you walk toward it, you change. It is a natural and exciting circle of growth.

Mitch was no accountant, and he certainly didn't fancy himself a good bill collector at the outset. But he learned. He went outside his comfort zone. As a result, he became a successful private practitioner.

You've already seen that most goals in life require the energy of money to bring them into existence. This is true whether they're big, such as buying a home or opening an office, or small, such as painting a picture or planting a garden. One way to prepare to get them is to see clearly how much of this form of energy we currently have at our command. We turn to this next.

GATHERING AND FOCUSING THE ENERGY OF MONEY

This section will tell you precisely how much money energy you currently have to work with. It will give you a sense of how well your current money game is going.

You will be gathering information about your money picture. Synonyms for gather are: collect, harvest, sort, and increase. When you increase your awareness of your current relationship with money, you increase your power. You also guard against engaging in driven behavior that wastes this energy. That's because you are dealing with the physical realm in a focused way.

When you gather something, you create an overview of it. To do this, I ask you to compute your net worth. Second, I suggest you obtain and correct your credit rating.

Take out your list of the Symptoms of Monkey Mind. Go ahead—I know you are having conversations in your head about skipping over this. What are they? Where do they fall on the symptom list? Take heart. Not everyone jumps out of their seats with enthusiasm when we come to this part of the You and Money Course.

What is the importance of taking those two actions? First, your net worth tells you the number of units of money energy you currently have available to you. It's a milestone in consciousness. It will truly wake you up to possibilities you never thought existed, not only with money, but also in all areas of your life. As you do this exercise, you'll get to work through any thoughts you have that your net worth is related to your worth as a human being. It isn't! It is simply a score. Do you want to increase it? Yes, but you must first see what that score is!

Second, your credit rating is a history of how well you've paid what you owe. Please breathe! It's time to see if your financial path is clear or if there are currently any barriers to progress that are based on your credit rating. These may be easier to correct than you think!

Finally, return to the model of life as a hologram: The goal is to become conscious and open, to experience breathing room, not needing to avoid any aspect of your journey. By experiencing a breakthrough in your relationship with your net worth and credit reports, you will free yourself of the strain of money worries. You'll have fortitude to face them. Don't take my word for it. Try it and see!

I've waited until now to coach you in taking these two steps because at this point you've had enough practice under your belt to handle any discomfort that may arise. You have what it takes to make uneasiness your ally and proceed anyway. Your increased awareness will cause a shift in your power that will enable you to pursue what you want with ease, to fund your goals with the money energy they need.

Exercise: Your Net Worth—Awakening a Powerful Relationship with Money

First, get a net worth form. They're easy to obtain from banks, real estate agencies, financial planners, and books about personal financing. You can also find them in computer programs on financial planning. Also have your notebook with you, since you will be answering some questions about what you have found.

The time it takes to fill out the net worth form varies. When in doubt, ask someone who has done one to help you out. It will make the process easier.

First, complete the net worth statement. Do it even if you have done one as recently as one year ago. You compute your net worth by subtracting what you owe from what you own. It is a snapshot in time and it's only true in this moment. Besides following any guidelines that might be included with the net worth statement you get, be sure you use these:

1. When figuring your net worth, be conservative. If you list your business as an asset, look to see if you really know you can sell it for a certain price.

2. Regarding furniture and personal items, compute how much you could get for them if you had to sell them within the next two weeks.

3. As you go over your assets, use this time to update your insurance to cover any items you have added or that have increased in value over the years.

4. If you are married, work with your spouse to find the best way for each of you to compute your own financial net worth statements. Do you have prenuptial agreements or anything that you owned individually before your marriage? What are the community property laws in your state? This may be difficult to discuss, but use this time to get conscious about your money.

Discovering your net worth gives your hero's journey a boost. Along the way it's natural for all sorts of thoughts and feelings to emerge as you do this work. Seeing what comes up is just as valuable as knowing your score. Whatever you see has been there all along. Write down your feeling and realizations in your notebook.

To dismantle some old structures of knowing, answer these questions, too, in your notebook. If possible, discuss them with a friend, your spouse, or in a group.

1. Does it feel as though this net worth statement is measuring your worth as a person? Tell the truth. Remember, one Monkey Mind symptom is "taking things personally." We all do this at some time. Get it out in the open. If this is true for you, now is the time to write and talk about it.

2. Were you pleasantly surprised at your net worth? Unpleasantly surprised? Does it help to know that it's just a snapshot in time? Seeing it is often a wake-up call.

3. Are you interested in increasing your net worth? Would it be all right for you to get a higher score? Are you satisfied with the score you currently have?

It's a good idea to revisit your net worth every six months. Some You and Money graduates have made graphs to show the increase in their net worth over time. They set targets for attaining a certain amount of money by a given time, then chart their results. This can be very rewarding. You may have more control than you think over how to spend or invest your money.

TOWARD A HIGHER SCORE

Would you like to increase your net worth score? There are four ways to do it:

1. Clear up debt.
2. Spend less.
3. Invest.
4. Earn more.

A fifth way, inheriting money, is not available to everyone but may affect you.

The most effective way to increase your score is to pay down debt, *especially unsecured debt, like credit cards.* Each time you pay an overdue bill or reduce your credit-card debt, you are increasing your net worth. You may think you have to earn more to increase your net worth, but that's probably the *least* effective means of increasing it.

As you think about spending less, recall the exercises you've done that make clear the difference between leaking money and spending it. Did you pick up some ways to stem the unconscious flow of money through your hands? This is a good time to use what you've learned. And it's a great time to simplify your life by focusing your resources on what's meaningful.

Exercise: Knowing Your Credit Rating

If your net worth is like a score, your credit rating is like your handicap—a golf handicap, for instance. It tells you how easily you can negotiate financial matters. This is important to know as you begin moving toward your goals. According to bank officers, one frequent obstacle in obtaining money is a credit rating that shows you are a poor investment risk. It can keep you from getting a loan. Your rating is independent of how much money you make—it's based on how promptly you pay your debts. It also reflects whether you owe more than you can comfortably pay back. I have known millionaires who have had difficulty negotiating financial matters because of poor credit ratings.

Your credit record is subject to inaccuracies and errors. For example, one woman found that, according to a credit agency, she was married to her adult son! Every time he wrote a bad check, it showed on her credit report. By writing a letter to the credit agency, she was able to get this error corrected, instantly improving her credit rating 100 percent! A man I know found he was being confused with someone with the same name, a person who lived three thousand miles across the country and had recently filed for bankruptcy. You, too, may find items you need to address on your credit reports.

Get reports from two different reporting agencies, such as Equifax, Experian, and Trans Union Consumer Relations. There are many such services. Lenders use one or more of them to check your rating when you apply for a loan. You can correct errors in one report, but they may not be changed in another.

But it helps if you can show a lender at least two corrected reports from respected agencies.

Each report may cost between $8 and $15, but it is money well spent. You will know *in advance* if there are any factors that will impede you from achieving your goal. These reports must be current. If you have one from more than three months ago, you are not necessarily getting the accurate information you need. Be sure you're working with bona fide credit reports, not computer printouts like the ones available at car dealerships and real estate agencies. Reports from credit-rating firms include rating codes that you should be aware of and understand, and give the methods each agency uses to clear credit items.

Do this exercise and see what you learn. I promise you'll have more power to go for your goals. It's all about waking up and lightening up! You are demonstrating the hero's courage. You will need your notebook for this exercise. Time requirements will vary, given the nature of your credit report. Expect to spend at least twenty minutes studying each document.

1. Look for any items that point to a question about your credit. You may have a poor credit rating because of your own mistakes or oversights. What are they? Can they be corrected? One mistake people often make is failing to close out accounts that they're not currently using. Simplify. Cancel old accounts and your rating may go up. Look at the back of your report for remedies suggested by the credit agency itself, and follow through on those suggestions.

2. If you are in doubt about any item, you may want professional consultation. Is this a legal issue? A mistake in accounting?

3. Write the items you need to clarify or rectify in your notebook under "Incomplete Money Business." Put a date next to each, noting when you will have taken the appropriate action. Take care of the items as soon as possible!

Share what you have found in this exercise with a friend or group. If you know precisely what is on your report, you can respond realistically when negotiating money matters. Often, a truthful, up-front account of the mistakes shown on your report will allow people to work with you in finding solutions. In addition, you can have the items removed by working with the agency that reported them.

What internal conversations did you notice while looking at your credit report? Were you relieved? Worried? Are you allowing your discomfort to be present, while at the same time handling what needs to be fixed?

The discomfort you may be feeling is natural. When you face discomfort, you actually diminish it; avoid it and you extend it. Facing it with compassion produces wisdom, because you will see how irrelevant it usually is to attaining your goals and dreams. This will help you cultivate the heart of the hero.

RUNNING THE OBSTACLE COURSE

By taking a measure of your money energy right now, you're more centered and better prepared for inevitable surprises. On our hero's path, we usually call them obstacles.

Do you ski? The first few times you try it, everything is an obstacle. How to use your poles, put on your skis, stand up and move—everything takes energy and deliberation. You start out with short, wide skis that are designed to take you over the patches of dried grass or dirt you might accidentally hit, and you go slowly.

As you improve, you use narrower skis. You begin to carve graceful turns around moguls. These skis will not carry you over grassy patches, however. Although they are made for grace and mastery, they're a lot less forgiving. When you ski more swiftly down the white slopes, the smaller patches of ice now become obstacles. At high speeds and precision, small imperfections on the trail can send you face-forward into the nearest snowdrift. You have seen this happen even with Olympic skiers in competition.

That's the nature of growth and progress toward your goals. The more powerful and knowledgeable you become, the more aware you are of the obstacles on your path. To continue to be powerful, you must clear them away. It helps if you can anticipate them, but that's not always possible.

Obstacles happen. They are often deflating, frustrating events. We rarely hear people say, "Oh, boy! Something else in the way! Whoopee!" Still, obstacles are necessary to the hero's journey. They define your lessons in life. No obstacles, no growth. No growth, no journey.

THE "OH SH–!" POINT, OR OSP

For a moment pretend that you want to buy a home for the first time. If this is actually true for you, so much the better. Your Life's Intentions for this goal are "to be financially successful" and "to be creative with your surroundings." You do some preliminary research and discover that because you are a first-time home buyer, you can purchase a home in the price range you want for $12,000 down.

You decide to go for it, determined to save $1,000 a month for twelve months. You get an extra job, tighten your belt, and begin the journey. In your mind it is supposed to look a particular way:

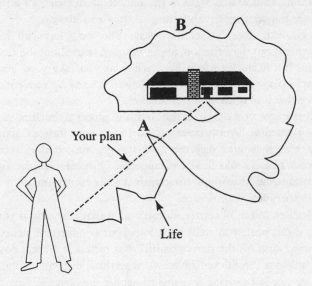

But then real life steps in with some surprises. Four months into this plan, at Point A, you have saved $4,000 and you're happy as a clam. Then, one day as you're driving to your second job, your car throws a rod. The engine is ruined. Your warranty's expired, and you have to shell out $2,300 for repairs. You really need this car. What a mess!

This is a real stopper in the hero's journey. What do you say to yourself as you look, for the first time, at the repair estimate for the car. Probably something profound, like "Oh, sh–!" It's a universal expression of distress. That's why we call Point A an OSP, meaning an "Oh, Sh–! Point." Monkey Mind leaps in with helpful comments like:

"There goes the house."

"Why does stuff like this always happen to me?"

"My universe is telling me something."

"This obviously wasn't meant to be."

"Back to square one. I'll have to start all over again."

In other words: "It wasn't supposed to work like this! This stop was definitely not on my itinerary."

Absolutely everyone hits a wall like this on the way to his or her goals. But if you find yourself at this point, consider this: when you are facing an obstacle, right in the middle of an OSP, it's a sign that you are fully engaged with your goal. It is a validation.

I know it doesn't feel that way. You may have all kinds of thoughts about the situation, about yourself, and about the rest of the world. But obstacles inevitably surface as you take your goal from metaphysical to physical reality. They're created by movement, like the ice that builds up on an icebreaker.

Every time you put an action into the physical domain, you meet with a reaction. If not, there would be no limit to your action and your energy would disperse just as light projected out into the heavens scatters and finally disappears. Obstacles are the sign that physical reality is pushing back against your efforts and adding form to the energy of your dream.

Monkey Mind, of course, doesn't see it that way, and if you listen to it, it can push you right back into your comfortable structures of knowing–and off the hero's path. What results is a breakdown–the psychological, emotional, physical, or spiritual discomfort that signals you've stopped moving forward to handle the obstacle. Breakdowns are not pleasant to experience, and they cannot be denied or glossed over in any way. So it's especially useful to know what to do with them when they happen.

With your car in the shop for that $2,300 engine repair, you look at the tatters of your work so far. You still have your intentions to be financially successful and creative. You still have your goal of buying a house, which reflects your intentions projected into physical reality.

Finally, you still have your plan, which is to save $1,000 a month. One, *and only one,* of these factors needs to be changed at this point. Which one is it?

Your first reaction might be to change your goal, or at least put it off for a while. After all, you don't have the money you said you'd have by now. It's four months down the road and you've managed to save only $1,700 for that original goal.

For the sake of illustration, let's make matters even worse. Let's say you've managed to get back on track. It is eleven months into the project to get your home. You have worked extra hard and saved $11,000. You've found a beautiful house and opened escrow on it. Then, a week before the close, your apartment is burglarized (Point B). More than $6,000 worth of computer equipment and software is stolen, and you need it to finish a job due in two weeks—the job that gave you much of that extra $11,000.

Let's return to the question What needs to be changed here? This time it's a three-part answer:

1. The intention need not change. External circumstances don't invalidate our intentions.

2. The goal may not need to change.

3. What may need changing or dismantling is your structure of knowing about the path. It's called your *plan.*

This may not seem like a revelation. But, in all the years I have coached people, I have noticed that when we hit obstacles, the first factor we sacrifice is the *goal,* not the plan! Most of us get hooked on our plans, almost addicted to them. We act as though it's less important to reach our goal than to achieve it in just the way we've mapped out for ourselves.

Our plans are created out of our mental models about what it will take for us to arrive at our goals. But a goal, if it is worth playing for, is a stretch. There is no way to create a plan that will never need to be adjusted or dismantled—especially when we are attempting something new to us. Many plans are flawed from the beginning because, in truth, they are only *approximations* of reality.

Consider the possibility that your plans or strategies for your life are holding you back from getting what you want. You have a picture in your mind of how your journey has to look. That picture may be insufficient to attain goals of your dreams. In the example of our house, the plan is to save $1,000 per month. Is this really the easiest, fastest way to attain the goal? Does the plan create more problems than it solves? Has it become inflexible?

People who are successful are willing to be flexible in their strategies. For them, attaining the goal itself is far more important than being right about what it takes to get there. They are willing to be incorrect about their original plans. They are willing to turn lead into gold—obstacles into miracles.

Brenda, a woman in the You and Money Course, had actually been following a plan to save $1,000 a month for a house when her car broke down.

> BRENDA: It felt like someone punched me in the stomach. I thought there was no way I was going to get my house, but then I remembered our work on obstacles. When I looked at what I'd been doing, I saw that I was trying to get this goal on my own, without help. I called together a group of friends who knew my goal and intentions and told them I was willing to be coached to go beyond my structure of knowing. Getting others to support me was a way to manifest my intention to be creative.
>
> We started brainstorming. We came up with four alternatives: the owner carrying paper, getting a loan from my uncle, a friend going in with me on an equity-sharing basis, and getting a $1,000 loan from each of six friends. I went to my real estate agent. Guess what! The owners were willing to carry a second mortgage if I paid $5,000 of the $12,000 I owed. It worked!

FOUR GUIDELINES FOR LOOKING AT OBSTACLES

When you encounter obstacles, the following guidelines can wake you up to the possibilities that lie before you:

1. *Obstacles and the resultant breakdowns are acknowledgments of your intentions, not invalidations of them.* Logically, you must have an intention for it to be blocked. For example, if you didn't have an intention to be financially successful, not qualifying for a home loan wouldn't matter to you. As one friend put it to me, "Sometimes you can tell the size of a person's intention by the size of their obstacles to manifesting it." Examples abound: Martin Luther King, Mother Teresa, the Dalai

Lama. Take heart. When you experience obstacles, you're in good company!

2. *If no obstacles ever appear on the path toward your goals, you may not be challenging yourself.* This has nothing to do with ease. Obstacles arise only when you face events outside your current structure of knowing. If you are operating within your current structure of knowing, no real learning is taking place. There is very little risk. You can afford to raise the bar. You'll have more of an occasion to come across miracles that way.

3. *If you experience only obstacles on the path toward your goals, you may be doing things the hard way.* A consistent flow of obstacles and breakdowns may be a signal you have chosen a goal that is out of your reach at this time. If you continue on this path without modifying your goal, you could wind up with evidence about the futility of going for what you want in life. This is pure Monkey Mind. Another sign that you may be caught up with reaching your goals the hard way is if you do not ask for support. "I need to do this alone" is one of the most insidious structures of knowing to dismantle.

4. *People who are successful consistently choose their goals and intentions over their plans.* Your plans are your best guess, given present information, about what it will take to achieve your goal. Real life rarely follows our plans. If you cling to them they may hold you back. You have big dreams, and they are important to you, more important than any plan. Your plans will always need to be modified—not your dreams. Grasp this and you have the golden key to success!

Exercise: Turning Lead into Gold

The process for turning lead into gold is an alchemical metaphor for turning obstacles into miracles. Alchemists were philosophers and sages. They saw life as a laboratory for the distillation of the human spirit from its unenlightened state (lead) to enlightenment (gold). If one could purify his or her own spirit, the reasoning went, he or she could then learn to transmute real lead into actual gold. Some may have learned to do this. Many attained an even greater treasure. They learned to use the stuff of everyday life, both the joys and sorrows, to awaken themselves to their own essence. They discovered that lead *is* gold.

You are going to learn to use your obstacles and breakdowns to expand your awareness of the miracles that surround you. This exercise is good for the times when you encounter what you perceive to be an obstacle. With practice, you can go through it rather quickly. I suggest you do the work with someone else at first so that you can support each other in implementing what you get out of this work. You can compare notes, discuss ideas, and keep each other going in the process. Share what you find at each step. Above all, make sure you take Authentic Action.

You will need your notebook and your Life's Intentions and Standards of Integrity. Initially, this exercise may take about thirty minutes to examine each obstacle. With practice, you can significantly shorten the process.

1. Identify an obstacle you currently face, something that you believe blocks you from reaching a goal. Write at least three sentences about the obstacle. This is your preliminary assessment.

2. Narrow your description of the obstacle. Look at what you just wrote. You want to state clearly the facts of what happened. Is your statement vague or general? For example, "I'm tired a lot" is a general statement. Be more specific and locate an incident that is blocking you from proceeding on your path. Let these statements help you:

> JOEL: I just got a notice from the bank that I didn't qualify for the loan to refinance my house. I was counting on it to help get out of debt.

> MEG: I failed my counselor's license exam. It's the third time I've taken it.

> KAREEM: We have a deadline on this construction project. I've worked with my supervisors, but they're still late on getting the specs to me. We may not execute the contract on time as I planned.

3. Examine your breakdown regarding the obstacle. A breakdown is your personal reaction to the obstacle. There are four areas in which you can experience a breakdown: your thoughts,

feelings, body sensations, and spirit. These factors are not independent of one another. They form your structure of knowing about the event/obstacle. You will sort out each area and look at your specific reactions. This is part of the dismantling process.

Take a page from your notebook and label it "Thoughts." Write out all of your thoughts about the obstacle. Include your explanations, reasons, and theories about why this situation happened.

> JOEL: The bank didn't give me the loan because they don't trust me. Economic times are tough. Banks are not lending money right now. This is going to set me back. This is my own fault. I have too many questionable items on my credit report. My ex-wife charged too much on credit cards before we divorced.

> MEG: I did my best. I can't pass the exam. I'm too old for this. I should have done this when I was younger. I waited too long after graduation to go back and study. The study course I took this time didn't prepare me.

> KAREEM: You can't count on construction supervisors. Everyone knows it. All they want is their paycheck. I have to do the spec work myself. It comes with the territory. If you want something done right, always do it yourself. They're all jerks.

When you write your thoughts, include any judgments you have about yourself, the situation, or other people. If you have tried and failed to fix the situation, write that down as well. Include any methods you used. Keep listing your thoughts until nothing more comes to mind.

Now do the same for your "Feelings." Are you sad, frustrated, bored, anxious, furious, panicked, dumbfounded, numb, enraged, or lonely? Do you feel betrayed, abandoned, or hurt? Be as articulate as possible about your feelings. It is important for you to get them all out in your writing. It might look like this:

> KAREEM: I feel disgusted with the whole situation. I am angry at those supervisors, and I'm panicked that I'll ruin my reputation if I can't deliver.

This process asks you to differentiate your *thoughts* from your *feelings*. You are taking the cover off and looking at the component parts of your structure of knowing about the obstacle at hand. This act makes the structure more permeable and flexible, easier to expand in order to include the miracles that currently wait outside.

Your "Body Sensations" come next. What do you perceive even as you write about this obstacle? Are you tired? Does your head, stomach, neck, or back ache? Is your heart racing or your chest tight? Do you have a sinking feeling in the pit of your stomach? Write down all your physical sensations.

"Spirit" is the fourth area to look at. Symptoms of your breakdown at this level are usually framed in terms of what is missing. You may experience a lack of inspiration, enthusiasm, hope, gratitude, belonging, and enjoyment. On occasion, people have the feeling that the future does not hold much for them.

> KAREEM: I am hopeless about this situation. No one is playing on my team. I know I am alone here. There's nothing to feel grateful or enthusiastic about. The future looks kind of dark. I used to be able to inspire people who work for me. Not now!

After you have completed this step, take a moment for rest and quiet reflection. Don't be put off by the negativity you've been expressing. It's a common response. We usually don't take the time to thoroughly acknowledge our breakdowns in life. We know that something is wrong or that we are angry and frustrated. Or we think the whole world is against us. But we remain vague in pinpointing the exact nature of the obstacle and breakdown. As a result, we remain where we are. Using this exercise will break that pattern.

4. Get some distance and perspective on the obstacle/breakdown/event.

a. Talk to someone about it. Read your symptoms. Ask them to simply listen to you without comment.

b. If no one is available at this moment, then take what you have written and put it faceup on a table or the floor and walk about five feet away. Turn around and look at it. Do this even if it seems silly. From where you stand, do you notice anything about what you wrote? Isn't it just like a little clump of energy? With a bit of imagination you can almost hear it hum like one of those high-tension-wire transformers. Whether you opt for a or b above, use the following questions to help you get a distance on these highly charged perceptions and interpretations:

- Do I see clearly that I am experiencing breakdown in this situation?
- Do I see that my best strategies are not working, or that they may be part of the problem?
- Have I been trying to solve this alone, without consultation or support from those who could help me?
- Am I willing to go on, even if it means doing things differently than I have done them before?
- Am I willing to give up plans that may no longer work?

5. Restate the obstacle. What really happened, the bare facts? This is where you distill the truth from your symptoms, like separating gold from lead. The truth is a statement about what happened in physical reality.

> JOEL: I didn't qualify for a loan. My credit report contains questionable items.

> MEG: I have not yet passed my counseling license exam.

> KAREEM: I am not meeting the deadline on this contract.

You may have seen the truth about the obstacle when you first read each person's story. But they did not. They were in the middle of it, with Monkey Mind cheering them on. This is why the above steps are so important. It's like clearing the bugs off your windshield so you can see what is really in front of you.

So, what is the truth about this obstacle? What really happened? What did you do or not do? Take a deep breath at this point and wave at Monkey Mind.

6. Look at any broken promises. A closer look at the above obstacles reveals that in each case the person has failed to keep a promise to themselves or others. They have not yet done something to correct or balance the situation. This is uncomfortable and is at least partly the reason for the intensity of their symptoms.

One way to get to the underlying promise is to look at your Standards of Integrity. Does your behavior in this situation go counter to any of your standards? Which? Write them down. What are the broken promises?

> JOEL: One of my Standards of Integrity is "intelligence." It is definitely not intelligent of me to have credit reports with questionable items that I have not personally cleared or accounted for. Another one is being "conscious." When I applied for the loan, I was not conscious that my credit reports would reflect what they did. The promise? It was to get refinancing on the house. I have not yet kept that promise.

Do you see the wisdom operating here? Joel is demonstrating the heart of a hero. You can sense his trustworthiness and intelligence. He has gotten off the side of the road and is back on his path. Be gentle with yourself as you do this work. Many of us never get to the point of looking at our promises, broken or not.

When you tell the truth about obstacles and broken promises, guilt melts away. You stop blaming yourself or others. Blame is a Monkey Mind response. Instead, you simply point to what is so, the bare fact. This is possible to do even if the obstacle was totally out of your control. A fire or flood, for example, can generate a host of unkept promises. The hero's path through this is clear: learn from the mess, clean it up, and keep going.

7. Look at your underlying Life's Intentions. Though it might look like it, obstacles and breakdowns do not erase intentions. To the contrary! As we said earlier, the fact that you consider a situation an obstacle means that you have an intention that is currently thwarted. It is a validation of the intention and you! If you didn't have an intention, this incident or circumstance would mean nothing to you.

JOEL: My intention is to be financially successful.

MEG: My intention is to be a competent professional counselor.

KAREEM: I have the intentions to be a successful entrepreneur and supervisor.

What Life's Intentions are being thwarted in your current situation? Write them down. If you have difficulty, enlist the support of someone who can be objective.

8. Identify the goals you've been striving to attain. Reacquaint yourself with your goal. It will help you face your obstacle. Having gotten this far, you may discover that you did not clearly define your goal, or that it was not a goal. Operating without a goal, or without a clearly defined one, is a little like being an archer shooting at no definable target. Your trajectory may be straight, but what is it headed toward?

JOEL: My goal? Buying a home, with ease!

MEG: I want to open my private practice nine months from today!

KAREEM: My goal is to complete this project in five weeks, and to give my team bonuses because they did so well.

Take time with this part of the exercise. You reward yourself with a real gift when you see your goals clearly. The goals are the benchmarks you choose so you can manifest your intentions.

9. Take Authentic Action. Line up your Life's Intention(s), your goal, your Standards of Integrity, and a statement of any broken promises you have. Ask yourself how a person with your Standards and Intention(s) would handle this situation.

a. First, what promises need to be kept? What is the next Authentic Action for that? By when?
b. Do you need help restating your goal so that it conforms to all the SMART criteria?
c. What's your next Authentic Action toward your goal?

d. From whom are you willing to get support? Talk with that person within the next twenty-four hours. Do it while this exercise is still fresh in your mind.

e. If people offer their support, are you willing to take it? Even if it's not necessarily how you'd do things?

Practice this exercise and it will become easier to face your obstacles and breakdowns than to let them stop you. You will soon find yourself moving both mindfully and quickly through the steps. The first two times may be the slowest. Nevertheless, do them fully. You are developing your ability to stay on your path.

Did you allow someone to accompany you at each step? How did it feel to let another person support you? Could you get used to it? Good work!

MUTUAL SUPPORT INCREASES
YOUR POWER

To a lot of us—especially if we've grown up in America—the word *hero* is synonymous with "rugged individual." We picture our travels toward our dreams as a lonely quest. We believe that the most admirable and successful people among us reached their achievements or status by going it alone, pulling themselves up by his or her own bootstraps. Yet I've found that behind every great success is a team of supporters.

Think for a moment about the most significant accomplishments in sports. Athletes, whether they're members of teams or not, are aided by coaches, sponsors, family, and friends. They openly acknowledge the pivotal role these people play in their lives. No important sports figure has turned his or her incredible talents into dazzling achievements without support every step of the way.

All of us deserve and can find the energy of support. Your life will be creative and easy if you give and receive that energy.

People who are successful have learned to help others and to be helped. This mutual support amplifies our own natural courage, faith, and confidence. Support structures remind us of the promises we've made and keep us focused on them as a part of our path. True support is larger and more powerful than Monkey Mind, and reminds us of our greatest skills, talents, and dreams.

Most of us share the myth that if we accept support we diminish our own achievements and don't deserve praise for what we have done. Somehow help looks like a crutch, even a personal defeat. But if we stick to this line of reasoning, we become old before our time. We run ourselves into the ground pursuing our dreams in isolation.

You don't have to do it alone! Support is all around you, and connecting with it will change your life in wonderful ways. It will allow you to do things the easy way. In this chapter we join hands with our fellow travelers, our allies, and the welcoming circle of hearts and hands.

"DOING IT ALONE"

There's a story, almost legendary by now, that is worth retelling here. It's humorous and also conveys a message about the hazards of "doing it alone." As the tale is told, the following report was submitted as part of a workers' compensation claim in the 1920s.

> I am writing in response to your request concerning Block #11 on the insurance form which asks for the cause of injuries, wherein I put, "Trying to do the job alone." You said you needed more information so I trust the following will be sufficient.
>
> I am a bricklayer by trade and on the date of injuries I was working alone laying brick around the top of a four-story building, when I realized that I had about 500 pounds of brick left over. Rather than carry them down by hand, I decided to put them into a barrel and lower them by a pulley, which was fastened to the top of the building. I secured the end of the rope at ground level and went up to the top of the building and loaded the bricks into the barrel and flung the barrel out with the bricks in it. I then went down and untied the rope, holding it securely to insure the slow descent of the barrel.
>
> As you will note on Block #6 of the insurance form, I weigh 145 pounds. Due to my shock at being jerked off the ground so swiftly I lost my presence of mind and forgot to let go of the rope. Between the second and third floors, I met the barrel coming down. This accounts for the bruises and lacerations on my upper body.
>
> Regaining my presence of mind, again I held tightly to the rope and proceeded rapidly up the side of the building, not stopping until my right hand was jammed in the pulley. This accounts for my broken thumb. Despite the pain, I retained my presence of mind and held tightly to the rope. At approximately the same time, however, the barrel of bricks hit the ground and the bottom fell out

of the barrel. Devoid of the weight of the bricks, the barrel now weighed about 50 pounds. I again refer you to Block #6 of the insurance form and my weight.

As you would guess, I began a rapid descent. In the vicinity of the second floor, I met the barrel coming up. This explains the injuries to my legs and lower back. Slowed only slightly, I continued my descent, landing on the pile of bricks. Fortunately, my back was only sprained and the internal injuries were only minimal. I am sorry to report, however, that at this point I again lost my presence of mind and let go of the rope. As you can imagine, the empty barrel crashed down on me.

I trust that this answers your concern. Please know that I am finished trying to do it alone.

WHAT IS SUPPORT, REALLY?

We all exist in an interdependent system. No matter how we feel about it, we're linked socially, economically, and biologically, like the cells of a giant organism. We are healthiest when all parts of our bodies and society are functioning together. Thich Naht Hahn, the Vietnamese Buddhist teacher, talks often about our "inter-being."

Take this book, for example. Think about the efforts of every person who put his or her energy into it. Recall the exercise in chapter 1 where you held a dollar bill in your hands and imagined all the lives that dollar has touched and will touch. It's easy to get a real picture of just how intimately we are all connected through webs of energy. Given that interdependence, it quickly becomes clear that our greatest success comes when all of us succeed together.

Most dictionaries say that support involves actively promoting the interests of, and giving assistance and sustenance to, another person. Yet some of us shun the whole idea of support. David, a workshop participant, and I explored this during one of the You and Money Courses.

DAVID: I hate the idea of being interdependent. I'm going on my own for a while. One of my goals is to get a 4 × 4, load it with food, and go up to the mountains to be by myself for a few months.

ME: Okay, how are you going to get up there?

DAVID: Like I said, in my 4 × 4.

ME: But, David, you're dependent on the manufacturer to make a good truck. And what about the roads? Who made them? And who produced the food you're carrying? And your shoes and clothes? How about the fuel you're using?

DAVID: Don't start confusing me. You know what I mean. I want to be my own person.

ME: But that's just it. We think that being our own person means isolating ourselves from the supportive energy of others. Look carefully at this, because it's the source of a lot of our suffering.

DAVID: (becoming thoughtful) I do spend a lot of time trying to prove I don't need anyone for anything. And I've got to admit I'm always complaining that nobody is ever there to help me out when I need it. But I was taught to be a rugged individualist. I believe in that.

ME: Be a rugged individual where it counts, by making your own unique contribution. Then get others to support you in realizing your dreams.

DAVID: (becoming reflective) I would like that. Then I'd get away in my 4 × 4 because I want to, not because I'm trying to escape from being interdependent. I'd be going toward having a good time, rather than trying to escape from people. I wouldn't be so driven all the time, trying to do it all alone!

You may be able to recall a time in your own life when you accomplished something great with the support or collaboration of others. Maybe you and a friend worked together on a science project in high school. Or a friend of the family helped you finance your college education. Or an art teacher encouraged you to paint, and you produced a beautiful work of art. Or you had a coach who helped you develop your athletic abilities. Or a friend taught you to drive a car.

Now look back on the times when you did it alone, without anyone's aid. Compare the quality of these two experiences and note any differences you recognize. Was there a contrast in how you felt emotionally? How about the amount of energy it required to be successful alone? Did support carry you more easily toward your goal? How did it feel to share that success, or not have someone to share it with?

THE BENEFITS ARE MUTUAL

When you ask another person for his support, you are actually giving him a gift. You are generously allowing the person to make a significant contribution in your life. By working together, you each benefit. His act of generosity comes full circle when you let him know the difference he has made.

Recall times in which you knew you had a positive effect on someone else's life. Perhaps it was the time you helped a friend through an emotional crisis. It could be the time you sat down with a relative and talked her through a business project. Maybe it was the time you became a mentor for a young person who just needed someone to listen to him.

When have you experienced yourself as being helpful to another person? Have you felt their relief or watched their sense of hope, self-esteem, and strength improve? You know it boosts your own sense of self-worth, increasing your own energy. In fact, most people, when asked to look back on their most significant achievements in life, name the times when they helped others and saw that their efforts made a positive difference.

I remember visiting my great-aunt Anna at the retirement home her first week there. Now, there was a woman! Ninety-five years old, sharp as a tack, and used to taking care of herself. She hated being at the home, but she was blind in one eye and too frail to be alone. She looked dismal.

I sat down beside her and listened to her complain. This was not her old, died-in-the-wool gutsy Socialist self. And all of a sudden I said to her, "Stop this, Aunt Anna. You're beginning to sound like an old woman!"

There was a pause. We both started laughing. She began to perk up immediately, and the gleam came back to her good eye. Then she became serious for a moment.

"Honey," she said, "I believe you've just saved my life."

That moment will be with me forever.

Aunt Anna gave me a gift by responding to me in that way. She let me know I had helped, and she taught me that letting others know their value to us is far more precious than any gift you could buy for them. It is returning the favor a thousandfold!

When someone supports your efforts, he or she does not have to act *for* you or *instead* of you. On the contrary. The best support comes from people who know who you are in your heart. They recognize that you are bigger than all of your doubts and fears. And they don't let *you* forget this! They don't collude with you in coming up with reasons why you did not keep your promises or why you can't fully realize your greatest talents and strengths. Instead of supporting Monkey Mind, they remind you of your greatest goals and dreams. In that way they feed you the energy to go way beyond where you would normally stop yourself.

It may be that many of us are uncomfortable with the support of others because we associate it with being like a young child. We've all had the experience of someone jumping in and taking a task away from us, rather than showing us how to do it for ourselves. We've even been on the giving end of that kind of "support," which is really frustration.

But watch the face of the little child who is shown how to tie her own shoelaces, for example, when she finally gets the knack of it. Her face lights up with pride, and if you are the one who's been coaching her, you are as proud as she! That's why most people seize the chance when we ask them to support us.

Robert Lewis, a columnist for *InfoWorld* magazine, suggests this experiment: Next time you have a task or new assignment that puts you in unfamiliar territory, call five people in your company whom you've never met, describe your project, and say, "I was told you may have some good insights on how to approach this problem. Can you spare an hour to help me get my thoughts together?"

"I guarantee you," he writes, "at least six of the five will offer more help than you have any right to expect. And when you're done, they'll thank you. People want to create value for other people—that's where self-esteem comes from." That's right, six of the five. People are that willing and eager to share what they know.

BEING SUPPORTIVE ISN'T BEING CO-DEPENDENT

In recent years much has been written about co-dependence. We have become sensitized to the potential problems associated with giving and receiving assistance. Supportive relationships, however, are different from co-dependence.

Co-dependence is in the eye of the supporter. When you're being co-dependent with another person, you view him or her as needing to be *fixed* in some way. You take care of him because you believe he would be lost without you. You believe he'd get into trouble on his own. In other words, you as a "helper" are dependent on his being dependent on *you*.

Monkey Mind evaluates others as broken in some way and believes it has to rescue them, or do something for them because they don't have the ability to do for themselves. You must supply them with answers to all their questions, because they don't have those answers inside. *That's* co-dependence!

In its most exaggerated form, co-dependence gives rise to a false sense of security. The other person needs you so much that he or she will never leave. He can't get along on his own. It's a limiting circumstance for both of you.

Helpers in a co-dependent dynamic quickly get exhausted. They often feel as though they are carrying the other person on their shoulders. This typically leads to resentment and frustration on both sides. There is no room for creativity and initiative for the person being helped in this type of relationship. He or she may get rescued over and over again, or be "protected" or prevented from having the opportunity to learn from his or her genuine failures.

Another way to separate a supportive from a co-dependent relationship is to ask if what you believe to be someone else's weaknesses, real or imagined, preoccupy you so much that you have little energy to keep promises to yourself about your own goals and dreams—or give you a good excuse for not keeping them!

Interestingly, when you are being co-dependent you do not allow other people to support you. Typical co-dependent slogans in this vein are:

- If I want to get something done right, I have to do it myself.
- If anyone tries to support me, they are just meddling.
- If anyone offers support, they think I'm not good enough to do it for myself.
- I'm too busy taking care of others to ask for anyone's help right now.
- No one understands how much I have to do, how hard I work.

You can just hear the driven quality of co-dependence. From this vantage point, you are caught in a vicious circle of doing the same things over and over again, with little or no satisfaction for either the helper or helpee. You feel isolated from others, and you usually end up working far harder than necessary.

SUPPORT MEANS WHOLENESS

There's a big difference when you are truly supporting someone else. You recognize that both of you are whole and complete. You are aware of the other person's courage, even when he or she doubts it. You are conscious of the hero standing before you. Most important, you see that he or she is much bigger than Monkey Mind, with goals and dreams worth playing for. You also see that she has a wellspring of wisdom and can find her own answers.

Supporting another person is not always comfortable. It may not seem polite or nice to remind him of promises he has made or goals he created. And it's not necessarily easy to be in a relationship where your partner expects the best from you. Monkey Mind chatter can become loud for both of you. You may worry that you are being pushy. You may think it is best just to let the promise slide. Or you may feel constantly challenged to reach within for the very best in yourself as you support them.

In an interdependent relationship you are companions, heroes traveling together but traveling your own paths. At times the other person's vision may be clouded, just as yours may be. But you realize that this says nothing about your ultimate abilities. You treat each other with respect, giving and receiving in equal measures. There is no energy drain here. The victories and accomplishments you celebrate together come from a place of generosity and strength, not from a place of fear and weakness.

Exercise: Getting Support for Your Hero's Journey

If you'd like to generate the energy of support, first take a moment to look at your current structure of knowing about getting support from others. If you were to map that structure right now, you might come up with phrases like:

• Only ninnies and wimps need support.
• If I ask for it, people will think I'm weak and don't know how to take care of myself.
• People can let you down. Why set myself up to be disappointed?
• I'm embarrassed to ask. I don't know how.
• Maybe it's okay to get support when I'm having a real hard time, but not when I'm going for a goal. I don't deserve it. It's selfish.

If you are willing to go beyond your structure of knowing about support, please do the following exercise. You will need your notebook, a pen, and your calendar. This exercise will take about ten minutes.

You are looking for a genuinely supportive person to help you attain your goals. This person should be someone you like, trust, and *cannot manipulate*. Rule out anyone who will be seduced by your mind chatter. Generally, a co-dependent "support" relationship is one in which two Monkey Minds play into each other's doubts and fears, drowning out everything else. So to be supportive of you, the other person must not collude with you about how you do not have the time, energy, or inclination to do what you said you would do. What you need at this point is someone who demonstrates ruthless compassion in reminding you of your promises. You need a person who will not put up with the mischief two Monkey Minds can create.

The person who supports you should not have a vested interest in the outcome. While you want to make sure that he or she is excited about your accomplishments, this person's own well-being and comfort should not be tied to your success. Such a relationship only complicates matters for both of you.

To find this person:

1. Make a list of any people in your life who fit the above description of a supportive person. Look at friends, co-workers and family members, minister, coach, or therapist.

2. If your list is very short, or nonexistent, take heart. The act of looking at how to get and give quality support for yourself will open up exciting possibilities. Give yourself a day or more to locate a person who would be a good support for you.

3. Pick a project in which you are willing to be supported. For example, in keeping with your incomplete money business list, you may have promised you'd make a dentist or medical appointment for weeks but not yet done so. You might have promised yourself that you'd walk one hour, three times a week. You may have pledged to balance your checkbook to the penny. You may have chosen to take the promotion exam at work but not yet begun to study for it. These and thousands of other examples qualify for support.

4. Choose someone from your support list. Ask yourself the question "Am I willing to let this person have success in supporting me?"

Do you recall times in the past when you didn't allow your coach or support person to be successful? Did you spend time and energy fending them off? What methods did you use?

DENISE: I stopped smoking four times last year. Each time I'd swear it was my last cigarette. The fourth time I asked my friend Jane to support me. I promised her I'd get some nicotine gum. I didn't. I promised I'd call her every morning and let her know how I was doing. That lasted for two days. On the third day I smoked two cigarettes. The next morning I didn't call her. That evening she called me. I could hear her voice on the machine. I didn't pick up the phone. I've had enough of doing it this way. Luckily Jane is generous. She forgave me.

What strategies did Denise use to avoid support? What do you use? One of the easiest ways to disable your strategies is to tell the truth about them up front. Do you:

- Make promises you know you will not keep?
- Avoid talking to your support person when you see them?
- Pretend you are too busy to talk to them when they call?
- Try to do things your way, even when it has not worked?
- "Nice" your coach to death? Example: "Thank you so much for caring. I appreciate what you're doing. Let's talk more later. Now is not a good time for me."
- Quickly turn the tables by asking how he or she is doing, when you know that you need support?
- Threaten to get irritated, annoyed, or downright angry when you are reminded of your promises?
- Lie about what you did or did not accomplish?

We all have favorite strategies that we use when we haven't done what we said we would do. These tactics keep us in the same rut, and they're embarrassing and uncomfortable to talk about. However, this momentary discomfort of self-disclosure is a small price to pay for having our goals and dreams become a reality.

5. Within the next forty-eight hours, invite the person you have chosen to support you on your project. Be frank with him or her. Tell him all the ways you have avoided or thwarted support in the past. When we do this in the You and Money Course, I often ask participants to exaggerate or dramatize their most prized methods. It is usually very funny. We all can relate.

Mary Kay screens her calls on her answering machine and doesn't pick up if it's the support person. When Ralph's support person calls and Ralph hasn't done what he said he'd do, he says, "I'm too busy to speak. I've got too much on my plate and I'll call you later." Betty says, "Sometimes I just say I'll do something to get them off my back. I have no intention of actually doing it."

6. Tell this person the nature of your project. Make a promise for an Authentic Action to be taken within the next forty-eight hours. Choose an action that's a stretch for you,

yet not obviously beyond your reach. We want to build in the conditions for success here. Give your support person permission to call you at a set time, either to support you before you take action or to congratulate you after you have taken it.

7. If you really want to stack the cards in your favor, give this person a copy of your Standards of Integrity. This will give her a special knowledge of the attributes you intend to demonstrate in life. Give him permission to call you on it when it appears that you are operating outside of these standards. Tell him you also want to know when it appears that you are manifesting these standards.

8. Keep your word! If you have not, tell the truth. Remake your promise. Keep going.

9. Acknowledge each other for this work. You are both demonstrating the attributes of successful people.

10. If you wish, make another promise for Authentic Action.

This experience of receiving support may have brought up a number of feelings and thoughts for you. What are they? Write about them in your notebook. Was this exercise difficult or easy? Did you pick an Authentic Action that was achievable, yet a stretch?

I usually advise people against supporting each other at the same time. You risk colluding with each other. And if one of you withdraws, the other will be left without support. You need to have someone whose own Authentic Actions are not in any way tied to supporting you.

FORMING A SUCCESS GROUP

As you consider the possibility of being supported by others, you may want to form a group of people with similar intentions. A success group is a form of self-help group, but with distinct characteristics:

• The focus is on success and moving forward on your hero's journey. This means each person is there to be supported in keeping their promises.

• You do not get extra points for struggling. That's because struggling usually means that you're trying to do things alone. In this group you get to work hard, but not to the point of exhaustion. You are there to get out of the pattern of being driven.

• You are willing to be supported by others, not just to be a supporter. It is often much easier for us to be a supporter than to allow others to support us. It makes us feel vulnerable.

• The group is not a substitute for therapy or any twelve-step program. The focus is on discovering how to take Authentic Action. Insight is considered to be the booby prize if it is unaccompanied by a demonstration in physical reality. In this format you come away from each session with promises that will be fulfilled by the next session. This could include seeking therapy or joining a twelve-step program, if that is appropriate.

• The group is committed to holding each member accountable for who they really are in their heart. For this reason, everyone's Standards of Integrity and Life's Intentions are a matter of group record.

Success Group Format: First Meeting

The format for creating a success group is simple. Have group members read the chapter of this book that you all want to work with before your first meeting. When you get together, open the floor for discussing the material. Make sure everyone gets a chance to speak on the topic. Stay away from being too theoretical; have people relate their lives to the subject at hand. Monkey Mind will want to get intellectual.

End each session with everyone declaring to the group what he or she will accomplish by the next session. Each member should choose a supporter from the group who will coach them between sessions.

THE COACHING CONTEXT: BLUEPRINT FOR SUCCESS

Groups become powerful when they occur within a context, an intentional space where certain activities and roles occur. We live in social contexts, professional contexts, spiritual contexts, occupational contexts, and so on. This is most vividly apparent when one context clashes with another. For example, have you ever gone to a friend's party, only to be surprised by the presence of your boss or psychotherapist? Have you noticed the embarrassed or awkward moments as you strive to find a way of relating that is appropriate in this situation?

The context of a success group revolves around coaching. Members are there because they are willing to be supported in going beyond their current structures of knowing and taking Authentic Action. They are willing to support others in doing the same. Protect this powerful space by ensuring that your sessions have a definite beginning and ending time. Then, if you want to socialize, make time for that after the meeting.

The coaching context is created only when everyone in the group answers the following questions out loud. These are important centering questions.

1. *What specific qualities am I willing to contribute to the group session today, so that all of us will be successful?*

For example, if you are tired, are you willing to be alert? If you are feeling defensive, are you willing to be open and receptive? If judgmental, are you willing to be compassionate? Each attribute or quality should be a bit of a stretch. This automatically takes you outside your structure of knowing. Make a list of these qualities. Declare what they are to the group. Do not use "non" words, such as "nonjudgmental." Say what you are going to contribute: "I will be open and compassionate."

Here are some more examples of attributes you can use to answer this question: open, kind, flexible, acknowledging, truthful, courageous, attentive, alert, receptive, grateful, clear, joyous, loving, focused, creative, supportive, gentle, empowering, appreciative, generous, compassionate.

You will notice that conceptual and emotional words are missing. That's because they don't reflect who you really are in your heart. You want to connect with more enduring qualities that can exist no matter what you think or feel.

You may also notice that the word "honest" is missing. Honesty is a way station on the road to being truthful. For more clarity on this, refer to our discussions of the difference between honesty and truth in Principle 1.

How does it feel to read those words? Do you notice a sense of spaciousness? When you invoke these qualities, it's a declaration of your intention to go beyond Monkey Mind. When a number of people do this at once, there's an incredible flow of energy. There's a synergistic effect, which is like linking a set of batteries or generators together. That's enough power to boost anyone through Trouble at the Border.

2. *Am I willing to dismantle my structures of knowing?*

This question asks if you are willing to go beyond your thoughts, opinions, judgments, and evaluations about what you think you know. You proceed toward miracles when you go outside your customary mental structures. A "Yes" answer says you're willing to go beyond your comfort zone. You may be apprehensive. Monkey Mind may be having a field day in your head. Nevertheless, you are willing.

3. *Am I willing to use everything that goes on in the group session as a personal lesson for myself?*

If you answer "Yes" to this, you are promising to create value and meaning for yourself out of whatever happens in the group. You are willing to get all the support you need today, even if it is from watching someone else get supported in the group. You are promising yourself that you will leave the session thoroughly satisfied that you received what you needed. This question puts *you* in charge of learning your own lessons. If you look, you will probably find that you can learn from any situation as long as you are willing.

4. *Am I willing to listen to the support of everyone in the group? Even if I do not agree with what they are saying . . . especially if I do not agree with them?*

If you are willing to suspend your structure of knowing and listen to the support of others, I promise you miracles. Your best efforts at solving problems without support may have gotten you far. But we all need the support of others to go beyond our self-created limitations. When you don't agree with what others are saying, look carefully. It may reveal where you have gotten stuck in a structure of knowing. You don't need to agree with the viewpoint of those who support you.

It is useful to use your disagreement with them to observe yourself.

Are you being defensive? Is Monkey Mind flexing its muscles? Have these symptoms stopped you in the past from going farther down your hero's path? Are you willing to experience the discomfort associated with suspending your judgment? Is it all right to get support you do not like from someone who you think has gotten it all wrong?

If you cannot answer "Yes" to each of these statements, take a deep breath. Sometimes we're not ready to interact with the group during a particular session. You might allow yourself to observe the group without interacting until you can authentically answer "Yes" to the above questions. If you remain unable to do so, use the following suggestions to trace possible causes:

• You may be exhausted because you have been struggling.

• You may have been operating outside your Standards of Integrity in some area of your life. If it is a matter of not having done what you said you would between sessions, use the current session to tell the truth. You'll be surprised at how people will identify with what you're going through.

• You may be facing an issue that needs some external support, such as therapy, a twelve-step group, or even a medical consultation.

In any case, allow yourself to get the help you need so that you can use the success group in a powerful way.

A SUGGESTED TIME AND FORMAT FOR THE GROUP

1. Opening. Have everyone answer the questions outlined above. (15 minutes)

2. Have everyone take 2 minutes to share a breakthrough since last session. (10–20 minutes, depending on group size)

3. Read from a selected chapter, doing exercises or sharing work on that chapter. (1 hour)

4. Form support pairs until the next session. This can be done by putting names in a box and randomly drawing the name of a person you will support until the next session. Or you may have someone work out a schedule so that everyone gets the opportunity to be supported by each group member at some point. Just make sure you do

not end up supporting someone who is supporting you. If you go into collusion with each other, nothing will get done.

5. Write down your promises for Authentic Action by the next session. Keep these in your notebook. They need to be specific. Examples of *vague* promises are:

• I'll be happier and more rested.
• I'll take care of myself.
• I'll be more careful about being on time.
• I'll be more trusting.

These promises are not measurable as they are stated. You do not know how to tell when you have accomplished them. Specific promises have more energy. There is a sense of being on the line for something:

• I'll have one appointment with a certified financial planner by next session.
• I'll create three goals and come to the next session ready to Treasure Map at least one of them.
• I'll call the travel agent and book that cruise.
• I'll take care of three items on my Incomplete Money Business list.
• I'll go to one Debtors Anonymous group.

Now, these promises have some teeth to them! They may be a stretch for you. Above all, they are specific actions that someone can support you in taking.

6. Pick four times between sessions in which your support person calls and/or meets with you to remind you of your promises. They might ask if you need any further assistance.

This is what is most important about a success group: *You are in the group to learn about being supported, not to frustrate your coaches.* You are in the group to learn to support others, not to be co-dependent with them.

If you are ready, be prepared for miracles in your life. You literally will not recognize yourself after going through this book with a support group.

My friend, Dr. Patricia Elliott, coined this motto after an especially

productive session. I invite you to take it with you on your journey:
"I did it myself, but I wasn't alone!"

Support opens the pathway to gratitude. You become thankful and
appreciative of those who have given their energy to uphold and sustain you on your hero's journey. You finally belong to a group whose
members are just as excited about the triumphs of others as they are
of their own. You begin to sense the presence of abundance.

The next chapter presents Principle 12: The Gateway to Abundance Is Gratitude. You will see there how to further develop and
unlock your power to be grateful.

THE GATEWAY TO ABUNDANCE IS GRATITUDE

I was regretting the past and fearing the future. Suddenly God was speaking. "My name is I Am." I waited. God continued, "I am not there. My name is not 'I was.' When you live in the future, with its problems and fears, it is hard. I am not there. My name is not 'I will be.' When you live in this moment, it is not hard. I am here. My name is 'I Am.'"
—HELLEN MELLICOST, ONE HUNDRED GATES

Abundance. The word has a life of its own. It is the promise that urges the hero onward. We are at a place to know what abundance means when we learn the lessons of money's energy, what frees it and what focuses it.

Thoughts of abundance can trigger visions of standing with arms outstretched as $100 bills rain down from the heavens, or jumping up and down as lottery numbers flash across the TV screen. In prosperity workshops, the word *abundance* glows with the promise of "more," which is always around the next bend, like a pot of gold at the end of a rainbow.

By now, however, we know that in traveling toward our dreams, "more" is not necessarily our goal. The desire for more is most often a conversation about scarcity. It's born of leaking and wasting money, or being driven, or thinking that amassing more stuff will substitute for having clear goals that represent our Life's Intentions. It's time to comprehend and grasp the true nature of abundance. If you're willing, you'll soon discover that you've known what it was all along. That's the power of all the work you've done to clear yourself as a conscious conduit of energy.

In order to imagine abundance, draw a circle on a clean piece of paper. Next, fill in the circle with examples of everything we experience in life: happiness and sadness, good and bad times, joy and sorrow, play and work, scarcity and plenty. You could spend the rest of your life filling in the circle, couldn't you? Our experience of life is infinite in its variety, isn't it?

This circle represents abundance. Abundance is everything. Every possible aspect of life's experience. All of it, including scarcity. From this perspective, you can see that scarcity is one of the manifestations of abundance.

We increase our power by embracing life's abundance—by saying yes. And we develop our ability to do this by practicing gratitude. In this chapter we complete our hero's journey by learning how to do so.

ABUNDANCE AND THE HERO'S JOURNEY

The idea of abundance as the totality of life is famously expressed in the Bible, Ecclesiastes 3:1–8: "To everything there is a season, and a time to every purpose under heaven. A time to be born, and a time to die; a time to plant, and a time to pluck up that which is planted . . ." Life teaches us that comfort and discomfort, joy and sadness are all qualities that will be expressed in the fullness of time. Abundance is all of it, even the bitter moments that serve to teach us and wake us up.

The well-lived life is a conscious life. When we are conscious, we're aware of everything, living fully. We don't choose what we want to become conscious of. We don't say "Let me be aware of this aspect of my life, but not that." As the veil lifts from our perception, we see both the miracles and the lessons that surround us. Every time you are willing to say "Yes" to everything on your path, you express the hero inside of you.

To answer "Yes"—an emphatic "Yes"—to everything is to put us in the position to experience prosperity. Prosperity comes when you participate fully in *every* aspect of your life. That's because you thrive when you participate. It's a state of growth. You're not pushing away anything, you're using everything as an opportunity to wake up and express who you are in your heart.

Take a deep breath. With this new understanding of abundance and prosperity, you can handle the flow of energy in your life. When you're not blocking anything, are willing to learn from everything, and are committed to expressing your true nature, you are *in that moment* prospering. From this we can see that prosperity is not something out there, waiting to happen in the future. Prosperity occurs now, every time you are willing to be fully present to your life. That's why "Yes" is the most powerful word you can utter.

Your work in this book has been designed to help you discern when to say "No" to your driven behavior, so that you gather energy and focus it on worthwhile pursuits. But using "No" to push away anything in our internal experience that we fear or dislike can limit our experience of abundance. Attempting to avoid unpleasant aspects of our lives, as we have seen, drains our energy and power. As American-born Buddhist abbess Pema Chödrön put it, "It doesn't do any good to get rid of our so-called negative aspects because in that process we also get rid of our basic wonderfulness."

One way to encounter abundance is through developing the art of gratitude. We turn to this next.

THE FINE ART OF GRATITUDE

Spiritual leaders tell us that it's important to develop gratefulness. Theologian Brother David Steindl-Rast says we have gotten what makes for a full life all backward by waiting for good circumstances to occur before we express gratitude. The key to growing into your goals is bringing gratefulness to your everyday circumstances, no matter what they may be.

To have a goal designed to try to get *away* from an uncomfortable or painful circumstance only prolongs the very circumstance you seek to escape. Trying to escape gives you no breathing room or creativity. Gratitude shifts your energy and takes you out of the fight, flight, or freeze mode. You breathe deeply and unclench from your fears. Your belly is soft and receptive. You are open to possibility.

How do you become grateful for everything? You may not want to be grateful for whatever is in your life. You may think it's a bad idea to be grateful for a difficult circumstance because it will empower that circumstance. For example, you may find you owe $1,000 more on your income tax than you thought, or you may lose your job to downsizing. How do you wrap gratitude around that?

You may also feel worried about making too much of the beneficial circumstances in your life and believe that there's no use tempting the Fates with your happiness. This is not logical, but it's human, and the superstition shows up in many cultures. My older Jewish relatives, for instance, would look at a healthy and beautiful baby and say loudly, "It's too bad she's so ugly and sickly." Tradition had it that evil spirits would ignore a sick, ugly child. It was best to fool them by feigning misfortune.

One woman in the You and Money Course was having difficulty coming up with goals. She finally told us she was recovering from breast cancer and was afraid to make goals, lest she not live to meet them. At the same time, she was terrified of expressing gratitude for the lessons that the illness taught her, because she feared that that kind of gratitude would bring the cancer back.

Gratitude does not mean that you jump for joy at whatever occurs in your life. Rather, it means that you note, bear witness to, and see whatever is put before you. You are willing to let it be there, doing nothing to postpone whatever lesson or opportunity comes from fortune *and* misfortune.

AFFIRMATIONS: AWAKENING
THE GRATEFUL HEART

One way to kindle gratitude is to practice paying attention to what's happening in our everyday physical reality. We ordinarily spend so much time with Monkey Mind as it chatters about the past or future that we don't linger long enough to see what is here in the present. As Hellen Mellicost puts it, when we live in the present moment, life is not hard.

The foundation of affirmation is staying in the present moment. To affirm is to literally make firm. We do this by observing what's before us and allowing it to be there just as it is. This takes guts. We don't always feel up to it. However, we can be willing, even with all our doubts and fears that we're not up to the challenge.

There are three ways to engage in creative affirmation. Creative affirmation is not wishful thinking or offering incantations to the Fates. *It's the simple process of shifting the way you observe the events in your life and imbuing them with gratitude.*

The first way to use affirmation is to note and welcome your daily lessons. This is sometimes difficult, because deepest lessons don't appear beneficial at first glance. To discover that you have lost a job seems more like a closing than an opening. It feels terrible. At the moment you experience this loss, it would be useless for anyone to tell you, "Oh, but you will learn so much from this! Be grateful!"

No, first you need to fret, complain, or get angry. Then, and only then, do you have the opportunity to say, "Yes. I am willing to experience this. I am willing for this to be a lesson for me."

The experience of first acknowledging, and then being open to a difficult lesson looks something like this, a dialogue that comes out of the You and Money Course:

MARK: I lost out on an organizational development consulting job.

ME: What happened?

MARK: I'm not sure. This really burns me. I thought I did a great job.

ME: Tell us about being "burned up." (I am not trying to use logic to talk him out of how he feels.)

MARK: I really wanted the job. Could have used the money, too. I feel like such a jerk. Maybe I came off really badly at the interview.

ME: Anything else that burns you up about this?

MARK: Maybe I'm not as great as I think I am. I've been in this business for eighteen years. Maybe I've just been fooling myself all along.

ME: What else burns you about this?

MARK: (Goes on for another two minutes emptying the Monkey Mind conversations out of his head. Then he pauses.)

ME: Take a deep breath. (He does.) Are you willing to have this be here? Are you willing to have this be a message or a lesson for you?

MARK: I don't think so. I feel so stupid.

ME: I don't mean do you *want* this lesson. Or even that you believe it can teach you anything. I'm asking if you're willing. This is above and beyond what Monkey Mind is telling you right now.

MARK: Okay. Then I'm willing. Something happened that I hate. But I'm willing to have it be here. (He pauses.) I'm even willing to be grateful for the wake-up call this mess created. I'm not grateful now. But I'm willing to be.

Mark decided to call the man who had interviewed him to ask him for feedback. Was there anything the man could tell him that might be helpful for future interviews? The interviewer was impressed. He told Mark the only thing disqualifying him was that he had not given enough details about his proposed program for the company. This had nothing to do with his skill or ability. Mark revamped his consultant brochure and presentation material. He landed a large contract within two months. It seemed like a miracle. For Mark, the true miracle was seeing the possibility of being grateful despite the discomfort.

The second form affirmation can take is being grateful for the pleasures we receive: a beautiful sunset, a letter from a dear friend, an unexpected raise in salary. You might think that affirming these gifts would be natural. After all, how much simpler can you get than being grateful for what brings you joy or happiness? Yet we don't often do it. In the normal course of events, we spend only a short time with them before Monkey Mind once again directs our attention to the past or future.

Gerry was an architect and felt great that he and his assistant had finished some critical preliminary renderings well and on time. He told me, "It was at the end of the day and I felt very proud and grateful that we had done such a good job, but no sooner did I feel that appreciation than Monkey Mind came in with 'But what if the clients don't like what you did? How many versions of these renderings are you going to have to go through? Don't be grateful too quickly.'"

AFFIRMING YOUR BASIC NATURE

The third form of affirmation I'd like to suggest is affirming the attributes that are inherent in your Standards of Integrity. You've probably noticed by now that we're not using affirmations to deny or escape difficult circumstances, but rather to help us stay with what is true.

Emilie Cady, in her pioneering book *Lessons in Truth*, said that "to affirm anything is to assert positively that it is so, even in the face of all contrary evidence." You have the qualities you've listed in your Standards of Integrity, and they express the genuine person you are. Affirming them will give power to that which already exists inside you. You can do this no matter what "contrary evidence" your Monkey Mind dishes up.

Affirming who you really are, your basic nature, is simple. It doesn't require a stretch of the imagination. You start by declaring that you are willing and follow it with the attribute you are willing to be. This attribute is taken from your Standards of Integrity. For instance, you say, "I am willing to be courageous," or "I am willing to be loyal," or whatever is true for you.

Will you try this right now? Just take out your Standards of Integrity, say, "I am willing to be . . ." and follow this with one of your Standards. Then go on to the next one, and the next. Say the words out loud. See how they feel on your tongue. Repeat them to yourself each night for at least one week. What do you perceive? Is a spark of gratitude present? I asked Alan to do this, and this is what he reported:

> ALAN: This was much easier for me than I expected. My mind didn't go nuts. In fact, it seemed natural. At first it felt like I wasn't saying that I was these qualities, only that I was willing to be. After a while something happened. One night when I was saying them, I got this flash! Of course I was courageous, truthful, loyal, and intelligent! That was not the question. The real question was Am I going to demonstrate that this is who I am? It does no good to have these attributes if I'm not doing something with them. I'm glad to be me. It's an adventure.

Affirming and then expressing your Standards of Integrity prepares you to say "Yes" to abundance, and to feel gratitude. Connecting

with your Standards gives you the fortitude to look and see and tell
the truth about everything on your path. That's the hero's way. And
recall that you're meant to do this with ease. Like Alan, you needn't
regard your Standards as an unreachable measure of perfection.
They reflect who you are now. They ask only that you use them to
guide you.

When you see that you are out of alignment with your Standards,
take Authentic Action to restore the balance that comes with
integrity. In fact, allow yourself to keep in touch with your Standards
so that the imbalance doesn't even occur. Ask yourself how you can
express your Standards in your everyday life. And acknowledge
yourself fully when you do!

I sometimes start the day by looking for ways to express trustworthiness and loyalty and compassion. Those are the qualities I
want to shine from my heart through my actions. By no means do I
do a perfect job. But I like to think that taking a proactive stance like
this gives me more of a footing as I dance with abun-dance.

CONTRIBUTION: THE CONSEQUENCE OF GRATITUDE

Gratitude allows you to experience the gifts of life. When you receive
gifts, you naturally want to give back. This maintains a flow of
energy, a balance between giving and receiving. Contribution is as
natural as breathing in and breathing out.

When your contribution is blocked, your energy gets backed up
like the waters behind a dam. You get cranky, tired, and uninspired.
Miracles are lost on you. The lessons you learn here about contributing money to others can be applied to all areas of your life.
Monkey Mind gets antsy when it considers giving money. Actually,
for the Monkey, giving away money is the real issue, as though
you're losing money in giving.

But here is a secret I have discovered that puts to rest a number of
my Monkey Mind conversations about donating money. You and I
are compensated *immediately* when we intentionally and generously
send energy away to others from ourselves. Our self-esteem rises.
There *may* be additional rewards for giving, but they are secondary to
the immediate knowledge that you have the ability to make a differ-

ence right now. You are bringing energy from the metaphysical into the physical.

Several years ago I listened to a talk by Lynn Twist, who spoke about raising money for The Hunger Project, a nonprofit organization whose mission is to end world hunger. Twist explained that in her fund-raising work, she'd seen how people want to contribute to causes such as hers because they consider them to be important. The act of giving empowered them. They thrived. Now I see she was describing prosperity to a T.

TITHING TROUBLES

It is a commonly accepted metaphysical principle that tithing brings prosperity. Tithing is giving one-tenth of your money to that which you consider to be your spiritual source. Charles Fillmore, cofounder of the Unity School of Christianity, wrote that tithing makes giving a methodical process and "brings into the consciousness a sense of order and fitness that will be manifested in one's outer life and affairs as increased efficiency and greater prosperity."

The act of giving establishes balance and allows energy to flow freely, coming in and going out. When you are balanced you naturally open to the miracles that surround you every moment of your life. You use opportunity. Your energy is free to create. You are open and present in the moment, open to possibilities, and you perceive your life as being blessed. You transmit this blessing to those around you, and you are prosperous.

But wait a moment before you rush out to give, expecting this wonderful surge of energy in return. Be aware of this pitfall: When we give with the thought that we will "get a return on our investment" in the future, we do not create balance. Rather, we're forming an imbalance. In fact, those conditions we place on our giving are nothing but extensions of our own sense of scarcity! This is usually at the heart of any difficulties we might have with contributing to spiritual causes.

. Giving with an expectation of return for our money is a setup for anger and pessimism. We don't feel that rise in self-esteem. Monkey Mind has us looking only for future rewards. This invalidates or diminishes our spiritual benefits.

Tithing, or any contribution of money, is a demonstration of our power. But often our experiences of contribution have been less than powerful, sometimes even torturous:

> WALLACE: I remember when I was a kid. My father gave a lot of money to our church. There were six of us in the family and we hardly had enough money to get by. One winter I wore a coat two sizes too small. I resented my father's giving away what little we had. He told us he was doing it to make sure we all went to Heaven. It was like he was afraid or something and this was his way of escaping his fear. Sort of an insurance policy. I don't give much to my church at all. I don't want the feeling I'm buying my way to salvation. I also don't want my kids ever to suffer the way we did.

You could point to flaws in Wallace's logic. He went to the opposite extreme from his father because he and his siblings had had to endure the effects of their father's driven behavior. If you recall, one aspect of driven behavior is that you can never do it well enough. When Wallace's father gave beyond his means, he created an imbalance of energy. His contribution carried a condition that was based on fear, not on the joys of giving freely. It was hard on his family.

When you contribute in a driven way, you're not really being generous. You're attempting to fill a void created by the absence of joy and gratitude. Contribution is authentic when it's a natural outgrowth of your Standards of Integrity.

TRUE GIVING

Greg owns an insurance agency and began tithing to his church. He told me that every month when he wrote out his tithe check and deposited it in the mail, he experienced a real sense of joy. He said that in contributing to and helping take care of a church that was a source of spiritual inspiration for him, he made it "his" church. It wasn't just a place he went to get value; he was directly participating in some miraculous kind of energy flow. He noticed that it affected how he conducted his business, and that his business grew as a result. He felt very clear and empowered.

When people give money in this clear, generous way, they often report a sense of empowerment. One reason is that they know they are wielding the energy of money powerfully enough to make the gift. Another reason is that they are in the energy flow of which Greg spoke.

Giving as a demonstration of your Standards of Integrity to support something that benefits you and others puts you in that flow. You don't hope for benefits in the future. You are actually *in that flow* in the moment that you give. And you are giving to empower others as well.

The interesting thing about energy is that when you are in the flow of it, it goes both ways. Have you ever noticed that when you feed or focus energy on something or someone, you get that energy back immediately? That is the nature of energy.

In the early chapters of this book we limited our discussion to your focusing energy on your goals and dreams. Now, as we talk about contribution, we can expand that discussion to include the mutual, two-way flow. We often think about energy in a strictly physical and Newtonian sense, that it flows only one way—in the same way that energy from batteries flows only one way, and that's why they get drained. But on the metaphysical level, energy goes both ways at the same time. It's part of the interconnectedness of things.

We close our journey together by looking at how to achieve ongoing balance in your money affairs. Using Standards of Integrity is one key. Enhancing the power to be grateful is the other. When your energy is balanced, you can give in a way that benefits the world and enriches your life.

These, then, are the final action steps we will take together on this journey: looking once more into our hearts to express our integrity, who we really are, and then looking outward, to experience all we see and encounter with gratitude.

Exercise: Integrity Aerobics

This exercise is designed to pump up your power to bring balance to your life. As you demonstrate your Standards of Integrity, you will notice increased freedom in your interactions with people and money. Please have compassion for yourself as you do this part. The work is important and sometimes difficult. You are demonstrating your willingness to dance with abundance, to be open to everything in your life. Because this will definitely make your perceptions finer, be prepared for miracles!

You will need your notebook, a personal calendar, and your Standards of Integrity.

This exercise is an ongoing process. Give yourself no more than forty minutes for the first step. You can always come back later and add items. The list you create won't be complete, but it will get you started. After that, each item you choose to examine can take from five to fifteen minutes. I recommend you take one hour with this exercise the first time you do it. Then rest.

1. Locate items in your life that represent an imbalance in integrity. Use the following questions to spur your memory:

- Regarding money, where have I lied, cheated, or stolen anything?
- Regarding my relationships with people and money, where have I bent the rules?
- Where have I been greedy, uncharitable, or ignorant in my personal and business dealings?

Be very specific about your behavior. Clearly describe what you did. Note the promises you didn't keep. Use the following examples, taken from people in the You and Money Course, to get you going:

> Lois: I filed a false claim on my insurance. When my house was burglarized, I reported that my mother's diamond ring had been stolen when it wasn't. It's there in the back of my mind every time I wear the ring.

> Don: I didn't report to the IRS $4,500 I made under the table at my mail-order business last year. I tell my wife I'm not worried and that everyone else does it. But whenever we get a letter from the IRS, I'm sure it's going to be a notice that they found out and I'm going to be audited.

ART: I make personal long-distance calls at work and charge it to the company. I've never told anyone, least of all my boss.

CHANTEL: I take pencils, pens, and paper from the stationery store where I work. I tell myself I deserve it because the owner pays me such a small salary. But it weighs on me. Lately I haven't wanted to go in to work. When she looks at me sometimes I'm just sure she knows.

SIDNEY: I haven't paid child support for the past two years. I know I'm ordered to by the court, but I'm really angry with my ex. She's been living with this other guy. I'm sure she's been trying to turn my kids against me.

Make sure you list even the smallest items. Monkey Mind may tell you that they do not make a difference. If they came up, they make a difference. What about the newspaper(s) you took without paying? The time a waitress gave you back too much change and you did not tell her? The item(s) you have shoplifted? The time you bought a dress or shirt, wore it to a party, and then returned it to the department store for a refund? Raiding your child's piggy bank without permission? Slipping into additional movies at multiple-screen theaters without paying?

We all have items like this. What are yours? Cough it all up. Also, no dawdling or wallowing allowed. If you hear Monkey Mind's chatter, give it a wave and keep on going.

If you have done the above, even if you have listed just one item, bravo! You are getting in shape to have a powerfully free and creative relationship with money, your goals, and your dreams.

2. Take one of the items you listed above. You might want to start with a relatively small item at first. Let's say that someone wrote, "The time I stole a tube of toothpaste from the supermarket." On a clean piece of paper from your notebook, draw a large box. Write this item on the top of the box. Write all the reasons, justifications, rationalizations, thoughts, theories, and feelings that went along with this behavior. Be real about it.

This is not the time to censor what you write. Write until you have emptied your entire structure of knowing onto the piece of paper. Get it all out of your head. Take a moment and look at all this stuff. How do you feel as you read it?

3. Draw another box and put in it "What it has cost me to have done this and not cleaned it up." The cost will show up in terms of money, time, physical energy, and emotional comfort. This is the imbalance. Be thorough with yourself. Did you return to that supermarket again? If so, did you feel tense? Did you use that toothpaste? How was your next dental checkup? If you are willing, you will encounter related costs that you never might have noticed. They have always been there.

4. Look at the two boxes. Do you see the energy that has gone into maintaining this imbalance? Now ask yourself the questions we all face in the You and Money Course:

- Have I had enough of doing my life this way?
- Am I willing to move on to more freedom?

5. If the answer is "No," remember that we are talking about willing, not wanting. You may be afraid to clear this up. You may not want to. Monkey Mind may be going a mile a minute here. Are you willing? The truth is, you know you are willing or else you would not have begun this exercise. So take a deep breath and just say "Yes."

6. Take out your Standards of Integrity. Look to see what specific Standards are missing from physical reality while this item goes uncollected. For example, what might be missing in the case of the stolen toothpaste are: honest, trustworthy, prosperous, and intelligent.

After you have assessed what is missing, ask yourself the following: "Since these are my Standards of Integrity, how would someone who is _____(fill in the word for the missing Standards) clean up this situation?"

The woman above completed the sentence this way: "Since these are my Standards of Integrity, how would someone who is honest, trustworthy, prosperous, and intelligent clean up this situation?"

7. Now we correct the imbalance. We clean up the mess. Regarding the current situation, the Authentic Action was rela-

tively simple. She went to the supermarket where she had stolen the toothpaste and told the cashier that she had not been charged for a tube of toothpaste on her last trip. She had the cost added to her present charges. She paid for it then and there. Balance was restored.

When you begin to correct items to restore integrity, follow these guidelines:

• Do not leave anything out. Taking Authentic Action means cleaning up every mess. This goes for income tax evasion, returning stolen goods, or making good on an old debt.

• Be persistent. One person had to work closely with his insurance company to get it to accept a check for an item he had misreported. There was no category in the computer for client reimbursements to them! A woman who had filed for bankruptcy retracted voluntarily before the final hearing. Her bank had already written off her credit-card debt, so she spent a few weeks and finally persuaded them to accept her payments on the defunct account. The result, however, was that they reinstated her credit. The bank had never before done this with customers who had filed for bankruptcy.

The results of taking these difficult actions often seem miraculous. Someone else returned $1,100 in disability overpayments from a county agency for which he had worked. A reporter soon called and wanted to interview him as one of a "dying breed of honest people." Another man reported that the IRS agent with whom he was working became visibly relieved when he openly admitted to her that he had not paid his full taxes the previous year. He told her he wasn't going to make any excuses for it, and took full responsibility for what he had done. Her response was to help him figure out a way to pay what he owed in the easiest, most painless way possible.

If you notice some cynicism creeping in as you read these accounts, with Monkey Mind actively commenting about these foolhardy do-gooders, take a deep breath. Ask yourself the question "What interests me more, holding on to my cynicism or having my goals and dreams become reality?" Pick one. You can't have both.

8. Clean items up in a way that works for you and will not get

you in any trouble. If you are going to clean up an item with legal implications, get advice from an attorney first. If you create more of a mess through your actions, you will have a perfect rationale for not correcting imbalances in the future. It may be necessary to get legal or human-resource consultation before you tell your boss about something like personal charges on a company phone bill. You may want to consult a tax attorney or CPA before going to the IRS. There are ways to clean up these situations without putting yourself or others in jeopardy.

9. If cleaning up the mess has to do with another person, get support. Use a friend, counselor, or loved one so that you do it in a way that demonstrates your Standards of Integrity. It does no good to lay your guilt at someone else's feet. Get proper coaching before you handle the situation. This is the way to bring about balance with integrity and compassion.

Also be mindful of the principle reflected in Alcoholics Anonymous's Ninth Step, "Make direct amends to such people wherever possible, except when to do so would injure them or others." As you clean up messes, keep your Standards of Integrity in mind so that you don't create more trouble by harming others.

10. Take specific Authentic Actions. In almost every instance, you know what to do. You have a wellspring of wisdom in your heart, and it's time to show it. Set a date by which you will take action, then do it! One man remembered a time twenty-five years earlier when he stole $16 from a summer camp's store. He also recalled that he never wanted to go back to that camp again. Or any camp, for that matter. The place itself no longer exists, so to create balance he took the $16 and added twenty-five years' worth of interest. Then he donated that $250 to a local charity. Balance and integrity were restored.

If no specific action comes to mind, sit with it for a while. Get counsel from someone you know who will support you in handling this matter. It does no good to talk with someone who might collude with you about not having to do anything.

11. Take a few minutes and acknowledge yourself every time you complete an item. Do not rush on to the next task. Every hero needs a moment of replenishment. Let someone

know what a good job you are doing; reward yourself with a little fun.

Do your Integrity Aerobics with increasingly difficult items. The more you resolve, the more balance and energy you will experience. Integrity Aerobics gets easier with time. As you experience more relief, you will see when your integrity is missing—before it shows up in your behavior. You can then cut it off at the pass. For right now, acknowledge yourself for being willing to see who you really are and taking action to express it.

What do you experience as you work through the items in this exercise? You may want to make a point of doing the exercise that follows this one, acknowledging instances for gratitude every night before you go to sleep. Do more instances seem to arise? Are there openings and opportunities where there seemed to be none? Were they always there, just waiting for you to be clear enough to perceive them?

One of my favorite stories comes from a woman who wanted to travel the world for her company but hadn't had the opportunity. She owed $6,000 in taxes she had not reported from consulting she did on the side. One month after she sent her check for this amount to the IRS, her company offered her a job that involved world travel—at a salary that more than made up for any money she had paid in taxes. One happy person!

The results of this work are best summed up by a man who said, "I sleep better at night. I'm not afraid to read my mail. I don't have to keep track of any lies I've told. My business has been expanding as never before. It's simple. And yes, it is just fine with me that things have gotten easier."

Exercise: The Active Demonstration of Integrity

This is a simple process. It can be implemented every day. I suggest you try it for at least two weeks.

1. Each morning when you arise, get a small piece of paper and write down the specific Standards of Integrity you're willing to demonstrate that day. Pick ones that you sense would bolster you on that day.

2. Carry that paper with you. Before any important or poten-
tially difficult meeting or interaction, take it out and look at the
specific Standards you said you'd demonstrate.

3. Note any breakthroughs you're having in your ability
to communicate in an empowering way. Are you noticing
miracles?

4. Finally, look at the places in your life in which contributing
money would be actively demonstrating your Standards of
Integrity: political causes, spiritual centers, medical research,
education, a local charity, animal welfare. Pick at least one that
calls out to you. Donate to it within the next week.

Exercise: Basic Affirmation Training

Restoring the balance in your life with Integrity Aerobics makes
room for gratitude. As you learn to look at your life with open
eyes and a grateful heart, you will notice your heart expanding
and allowing you to experience even the uncomfortable aspects
of abundance without pushing them away.

For this exercise you will need your notebook and inspirational writings by your favorite authors or poets. It will take
about ten minutes of quiet time at the end of each day. You
may do this for one week, but for best results do this exercise
for thirty days. Please note that for some of us, just engineer-
ing ten minutes of quiet time at the close of the day is a miracle. Try it!

1. Each night before you go to sleep, list three instances from
your day that evoke a sense of gratitude within you. It does not
matter how big or small they may seem. Keep your notebook by
your bed and make your list before you turn out the light. You
may find situations for which gratitude is an easy and ready
response—a job well done, the smile of a child, or a good meal.

2. You may notice that you are unable to come up with three
instances of gratefulness. This may be especially true during the
first days of this practice. Ask yourself, "What doubts, worries
or other thoughts am I listening to instead?" Write your
answers on a sheet of paper that is not part of the notebook.

Then throw that paper away and go back and list three instances for which you are grateful.

3. You will probably have times in which gratitude seems a highly unlikely response, as in the case of difficult or distressing events in your life. This is where the exercise becomes more challenging. Try asking yourself, "Am I willing to discover a way to respond with gratitude, even in this situation? Am I willing to see the important lessons here?" If the answer is "No," don't push yourself into saying "Yes." It is sufficient that you were willing to ask the above questions and answer truthfully. You can try again tomorrow with the same incident.

4. Find some writing that inspires you and read it. It might be a sonnet, a verse from the Bible, the Upanishads, poetry, or a passage written by your favorite motivational or spiritual author. Anything. Just allow yourself to read for ten minutes. That is usually sufficient to raise the gratitude quotient. Then return to the situation and ask yourself; "What is there about the situation that could evoke gratefulness? What might I learn from this?" If you find something about which to be grateful, write it down. If not, give it and yourself a rest until the next day.

Review what you have written after the first week. Are there any patterns? How do you feel as you look over your writing?

RON: It felt good to read what I'd written. One night I came home after a particularly lousy day at work. On my way to change clothes, I passed by the notebook. I opened it and began to read my notations on gratefulness. I felt better immediately and had a great evening with my family.

SUZ: I was just about to lead a difficult staff meeting. We had found we were $10,000 over budget on a $50,000 project. Ordinarily I'd be agitated and everyone would be walking on eggshells around me. I happened to have my notebook with me that morning and spent three minutes reading over some of my entries. By the time I entered the meeting room, I was calmer. We solved the problem in record time. I got to use it as one of my manifestations of gratefulness.

Share your results with a friend. Are you willing to carry this exercise forward for a total of thirty days?   .

Exercise: Contemplating Gratitude

The final process I'd like to share with you will increase your ability to bring gratitude into the present moment, the space where miracles are possible. It is very simple to do. Although I recommend that you begin with ten minutes, you may find you can increase this to twenty minutes over time. Remember, these processes are designed to open your heart to experiencing the true nature of abundance, and as you do them you will evoke gratitude in everyday events.

You will need a small spiral pad that fits in your purse or pocket. Give yourself thirty minutes for this exercise.

1. Stand in a place, at home or outside, where you feel comfortable. If you do this in a group, make sure you are someplace where you have enough room to walk around without bumping into one another. Begin a slow walk, exploring your environment. Make sure you are breathing easily and deeply.

2. Begin to search consciously for objects or scenes that bring you a sense of joy, peace, or happy surprise. As you do this, note your experience in your small spiral pad. Be sure to describe what is going on both outside and inside of you. Look closely at ordinary items. Do you see dew on leaves? Have you noticed the texture on the covering of your favorite pillow?

You might make notes that look like this:

- I see the shell of an acorn, with two leaves attached.
- It looks like the leavings of a squirrel. I love squirrels.
- I smell a rose. Its outer petals are red, but the inner ones are pink. It's so soft. I'm glad I found it.
- I am looking at the photo of my great-aunt Anna. She is smiling at me.
- My heart feels warm.

3. Continue this exercise for ten minutes. This is a form of walking meditation. It requires attention. Every time your inner

conversations take you away, pause. Take one or two deep breaths. Keep your stomach loose. Bring yourself back to the present moment. Search for what brings you joy, peace, or happy surprise.

4. You may find that nothing evokes these reactions in you. Take another deep breath. That you are even engaging in this exercise means you are opening the way for the experience of gratefulness. It will come, most probably when you least expect it. Recall what happens when you're trying unsuccessfully to remember a name. The more you struggle with it, the more elusive it becomes. When you let go of the struggle, the name appears in your consciousness. That's what will happen here for you. Just being willing to do this exercise may be a special opportunity for gratitude.

5. If you continue to have difficulty discovering the joy in ordinary items, try this: Take an orange or banana. Sit down and hold it in your hands. Look closely at the fine lines or marks on the skin, its texture and color. Remove the peel and look at the fruit within. Breathe in its smell. Now take a section of the fruit. Hold it to up to light. Taste it. What do you notice? Is gratitude beginning to peek out from between your taste buds?

6. Look at what you have written. In your own words, write what gratitude is for you. Your heart is full and wise. Let your wisdom surface. How do you describe this phenomenon in a way that is meaningful for you?

7. How would it affect you and those around you if you were to recognize the gifts each day brings? How would this simplify how you live?

How does your heart feel at the end of this practice? Would it be all right with you to feel this way most of the time? Or would Monkey Mind tell you, "Life is passing you by when you feel this good. This isn't real life. We're supposed to be struggling here." Given that the chatter may never go away, you have an important choice to make:

• Am I more interested in engaging with Monkey Mind or my heart? Which brings me a sense of peace?
• Have I had enough of doing life the hard way?
• Am I ready to experience gratitude every day?

Share your results with a friend. It is valuable to hear yourself talking about your discoveries regarding gratitude.

Franz Kafka once wrote: "You need not do anything. Remain sitting at your table and listen, and you need not even listen, just wait, and you need not even wait, just become quiet, still, and solitary, and the world will offer itself to you to be unmasked; it has no choice. It will roll in ecstasy at your feet."

I wish you the ecstasy of discovering gratitude in every day of your life. I wish you the joy of living fully and openly with abundance.

EPILOGUE

Working wisely with energy and opening yourself to its power will change you. At the beginning of our journey together, it may have seemed that the goal of our work was to claim a prize—to lay hands on things, or perhaps the cold hard cash, that would finally make us feel safe and secure. But the real rewards you've earned on the way to your dreams are much larger.

Emmet Fox once wrote an allegory about fools' gold, the shiny material that looks so much like gold that you can't tell the difference. He said new prospectors waste time and hard work before they see that it's not the genuine article. How could you tell the real thing? Advice from experienced miners to the novice was that if they *thought* they'd found gold, they probably hadn't, because when then did find gold, they would *know* it for sure.

Fox wrote that there are many kinds of fools' gold to be found in life. But when we meet up with the real thing, there will be no doubt in our minds. The true gold we seek gives us peace and clarity. It gives us a sense of freedom and power because we're no longer in "bondage to passing material things." Fools' gold, he said, usually takes the form of material riches, social prominence, power over others, and the gratification of whims. True gold is the sense of a Presence much larger than ourselves, which is the true purpose of our lives.

The work you've done has given you the power to unearth the true gold of your life. That's the real reward you've earned on the way to your dreams. To look at your life, to see it, and to tell the truth about it is an act of raw courage. It is daring to take Authentic Action in order to transform your life, despite everything you've always believed about who and what you are. And to continue, fully awake, with gentleness toward yourself and the people in your life, requires deep compassion. You've demonstrated these things, time and again, by doing the work in this book.

Draw your dreams from your heart—the ones that bring you joy, the ones that seem just out of your grasp—and make them real with the energy of your life and the energy of money.

The Treasure Maps you've created are filled with the radiant energy of your own passion. Let them remind you of the joy that's pulling you forward. The Standards of Integrity you've established are true reflections of what you value most in life. Let them be the firm ground that you walk on. Use everything you've learned to contribute to the world and the visions that only you can offer, the full expression of your talents and who you really are. Your greatest lessons are disguised as obstacles. Embrace them, too, for the gifts they are.

We can see the hero as a mythological character so far removed from everyday life that the concept has no relevance for us. But would it be all right with you if you recognized the hero in everyone, including yourself? That, I think, is the basis of a life well lived. You are a hero. We all are.

My hope for you is that you will connect not only with your dreams but with the sense of ease that you were designed to have. Would it be all right with you if life got easier?

I hope you will use the 12 Principles to remind you that money's true purpose is to serve the larger purpose of your life. May you stay on the hero's path to create a life for yourself that is adventurous instead of safe, thoughtful instead of expedient.

May it be a life that is lived awake in each moment, a life that is, in all ways, rich.

INDEX

Cooper, David, 198–99
Creative Visualization (Gawain),
    135
Credit-card debt, 229, 253–54
Credit rating, 251, 254–56

Deprivation cycle of spending,
    139–42
Discomfort, facing, 31–32
Dishonesty, 150
Donations of money, 294–97
Driven behavior, 107–29
    addictive, 117–18
    binge and purge spending,
        119–20
    busyholism, 127–29
    cost of, 110
    cycle of, 109–10
    gambling, 120–22
    and Internet, 122
    limited satisfaction in, 113–14
    obsessive-compulsive, 116–17
    perfectionism as, 114–16
    repetition of, 111–13
    spending urge, 44, 118–19
    workaholism, 123–27

Einstein, Albert, 77
Energy
    forms of, 29–30
    infinite supply of, 221–22
    in metaphysical realm, 20, 21, 26
    in physical realm, 20–21, 26
    in quantum realm, 22
    See also Money energy
Enlightened Mind, The (Mitchell),
    181
Enlightenment, 198–99
Error, 150
Estate planning, taking care of,
    229, 240–42

Failure-phobia, 31
Family money-handling
    with children, 241–43
    and inheritance, 240–41
    loan repayment, 208, 229, 238–39
    partner decision making, 240
    unfinished business, 227–31
Fear
    defined, 150
    facing, 108
    of failing, 31, 63–64
    of scarcity, 132–35
    as teacher, 32
    of true nature, 63–64
Fee. *See* Work
Flight-or-fight response, 166, 170
Fools' gold, 309
Forgiveness, 200–217
    and characterizations, 202–6
    empowering, 210
    vs. forgetting, 206, 209
    and letting go, 201–2
    and Monkey Mind thinking,
        207–8
    negative effect of announcing,
        209
    practicing, 210–17
    as teacher, 209–10
    willing to forgive, 206–7, 215–16
Fox, Emmet, 309

Gambling, 120–22
Gawain, Shakti, 135
Giving, 294–97
Goals, 83–104
    of abundance, 287–89
    creating, 87–90, 91–96
    defined, 84–85
    energizing, 29–30
    with Life's Intentions, 20, 22, 23,
        24–27, 59–60

ABOUT THE AUTHOR

MARIA NEMETH, a UCLA graduate, is a licensed clinical psychologist and a nationally recognized seminar leader and speaker. Dr. Nemeth kept a private practice for twenty-eight years, during which she worked with individuals, couples, and families. She has over thirty years' experience in working with alcoholism, drug abuse, and community-based crisis intervention programs around the country. She has trained people and teams in communication skills in the public, private, military, and nonprofit sectors. She was an associate clinical professor at UC Davis School of Medicine, Department of Psychiatry, and an assistant professor in psychology at California State University, Dominquez Hills. For seven years she served as a governor's appointee to the state licensing board for clinical psychologists.

Maria is the founder of You and Money, a personal and professional development/transformational seminar that shows people how to shift their relationship with money from scarcity to abundance. Her work is directed to successful communication, authentic action, partnership, and extraordinary results with ease. Thousands of people have taken this course. She teaches seminars at Esalen Institute, Mt. Madonna Conference Center, the Institute of Noetic Sciences, Reverend Johnnie Colemon's Universal Foundation for Better Living, and the Association of Unity Churches Regional and National Conferences. Maria also travels around the United States and Canada conducting her courses for local Unity and other New Thought churches. Courses that Maria Nemeth Associates conduct include: You and Money, The Heart of Your Money Matters, Life's

Work, Being Coach, Forgiveness, Befriending Your Body, The TeamWorks Series, and Gifted Communication.

Maria is a former columnist for the *Sacramento Business Journal*, where her column, "Mind Over Money," appeared for two years.

Maria's first book, *You and Money: Would It Be All Right with You If Life Got Easier?* was published in 1997. Her first audio cassette series, *The Energy of Money*, was produced by Sounds True in 1997.

For information about and registration in courses offered by Maria Nemeth Associates, including the You and Money Course, visit www.youandmoney.com or call 800-835-9782.

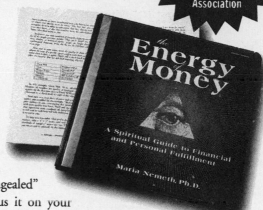